"I started hurting on the bottom of my stomach. The pain was unbelievable. It was like, Oh, God, why doesn't he call? I didn't go to work. I'd just sit and drink wine cooler after wine cooler . . . all the time thinking about him."

"I waited patiently for two years for her to leave her husband, but nothing changed. I kept telling myself, well, if I'm just patient . . . I felt like I was on a torture rack."

"It was very melodramatic, like something out of a bad movie. I knew I wasn't about to actually burn his house down but I couldn't stop thinking about it."

"I'm afraid of the emptiness I used to feel. I'm afraid it'll come back. Just total emptiness."

"I kept calling into the night, but she wouldn't answer the phone. So I just kept going at it on and on, over and over. Like a robot."

These people regained their emotional wholeness and freedom. You can, too. This compassionate and practical book will show you the way.

OBSESSIVE LOVE

DR. SUSAN FORWARD
and Craig Buck

BANTAM BOOKS
NEW YORK • TORONTO • LONDON • SYDNEY • AUCKLAND

OBSESSIVE LOVE

A Bantam Book

PUBLISHING HISTORY
Bantam hardcover edition published June 1991
Bantam paperback edition / June 1992

ISBN 0-553-29674-4

Published simultaneously in the United States and Canada

Bantam Books are published by Bantam Books, a division of Bantam Doubleday
Dell Publishing Group, Inc. Its trademark, consisting of the words "Bantam
Books" and the portrayal of a rooster, is Registered in U.S. Patent and Trademark
Office and in other countries. Marca Registrada. Bantam Books, 666 Fifth Avenue,
New York, New York 10103.

PRINTED IN THE UNITED STATES OF AMERICA

RAD   0 9 8 7 6 5 4 3 2 1

ACKNOWLEDGMENTS

I'd like to thank several people who helped make this book become a reality.

First and foremost, my treasured collaborator and friend, Craig Buck. This is our third book together and his insights, talent, skill, patience, and never-failing good humor continue to amaze me.

This is also the third book I've done with my editor, Toni Burbank. I wish I could tell you how brilliant, knowledgeable, caring, dedicated, and extraordinarily competent she is, but she's far too modest to allow me to be so laudatory.

I'd also like to thank Linda Grey, Stuart Applebaum, and all the other wonderful people at Bantam Books who always go the extra mile for me. And my agents, Lynn Nesbit and Ken Sherman, for their continued support and encouragement.

My colleague and dear friend Nina Miller, M.F.C.C., and Marty Farash, M.F.C.C., have been more than generous in allowing me to pick their brains to enrich the conceptual foundation of this book.

As always, my family and friends—especially my daughter, Wendy, and my mother, Harriet Peterson—have been there for me throughout the creation of this book to lend their moral and emotional support as I confronted daily the inevitable anguish of writing. And some friends, both new and old, have been notably loving and supportive—Dr.

Barbara De Angelis, Madelyn Cain, Lynn Fischer, Dorris Gathrid, Mona Golabek, Roy Johnston, Paul Kent, Diana Markes Levitt, Lisa Rafel, Neil Stearns, Dr. Shelley Ventura, and Don Weisberg.

Karina Friend Buck wins the patience and generosity award for permitting me to monopolize Craig, use up her Earl Grey tea, and coopt her home for our 19-month wrestle with the blank page. Our task was lightened considerably by four-year-old Zoe Buck's hugs and spritely comic relief.

Finally, I'd like to offer my heartfelt thanks and appreciation to the wonderful women and men without whom this book truly could not have been written—the clients, friends, and acquaintances who so graciously allowed me to use their stories. Whether they have been tortured by obsession themselves or have struggled to escape obsessive lovers, their courageous battles with obsessive love, and their successes in overcoming it, inspired me to write this book.

CONTENTS

INTRODUCTION

Something wasn't right when Gloria arrived at work. All eyes were on her as she walked through the newsroom toward her office. Many of her co-workers were smiling like guests at a surprise party knowing the birthday girl has arrived at the door. Her adrenaline began to pump. Was she getting a promotion? Did her brother and sister-in-law have their baby? Did her vacation request come through?

As Gloria swung open the door to her office she was overwhelmed by the smell of roses. Covering the entire surface of her desk was a breathtaking arrangement of at least six dozen of the most beautiful red roses she had ever seen. What was the occasion? She checked the calendar on her watch. May 2. The date meant nothing.

Then it dawned on her. They were from Jim.

The fear and anger hit her like a train. Why couldn't Jim understand that she didn't want to see him anymore? Why wouldn't he leave her alone? She leaned helplessly against the doorjamb and began to cry.

In his modest law office, several miles away, Jim waited by the phone. His nerves felt like they were plugged into an electric socket. On the one hand he was certain that it would be only a matter of time before Gloria called. The flowers marked a sacred occasion: the anniversary of the night they'd met. He was certain the roses would awaken in her the same lush romantic memories that they did in him—the night they'd made love under the stars overlooking Big Sur, the photo she'd secretly taken and then had framed for her bedroom of him sleeping blissfully in her garden, the horseback ride through the orchid-covered trail that led down to the beach in Puerto Vallarta. . . .

He knew she didn't really want to break up with him. How could she? Their love was so right. It was clear to him that she was just afraid because her feelings for him were so powerful. The kind of love and passion he offered her was a once-in-a-lifetime gift, and he knew that sooner or later she would allow herself to accept how perfect it was.

On the other hand, he was terrified that she might not call. When she'd first told him she didn't want to see him anymore, the pain had been so great that he thought he would die. For the past two months she'd been returning his gifts and love letters unopened. He had reduced his phone calls to two a day because she had started hanging up. He had taken to driving by her house almost every night, but on those few occasions when he had been unable to resist knocking, she had become angry. The last time, she had actually slammed the door in his face without a word. So he was terrified of how he would feel if she didn't respond to the roses, and the opposing forces of hope and fear were tearing him apart.

Gloria knew that Jim needed her, and she felt guilty at not being able to reciprocate, but she couldn't. And she'd been painfully clear about telling him so. She hated to see him suffer, they had once been so close, they had once shared so many hopes for a future together. But little by little, Jim's love had become so fraught with jealousy that she felt suffocated. What had started out as passion began to feel more like prison. She had tried to get him to understand her feelings, to understand that she needed to have more independence, to feel less like a possession, but nothing she said seemed to make any difference. Finally, she lost patience and told him she didn't want to see him anymore. When he begged her to reconsider, she tried to let him down easy, but she still held firm.

In the ensuing months, he had refused to give up. She felt driven, by his never-ending campaign to win her back, to become increasingly assertive. She was convinced that the kindest thing she could do was to get him to give up on her so that he could offer his enormous passion to someone who would appreciate it.

Jim sat at his desk, waiting for Gloria's call, rehearsing the words he would use. He opened a file to appear to be studying a contract should anyone walk into his office. But work was the last thing on his mind. After three hours of bouncing between hope and anxiety, he sensed his growing anger over Gloria's blindness to his love and to her own true desires. He fought off this anger by rationalizing that she wasn't calling from her office because she wouldn't have time for all the catching up they'd have to do. But his head was so full of things he wanted to tell her that he picked up a pen and began to write her a letter. By the time he finished, he had filled twelve pages.

Gloria couldn't concentrate on work either. Whenever she tried to edit the story on her desk, her thoughts returned to Jim. Was she encouraging him without realizing it? When she broke up with him, she may have given him double messages in trying to spare his feelings, but she had become painfully blunt since. A chilling thought seized her: what if he tried to kill himself? Would it be her fault? Her head began to ache.

About eight o'clock that night, Jim finally decided that he couldn't wait any longer. The roses had apparently not done the job, but he didn't care anymore. He felt like he was about to explode from the pressure of his own anxiety. He had to hear her voice. So he called her. She hung up. He was devastated.

When Gloria woke up the next morning, she looked out the window to see Jim sitting on her front step. In desperation, she called the police, but because it wasn't an emergency, they told her it might take several hours before they could respond. She felt trapped in her own apartment, afraid even to open the door to get the morning paper. She was determined to skip work if she had to in order to avoid contact with him, but to her surprise, after about an hour Jim decided to leave.

Gloria arrived late to work to find Jim waiting by her parking space. She was so frustrated and furious that she started screaming at him to leave her alone. As she railed, Jim just smiled understandingly, urging her to calm down. Passersby stared at her as if *she* were the crazy one. She arrived at her office in tears. Her headache was back with a vengeance.

Jim went home upset with himself for being unable to find the key that would open her up to her own love for him. He knew that if he could just get her to go out with him one more time, his love would melt her resistance to their mutual destiny.

Jim and Gloria's story is a classic case of obsessive love. Jim's suffocating behavior and unwillingness to accept that Gloria didn't want to be in a relationship with him anymore was, in different ways, destroying both of their lives. Obsessive love is a prison, both for obsessors and for the men and women who are "targets" of their relentless love.

Why I Decided to Write This Book

Jim came to see me about a month after the incident with the roses. Intellectually, he knew he had to give up on Gloria, but emotionally, he could not. He begged me to help him.

As I listened to Jim pour his heart out I was struck by how much both he and Gloria had suffered, and were still suffering, from the burden of his obsession. How had such a promising and romantic relationship sunk to this point? Jim was desperate for answers.

Jim

What makes me do these things? I'm a lawyer—I'm supposed to act logically. But when it comes to Gloria, I just can't. Am I going to be like this forever? I feel like I'm never going to get over her. Am I going to be screwing up my relationships for the rest of my life? I can't go on like this. It's too painful. Is there anything I can do?

I told Jim that I understood how alone, confused, and out of control he felt. Most obsessors feel this way, yet they often have nowhere to turn for support. Their friends and family can't understand why they don't just "forget about" their lover and get on with their lives. Because their behavior is so often oppressive, they rarely find a sympathetic ear unless they seek professional treatment, and sometimes not even then. I assured Jim that if he really wanted to change, I wanted to help. The fact that he had chosen to come in to see me was an important first step.

As I began to work with Jim to find answers to his questions, I realized that these same questions must be going through the minds of millions of other troubled, hurting obsessive lovers.

By the same token, I knew that Gloria must be plagued by questions of her own. Shouldn't she have known early on that something was wrong? Was she unwittingly feeding Jim's obsession? Why couldn't she get him to take her seriously? Would she ever be able to trust another lover? While I sympathized with Jim's pain, I also felt a lot of compassion for Gloria. Targets of obsessive love are often forgotten victims. Their confidants often find their plight amusing or accuse them of exaggerating their lover's behavior.

After Jim left, I thought about the hundreds of obsessors and many targets of obsessive love I had treated over the years. I had been repeatedly moved by these men and women whose lives had been dramatically altered by this particularly destructive type of obsession. Many of the obsessors were intelligent, attractive, successful people, who had been shocked and ashamed by their own behavior yet had felt powerless to do anything about it. They had often described themselves as feeling "possessed" or "out of control," succumbing to impulses that they *knew* were self-defeating.

There are few of us who haven't experienced either the painful longing and frustration of being obsessed with someone we desperately want but can't have or the stress and anxiety of being the target of someone's obsession, or both. I wanted to help both obsessors and targets learn to deal with and get beyond the obsessive love that monopolizes their thoughts, distorts their judgment, and takes over their lives. Because of this, I decided to write this book.

Once Craig and I began writing, I was astounded at the numbers of friends, colleagues, clients, and even casual acquaintances who urged me to use their stories. Though this has happened with every book I've written, it has never happened with such frequency or passion. Obsessive love touches a nerve in us all.

All the stories in this book are real. Though I've changed the names, professions, and other identifying characteristics of all the people who talked to me (and of the people in their lives) in order to protect their identities, I've reproduced their words and their experiences as accurately as possible.

What Is Obsessive Love?

After two decades of practice, I have discovered four conditions that help me clarify, both for myself and for my clients, whether they are struggling with obsessive love:

1. They must have a painful, all-consuming preoccupation with a real or wished-for lover.

2. They must have an insatiable longing either to possess or to be possessed by the target of their obsession.

3. Their target must have rejected them or be unavailable in some way, either physically or emotionally.

4. Their target's unavailability or rejection must drive them to behave in self-defeating ways.

Throughout this book I will be using the word "obsessive" to describe certain behavior. This is technically incorrect since the term "obsessive" traditionally refers only to *thoughts*. The correct psychological adjective for behavior driven by obsession is "compulsive." However, for simplicity's sake, in this book I have chosen to use the one adjective, "obsessive," to describe behavior as well as thoughts.

Obsessive love knows no gender. Both men and women can become obsessed, and both men and women can be targets. Obsessors may be completely rational in other areas of their lives or may be involved in other driven behaviors. These behaviors can range from alcoholism, drug addiction, or compulsive gambling to less publicized compulsions like workaholism or rigid perfectionism. Anyone can be an obsessor.

Likewise, there are no rules about what kinds of people get singled out as targets. Some targets encourage their obsessive lover, others bluntly refuse all contact. Some targets initially share their lover's passion, others reject it out of hand. Some targets are married to their obsessor, others barely know him or her. The only thing all targets have in common is an unwanted, tireless pursuer.

The Myth of the Ultimate Passion

Popular culture has long cultivated a romantic fascination for obsessive love. In the miniseries "Napoleon and Josephine" there is a wonderfully erotic scene during which Armand Assante (Napoleon) expresses the power of his love for Jacqueline Bisset (Josephine) by telling her, "You are my obsession." A popular perfume uses the same line in its TV ads to promise a shortcut to passion and romance for its users. In the best-selling book *Presumed Innocent* (and in the subsequent movie), the main character still longs for the hot sexuality of his obsessive love affair, even after his lover's death. Even such movies as *Play Misty for Me*, *Star 80*, and *Fatal Attraction*, which present a black and psychotic portrait of obsessive love, still manage to paint obsession as a state of unsurpassable passion.

Compared to obsession, all other love seems humdrum and mundane. Obsessive love appears to be a sultry, seductive world of heightened emotionality and transcendent sexuality. Movies, television, advertisements, popular songs—they all collude to persuade us that love is not real unless it is all-consuming. Even when obsessive love goes sour, no matter how much fictionalized lovers may suffer, the underlying message is that it was still the most intense experience they—or we—will ever know. These lovers seem to have found some source of emotional fuel to keep the fires of passion burning long past the point at which most real relationships cool down.

Obsessive love appears to be the ultimate passion, but this romanticized view obscures the dark side of obsession. In the real world, obsessive lovers ride the crest of exhilarating hope and heightened sensuality, but they inevitably pay for their unreal expectations with disappointment, emptiness, and desperation.

For targets, obsessive love may at first seem flattering and even exciting, but it inevitably becomes suffocating. Once that happens, the target's life often disintegrates into emotional turmoil, anxiety, powerlessness, and fear of harassment. Many targets literally become hostages of unwanted, oppressive devotion.

Obsessive Love:
A Contradiction in Terms

In reality, obsessive love has little to do with love at all—it has to do with longing. Longing is wanting something you don't have. Even when obsessive lovers are in a relationship, they don't have enough of what they want. They always long for more love, more attention, more commitment, more reassurance. No matter how promising the relationship may seem in the beginning, the insatiable demanding nature of obsession will drive most targets away. No matter how loving obsessive lovers may feel, they are controlled by their own needs and desires, often at the expense of the needs and desires of their target.

Healthy love aspires to trust, caring, and mutual respect. Obsessive love, on the other hand, is dominated by fear, possessiveness, and jealousy. Obsessive love is volatile and sometimes even dangerous. Ultimately, it never satisfies, it never nourishes, and it rarely feels good.

Are You an Obsessive Lover?

I certainly don't mean to label every intense, romantic relationship as obsessive. I'm an extremely romantic person myself. I'm a pushover for a candlelit dinner, a beautiful opera, or an evening of dancing. In the first bloom of passion I—like almost everyone else—go through a stage that seems very much like obsessive love. It is possible to become very preoccupied with a new lover without being driven by obsession.

But obsessive lovers never outgrow that state of preoccupation. Their world becomes increasingly narrow as they neglect family, friends, and activities that were previously important to them in order to focus all of their attention on their lover. And as their world narrows, their need for their lover increases accordingly. Should their lover not continue to reciprocate their feelings, the blow is unbearable. Rejection is the obsessor's ultimate nightmare.

When confronted with the loss or growing disinterest of a lover, obsessors do not let go. Instead, they grow more desperate for their target's love. This is key to understanding obsession:

Rejection is the trigger of obsessive love.

Obsessive lovers are so caught up in the maelstrom of their passions that they simply refuse to accept when a relationship is over.

Many of you already know that you are obsessive. Others of you may be in a lot of pain over a relationship, and may even be appalled by your own behavior, but haven't yet clarified for yourself what may really be going on. To help you sort out whether you are obsessive in your relationship with a lover, ex-lover, or acquaintance, I have developed the following checklist.

Some of these questions may hit a nerve and make you feel understandably embarrassed, guilty, sad, or angry. Please hang in there if this happens. The discomfort is a positive sign that something is being stirred up inside you and being brought to the surface. Once you know what it is you can choose to do something about it.

1. Do you constantly yearn for someone who is not physically or emotionally available to you?

2. Do you live for the day when this person will be available to you?

3. Do you believe that if you want this person enough he or she will have to love you?

4. Do you believe that if you pursue this person hard enough (or in the right way) he or she will have to accept you?

5. When you are rejected, does it drive you only to want this person more?

6. If you are repeatedly rejected, does your excitement about this person turn to brooding or rage?

7. Do you feel like a victim because this person won't give you what you want?

8. Is your preoccupation with this person so intense that it affects your eating and sleeping habits or your ability to work?

9. Do you believe that this person is the only one who can make your life worthwhile?

10. Do you find yourself calling this person incessantly, often at odd hours, or waiting long hours for him or her to call you?

11. Do you show up unannounced at this person's home or office?

12. Do you check up on where this person is supposed to be and whom he or she is with? Have you ever secretly followed this person?

13. Have you crossed the line to vandalism or even violence against this person or against yourself?

If you answered "yes" to three or more of these questions, you are an obsessive lover. But don't despair—obsessive love is not a genetic flaw but a way you and a lot of other people learned to try and meet normal needs for loving and being loved. You *can* overcome obsession. Anything learned can be unlearned.

Before you can free yourself from the demons of obsessive love you must recognize how much control they've been exerting over your life. I know this is easier said than done. Obsession creates its own shell of denial and confusion and then hides inside. But I promise you that this recognition will help you make positive changes in your life.

(NOTE: If you answered "yes" to the last checklist

question, in addition to reading this book, you *must* seek professional help immediately, before you permanently harm yourself or someone else.)

Are You the Target of Obsession?

If you are in a troubled relationship or if you are the object of someone's unwanted attentions, the first step toward dealing effectively with your situation is to determine whether your lover or admirer is in fact obsessive. The following checklist will help you make that determination. Once you've made it, you'll be able to adopt appropriate strategies for taking back control of your life.

1. Do you feel suffocated by your partner's behavior?

2. Does someone you have discouraged try repeatedly to convince you that you don't know your own feelings or desires, that you really love him or her?

3. Does an ex-lover or ex-spouse refuse to believe that it's over and continue to pursue you despite your objections?

4. Do you receive *unwanted* phone calls, letters, presents, or visits from this person?

5. Is this person's pursuit of you creating so much anxiety in your life that it affects your physical or emotional well-being or your ability to concentrate on work?

6. When you reject this person, does it make him or her more desperate to have you?

7. When you reject this person, does he or she brood or become angry?

8. Does this person check up on your whereabouts and the people you see? Have you caught him or her following you?

9. Are you afraid to leave your house because this person may be waiting for you?

10. Do you feel like a hostage to this person's pursuit?

11. Are you afraid that this person may hurt you or become self-destructive?

12. Has this person threatened violence or become violent?

If you've answered "yes" to even one of these questions, you are most likely the target of obsessive love. While some of you may find an obsessor's unwanted attentions merely annoying, others may feel smothered by an obsessor's oppression and mood swings. Still others may be in real danger and mustn't underestimate that possibility. With this book you will gain a clearer understanding of your situation and learn ways to begin to work your way out.

What Can This Book Do for You?

Obsessive love has many faces—from the nurse who couldn't do her job because of incessant sexual fantasies about a married doctor at work, to the husband who stalked his faithful wife day and night to be sure she wasn't cheating, to the newly married producer whose former lover, in a pathetic attempt to win him back, showed up at his apartment naked underneath her coat, to the gay woman who was coerced into a sexual affair by the woman who was her supervisor at work, to the woman who miscarried when she was thrown down the stairs by her estranged husband.

If you know that you are, or suspect that you might be, an obsessor, I want to help you get past your pain, confusion, and anxiety.

In this book I will give you specific new techniques and strategies that will allow you to regain control of your emotions, rather than having them control you. I know some of you are thinking "that's impossible," but I assure you it isn't. You can learn to reason, to perceive, and to make rational judgments without being misguided by your obsession. You can learn to relate to other people in less desperate and driven ways. By confronting the source of your obsession, you can significantly lessen your need to possess or be possessed by another human being in order to feel whole.

If you are the target of someone's obsessive love, this book will reassure you that you are not alone and show you how to reestablish some normalcy in your life. The people you will meet in these pages will help you understand what you're dealing with and, in some cases, what you may be doing to inadvertently encourage your obsessor's attentions. You will learn to face the difficult decisions you must make to put a stop to your obsessor's invasive behavior. This book offers specific communication, behavioral, and legal strategies to enable you to free yourself from your obsessor's oppression, whether it is merely annoying or actually dangerous.

Though obsessors and targets may appear to have different problems, they share a strong sense of powerlessness over their lives. The obsessor's life is dominated by seemingly uncontrollable impulses, passions, and fantasies, while the target's life is often dominated by the need to escape oppressive and relentless pursuit. With this book, I hope to help both obsessors and their targets escape from the intensity, the pain, the chaos, the yearning, the powerlessness, and the power of obsessive love.

PART ONE

Obsessive
Lovers

ONE

The One Magic Person

I can't believe I did all those things. The phone calls, the drive-bys, the letters, the tantrums, the threats . . . it just wasn't me. But it took me so long to get him out of my head. The way he looked, the way he smelled, the way he touched me . . . he drove me crazy.

—*Margaret*

It was Margaret's last day of therapy. She had worked hard to break free from the painful obsessive patterns that had been plaguing her for the past three years, and she had largely succeeded. She was a very different woman from the depressed, desperate, volatile Margaret I had first met a year and a half earlier.

Margaret is a willowy, red-haired, thirty-four-year-old divorcée who works as a paralegal with a large law firm. She came to see me because her preoccupation with Phil—a lover who was clearly not interested in a monogamous relationship—was making her feel like she was losing

19

control of both her personal and her professional life. She was becoming increasingly short-tempered with her ten-year-old son. She was making careless mistakes at work. And she was alienating her friends by avoiding them, not only because she wanted to be available in case Phil called, but also because her friends were virtually unanimous in their criticism of Phil.

The Thrill of a New Romance

Margaret met Phil about six years after she divorced her husband. She had been dating on and off but had been unable to find anyone with whom she was interested in establishing a serious relationship. After six years, she was getting pretty discouraged. She hated the bar scene. She had already met most of the single men her friends knew, but nothing had developed. She had even gone to a video dating service—both the dates she'd had as a result had been disappointing.

Margaret met Phil at the courthouse while she was assisting her boss in the defense of an embezzlement suspect. Phil was a police officer, testifying in a highly publicized murder case. Margaret first saw him in the cafeteria during the lunch break.

Margaret

This gorgeous hunk sat down across from me and it was lust at first sight, which hadn't happened to me in years. We started talking and he asked me out that same night. I remember coming home after that date and as soon as I closed the door I broke into this little victory dance. Within a week we were seeing each other almost every night. It was an incredible

high. During the day he'd call me at work and I'd
get the most delicious butterflies in my stomach just
hearing his voice. I was really in heaven.

Even though Margaret was describing the beginnings of
what was to become an intensely obsessive relationship,
there is nothing in her description that could not just as
easily describe the beginnings of some healthy relationships. Most of us relish the giddy feelings that Margaret
talked about. When we first fall in love, we feel like we're
walking on air. Flowers smell more fragrant, music sounds
more beautiful, the sky seems bluer, our pulse quickens,
our mood soars.

These heightened sensations are not just imaginary. Physical changes *are* triggered in our bodies by romantic feelings, hopes, and fantasies. Our heartbeat quickens, we
become flushed, our adrenaline pumps, we experience
hormonal changes, and our brains release endorphins—the
body's natural opiate. As a result of all this chemical
activity, love is a physical state as well as a state of mind.

The Idealized Lover

In the thrill and passion of a new romance, it is only
natural to see a lover through rose-colored glasses. We go
out of our way to see only what we want to see, filtering
our perceptions through romantic expectations and dreams.
This optimistic filtering of reality is called "idealization."

You can see idealization at work in Margaret's description of Phil.

Margaret
After a couple weeks, he told me he was in love
with me. I was ecstatic. He was so perfect. I felt like

my life was finally rounding out. Not only did I have a job I liked, and my son seemed to be doing okay, but now, finally, I had this fantastic guy. The sex was great, the talk was great, he cooked these romantic meals, he even fixed my car for me. I felt totally safe with him, not just physically but emotionally. I'd finally found the man I was going to spend the rest of my life with. He made me feel like I was more than I'd ever been before, like I was finally a whole person. And I knew there was no one else on earth who could make me feel that way.

Margaret jumped to a lot of conclusions about Phil simply because he was a good lover and fun to be with. She really didn't know much about him. It would have been impossible for her to have learned much about his character or his past relationships in the two short weeks of passion that they'd shared. Yet she was convinced that he was "perfect," that he would make a lifetime commitment to her, and that he—and only he—had the power to make her feel like "a whole person."

I certainly don't mean to imply that Margaret did anything unusual. We all idealize. This is especially easy to do in the early stages of a relationship, since new lovers are typically on their best behavior. We all put on our best face when we are attracted to a new person. We make a special effort to be as alluring, charming, witty, sympathetic, flattering, and accommodating as we can. This is part of our mating ritual.

However, while this behavior might reveal certain facets of our personality, it can't possibly tell the whole story. We all have our moody days, our petty jealousies, our knee-jerk reactions, our rigid opinions, and our unattractive habits. And we certainly don't want to reveal any of these to a new lover.

In the heat of a new relationship, as we downplay our own shortcomings, we don't give much thought to the fact that our lover is doing the same. Under these conditions idealization can't help but thrive.

THE ONE AND ONLY

In healthy relationships, idealization helps lovers believe that—maybe—they have found the person of their dreams. But healthy lovers give themselves a safety net called reality. They hope their relationship will work out but also recognize that it may not.

Obsessive lovers, on the other hand, work without this net as they struggle for balance on the high wire of romantic expectations. In the heightened reality of obsessive passion there is no room for doubt. Obsessive lovers live by an unshakable credo:

This is the
one—and only one—magic person
who can meet all my needs.

Obsessive lovers truly believe—sometimes without realizing it—that their "One Magic Person" alone can make them feel happy and fulfilled, solve all their problems, give them the passion they've yearned for, and make them feel more wanted and loved than they've ever felt before. With all this power, the One Magic Person becomes more than a lover—he or she becomes a necessity of life.

There are no prerequisites for the One Magic Person. It is not necessary that he or she be especially attractive, intelligent, witty, or successful or possess any other qualities we usually associate with desirability.

In fact, some obsessors fall in love with deeply troubled or even addicted lovers. These obsessors are irresistibly drawn into relationships by a deep-seated need to be needed and a belief that they alone can save their lover (as we'll see in Chapter Four).

Obsessors' fantasies and expectations about their One Magic Person may have little to do with who that person really is and everything to do with what they themselves need and how they expect that person to fulfill those needs. No one really knows with absolute certainty why one person has such a powerful effect on another. But something about the One Magic Person clearly taps into the individual needs and yearnings that lie deeply embedded in the obsessive lover's unconscious.

The Mental Sculptor

In healthy relationships, as lovers grow more emotionally intimate, they begin to feel secure enough to reveal themselves as real people with shortcomings. The romantic expectations of these lovers naturally evolve to reflect the changes that this increased honesty brings to their relationship. If they don't like what they find, they have the choice to leave the relationship.

But leaving is not an option for obsessive lovers. No matter what the reality may be, they create the relationship they want in their minds. Like mental sculptors, they shape their expectations, using wishes, rather than truth, as their clay. These expectations are remarkably resistent to the inevitable hammer blows of reality.

My friend Don is a regular Rodin when it comes to mental sculpting. Don is a stocky, balding, soft-spoken, forty-two-year-old attorney whose James Joyce glasses give him a distinctly academic look. He was born and raised in Georgia and still retains a charming trace of a southern drawl. When he heard I was working on this book, he told me the story of his torturous, on-again-off-again, five-year-long obsessive affair with a married woman.

Don

I met her when I was in my last year of law school. I was working part-time in a bookstore and she came in—the most gracious, elegant, gorgeous woman I had ever seen. I was captivated from the moment I saw her. My first response was "God, I would love to be involved with her." As fate had it, I was talking to a friend when she walked over and just kind of entered into the conversation. She had this gorgeous British accent and this beautiful translucent skin and these eyes . . . she just knocked me out. We talked for a while, then my friend left and I suddenly had this impulse to ask if I could take her to dinner. She looked at me, and said, "I'm sorry, but I'm married." Normally, that would have been the end of it, but this time the words didn't matter to me. I couldn't just let her walk out of my life. I needed to find a way to spend time with her, no matter what. So I asked her if she'd be willing to join me for a cup of coffee, just to talk. When she said "okay," I thought I'd died and gone to heaven.

Don fell in love at first sight, just like in the movies. But there was a problem—from the first moments of their meeting, Don knew Cynthia was married. In other circumstances this would have discouraged him, but Don was convinced that he had found his One Magic Person. So he began to mold his own reality to eclipse the magnitude of this stumbling block.

Don

We began to have lunch together pretty regularly, and we'd talk and talk and talk. She was very British, so she wasn't used to discussing her feelings openly, but that only intrigued me more. Then one day we took a walk on the beach. The sun was shining, the water was shimmering. . . . I looked at her and I just . . . leaned over and kissed her. It was the most amazing moment of my life. After that, all I wanted to do was be with her, all I could do was think about her. As we got to know each other a little better, she finally began to talk more about herself and her marriage.

Cynthia had come to the United States when she was eighteen to study piano at Juilliard. A year later, she had met her husband, a physician fifteen years older than she. They married, and she gave up her studies to move to the West Coast with him.

Don

She'd always resented giving up the music, but she never talked to her husband about it. She never talked to him about anything. She said she'd never been able to open up to him like she could with me. She said no man had ever been so tender and warm and caring and sincere with her as I was. Here was the woman I'd dreamed of since I was a teenager, and she was making me feel like I was the only man for her. I knew it was only a matter of time before she'd leave her husband, even though she never talked about it. I started checking the paper to see how much it would cost to get a bigger apartment when she was ready to move in with me. I even asked around for the name of a good divorce attorney so I could give her a reference when she was ready.

At this point in their relationship, Don had only established a platonic friendship with Cynthia. They had ventured as far as a kiss on the beach, but that was it. But from this one kiss and a few tender words, Don had become convinced that he and Cynthia were destined to be together.

Don began to fantasize extensively about what their life together would be like. First he would help her through her divorce and settle into an apartment with her. She would continue working as a travel agent until he finished law school. Then he would be able to support them both, freeing her to quit her job and go back to her music. He pictured her sitting in their living room at the piano, beside a blazing fire, bewitching him with the sensual strains of Chopin and Brahms. He saw them jetting to London to visit her family, then hopping over to Paris to share a bottle of young Beaujolais on the banks of the Seine. And always, always, these scenes would culminate in a frenzy of passionate lovemaking.

Cynthia gave Don no indication that she was inclined to leave her husband, but this in no way prevented him from developing the conviction that she would. Don's extravagant fantasy constructions reduced the fact of her marriage to little more than a minor annoyance.

WORSHIPERS FROM AFAR

Most mental sculptors have at least some romantic encouragement from which to springboard their fantasies, even if it's only a few dates. But it is not necessary for a target to encourage his or her obsessor. In some extreme cases, the One Magic Person may not even know the obsessor's name.

Laurie, a registered nurse in a large midwestern hospital, called in to my radio program one morning in tears.

She told me she was in her early thirties and had left an abusive marriage two years earlier. She hadn't been involved with anyone since. But now she was madly in love with a doctor at the hospital where she worked—a doctor who may have seen her in the hallways but otherwise had no direct contact with her.

Laurie

I don't know what to do. This feels so crazy . . . he doesn't even know I exist. I'm just one of a million nurses to him. He's gorgeous, he's charming, he's witty, he's perfect. I can't get my mind off him. I think about making him candlelight dinners; I think about us naked together, about him putting his arms around me, holding me, making love to me. . . . And the worst part of it is, I know he's happily married. The other day his wife came in to have lunch with him and I couldn't stop crying. My supervisor finally told me to go home early. Every time I go out with somebody else, I have a horrible time because I just think of him all the time. But I could never bring myself to ask him out, you know, for a drink or even a cup of coffee or something. I mean he's married; it just wouldn't be right. I know it's stupid, but some nights I just can't stop crying about it. I'm losing so much weight that my friends are all worried about me. It's like this guy has taken over my life and he doesn't even know it.

Laurie's romance was sculpted *entirely* from imaginary components. She had no reason to expect that her fantasy lover would ever be even remotely interested in her. In fact, all the evidence pointed to the contrary. Yet, although she knew she had no hope of a relationship, she still remained totally fixated on her One Magic Person.

I call people like Laurie "worshipers from afar," obsessive lovers who have no romantic or sexual involvement with the targets of their obsession. These obsessive lovers build elaborate relationships in their minds, sometimes with targets whom they've never even met (often movie stars or other celebrities).

While this form of obsessive love may sound benign, its power should not be underestimated. It can be just as destructive to an obsessor's emotional well-being as any other type of obsessive love and, if left unchecked, can escalate into obsessive behavior, drastically affecting the lives of both the obsessor and the target.

The Power of Great Sex

Worshipers from afar are the exceptions, not the rule. Most obsessors *do* have some sort of relationship with their One Magic Person, ranging from infrequent dating to marriage. But whatever the nature of the relationship, sex almost always plays a major part. And obsessive lovers often report incredible sexual experiences with their target.

Margaret

The first time we slept together I felt like I was discovering sex for the first time. He actually asked me what I liked *while he was doing it*, which no one had ever done with me before. By the time we finished he knew everything about me, and I mean *everything*. He did things to me with his tongue that made me feel like I was going to *explode*. We kept going for like three hours, and it just kept getting better. And it was like that every time.

Margaret's heightened emotions, romantic fantasies, and extreme expectations helped stoke her sexual encounters with Phil to a fever pitch. The intoxicating pleasure she experienced from their hot-blooded lovemaking led her to idealize Phil even more. This, in turn, made him seem increasingly alluring and irreplaceable to her, which turned up the sexual heat still further.

This steamy cycle of sex, idealization, and enchantment hooks obsessors even more deeply into their relationships. Obsessors view their torrid sexuality as some sort of cosmic sign that they and their lovers were made for each other.

Margaret

There was no way this was just another guy, we were definitely meant to be together. I felt like we were melting into each other when we made love, it brought us so close together. I mean, it was the only time I really *felt* his love . . . he'd always clam up when I'd try to *talk* about our relationship.

Margaret believed that she and Phil had a close, loving relationship even though he never verbally expressed his feelings for her. She was convinced that the intensity of his sexuality was his way of expressing the intensity of his feelings. Only a man who truly loved her could make her feel so fantastic in bed. As so many obsessive lovers do, Margaret was confusing sexual passion for love, and in so doing, she was setting herself up for a painful fall.

From Romance to Rejection

The feelings that Margaret found so delicious were no different from the feelings that many of us experience during the heady tidal wave of new love. Because of this, a potentially obsessive relationship is virtually impossible to spot in the early stages. Almost all of us become preoccupied by thoughts and fantasies of a new lover at the beginning of a romantic relationship. Almost all of us disrupt our lives to spend as much time as possible with him or her. This mild form of obsession is perfectly healthy as long as it is generally a temporary phase and the feelings are reciprocal.

But when lovers are truly obsessive, there's nothing temporary about their preoccupation. And if, after the first flush of romance, their target begins to withdraw, falls in love with someone else, or simply walks away, their preoccupation fans their feelings of rejection into an emotional inferno.

REJECTION: THE OBSESSOR'S NIGHTMARE

The difference between healthy and obsessive lovers becomes apparent when rejection enters the picture. If healthy lovers are rejected, they generally grieve the loss of the relationship and get on with their lives. But obsessive lovers become flooded with panic, insecurity, fear, and pain, which drive them to resist tooth and nail the deterioration of the relationship.

Rejection unleashes obsession.

Rejection can be blatant or it can be implied, it can be real or imagined, current or anticipated, constant or intermittent. It can strike swiftly and decisively, like a flash flood, or it can be slow and subtle, like the Chinese water torture. Any form of rejection can unleash obsessive love.

REJECTION ANXIETY

Nobody likes to be rejected. It hurts a lot. But it happens to almost everyone at least once. Rejection is the risk we all take when we open ourselves up to a new relationship. Most of us feel occasional insecurities about the possibility of a lover leaving. I call this "rejection anxiety."

As healthy relationships progress, and lovers develop trust in one another, this anxiety tends to diminish. Unfortunately, most obsessors, if they are in a relationship, live with an almost constant fear that their One Magic Person will leave them.

Despite her excitement, Margaret was in a state of anxiety from the very beginning of her relationship with Phil. When he agreed to move in with her after three months together, she hoped this change would make her feel more secure about his commitment. But, to her dismay, just the opposite occurred.

Margaret

One night he called to tell me he'd be out late playing poker with the guys. He didn't roll in till three in the morning, and the whole time I kept thinking, why does he want to be with them and not me? Was he getting bored with me? Was he getting antsy? I tried to stuff my feelings, but it really scared me. I started asking him every time he'd leave the house if he really loved me. I knew it bugged him but I couldn't help myself—I had to hear him say it. I was so much in love with this man. I started hating it when he had to go to work; I wanted to be with him every second. When he wasn't there I was terrified that he wouldn't come home.

When Margaret's rejection anxiety kicked into high gear, her need for reassurance became insatiable. She felt threatened by anything and everything that took Phil away from her. She became clingy and demanding, which only increased her fear because she knew such behavior would alienate Phil. But she couldn't help herself. Her obsessive tendencies, brought to the surface by rejection anxiety, had taken on a life of their own. Margaret's better judgment was no match for the power of her obsessive love.

Because obsessors believe that their emotional survival depends on the success of their relationship, they often become hypersensitive to every nuance of their lover's behavior—whether it be a changed tone of voice, a broken date, or a new hobby. Anything short of their target's complete devotion and attention can make an obsessor feel shut out in the cold.

In an attempt to protect against rejection they fear, many obsessors try to second-guess what kind of person their lover wants them to be. They agonize over how they look, how they speak, how they perform in bed, how intelligent they appear—twisting themselves into pretzels in their attempt to be desirable to their One Magic Person. Anything to avoid rejection.

TIME DOESN'T HELP

Rejection anxiety is not limited to new relationships. My client Hal struggled with it for almost two decades. Hal was a slightly built forty-two-year-old dentist with thinning brown hair and a disarming smile. He came to see me because his obsession with his own wife had just about destroyed his marriage.

Hal and Fran had been married for nineteen years. Hal had always felt insecure in their relationship. Fran was so witty and outgoing that people always sparked to her, while he, on the other hand, tended to be shy and with-drawn. Hal had always worried that Fran would enchant some man who would persuade her to leave her marriage, but through the years he had managed to keep his fears in check. Then their only daughter entered high school and Fran returned to her former occupation as a real estate agent. With Fran out in the world, Hal's rejection anxiety began to escalate dramatically.

As he talked about his fears, Hal played nervously with his wedding ring.

Hal

As soon as she started the job I noticed she was talking a lot about all these guys she was working with. And then she started getting clients, and if it was a guy and she'd be meeting him in all these empty houses all day. . . . It was like fingernails on a blackboard. I couldn't stand it. I was sure she'd be taking off with one of these guys any day.

Hal had no reason to suspect that Fran was doing anything in the least bit inappropriate, or that she intended to. He was being tortured by possibilities that were not borne out by any evidence.

But Hal didn't need evidence. Like Margaret, Hal sub-stituted fears for evidence. And as a result of his fears that Fran would leave him, he created an atmosphere of suspi-cion and jealousy at home that ultimately drove an emo-tional wedge between Fran and himself.

For obsessive lovers, *fear* of rejection can have much the same effect as *actual* rejection. In this way, rejection anxiety often leads obsessive lovers to behavior that angers their target and provokes the very rejection obsessors fear. All too often, the obsessor's rejection anxiety becomes a self-fulfilling prophecy.

SPORADIC REJECTION

Rejection isn't always constant. When targets aren't sure about their feelings they often act rejecting one minute and loving the next. Like rejection anxiety, this kind of sporadic rejection is just as powerful a trigger for obsessors as is the blunt "I-never-want-to-see-you-again" variety.

Don experienced sporadic rejection more and more as his relationship with Cynthia developed. After their first kiss, their attraction escalated swiftly into an intense affair. They would meet three or four times a week at Don's apartment for furtive afternoon lovemaking. But Don was becoming increasingly restless with this arrangement. He wanted more than a part-time affair—he wanted to make a life with his One Magic Person. And he was sure Cynthia wanted the same thing. After all, she professed her love for him.

Don

I waited patiently for two years for her to leave her husband, but nothing changed. I kept telling myself, well, if I'm just patient, if I'm just patient . . . but she wouldn't leave him. I felt like I was on a torture rack, being torn apart. One minute she was mine, the next she was with him. One week I'd feel us growing closer, the next week I'd feel like she wanted to end it. I couldn't stand it. One day she'd be making love to me, and the next day she'd be making excuses about why she couldn't see me. I didn't know if I was coming or going, and it was driving me crazy.

By bouncing back and forth between being loving one moment and rejecting the next, Cynthia was giving Don what in my business we call "intermittent reinforcement." Perhaps she was being manipulative in order to keep both men, perhaps she couldn't make up her mind, perhaps she was using Don to prop up her marriage, or perhaps she simply lacked the strength to leave her husband. Whatever her motives, for Don the net result was the same. The good times gave him encouraging glimpses of what he yearned for while the bad times escalated his rejection anxiety.

Sporadic rejection keeps obsessors on an emotional see-saw, teetering between the dread of life without their One Magic Person and the refusal to accept the possibility their relationship might not work out.

SHORT-TERM PASSION, LONG-TERM PAIN

In Don's case, the affair that fed his obsessive fantasies continued several years. For many obsessive lovers, though, a few nights of passion are enough to persuade them the relationship is real. If their target loses interest after a few dates, they react as if they have been dumped after a long-term relationship.

This happened to my client Nora, a stunning black-haired, green-eyed twenty-nine-year-old who manages an exclusive dress shop in Beverly Hills. Nora came from an extremely troubled background. She became pregnant at fourteen and dropped out of school to be a single mother. To support herself and her child, she held down two jobs, making it almost impossible for her to manage a social life. Later, she quit her night job and enrolled in evening classes to get her high school diploma. Though she had gone on occasional dates during these years, she had not been involved in a relationship.

When Nora's daughter entered high school and became more independent, Nora began to feel increasingly lonely.

She put the word out to friends that she was ready for a serious relationship. Several of her friends set her up on blind dates, and it was on one of these that she met Tom.

Nora and Tom went on a few dates and really seemed to hit it off. Nora called the friend who had introduced them and told her that she was convinced she was going to spend the rest of her life with Tom.

Nora came into therapy soon thereafter. She had not seen Tom in five weeks and was beside herself with confusion and depression.

Nora

He's the only thing I can think about. I sit at home and eat and wait for the telephone to ring. I mean, when I met him, he made me feel so good, I really thought this was it. I slept with him on the first night and it was wonderful. I felt like our bodies just fit together like yin and yang. He said he felt the same way. I just knew this was it. It *had* to be. We went out a couple more times and everything seemed to just keep heating up. And then he just stopped calling. Just like that. I left a few messages on his machine, but he never returned my calls. How could he treat me like this after all we had?

What they "had" were four dates and some good sex, but Nora had become convinced that Tom was her One Magic Person. When he stopped calling and refused to return her calls, she truly felt like she had lost a meaningful relationship. Like Margaret, Nora had mistaken sex for love.

It is astounding how little real emotional connection some obsessive lovers need in order to turn a few crumbs of affection into a whole loaf. For Nora, the pain of rejection was every bit as great after four dates as it might have been after four years. Clearly, the depth of her pain was not determined by the depth of her relationship. It was determined by the depth of her obsession. Obsessive love distorts time and magnifies feelings, creating a reality all its own.

Denying the Undeniable

When rejection darkens the landscape of the obsessive lover's reality, he or she invariably seeks refuge in denial. Denial is one of our most basic, potent defense mechanisms. In its most extreme form, denial can be used to totally negate reality—to believe that the truth isn't true. But most people use less extreme forms of denial:

1. They *rationalize* what is happening with seemingly reasonable excuses or explanations.

2. They *minimize* the importance of what is happening.

Denial may seem to protect us from painful feelings, but it doesn't make them go away—it just helps us avoid them temporarily. You can only kid yourself for so long. Generally, the longer you deny the truth, the more pain it causes until it finally becomes impossible to ignore. Denial always turns out to be self-defeating.

RATIONALIZING REJECTION

Rationalization is the most common form of denial. It is a process of self-persuasion. If confronted by rejection, obsessors can be extremely creative in coming up with rationalizations to excuse, dismiss, or justify their lover's behavior.

Here are a few examples of rationalizations I've known obsessive lovers to use:

"I know he's seeing other women, but they don't mean anything to him. I'm the only one he really cares about."

"She keeps hanging up on me, but it's only because she can't handle how strong her feelings are for me."

"I know he doesn't act very loving, but he will once I get him to stop drinking."

"I haven't heard from him in three weeks. He must be working really long hours."

"She moved in with this other guy, but I know she's just doing it to make me jealous."

Though this form of denial is by no means unique to obsessive lovers, obsessors tend to continue trying to rationalize away the trauma of rejection long after it is evident that their relationship has gone sour. Nora was especially creative at this.

Nora

Maybe he'll call one day and say, "I was waiting just to see what you would do to get me." It's like a game. He's putting me to a test and one day I'll pick up the phone and he'll say, "Okay, let's get married." Because I know that that's got to be on his mind. I know him better than he knows himself.

Nora's rationalizations were keeping her from doing what she needed to do to deal with her pain, disappointment, and frustration. Instead of facing the reality of Tom's rejection, she was clinging to a stubborn belief:

He really loves me, he just doesn't know it.

Obsessive lovers often believe that they know far better than their targets how their targets really feel: They believe that if they can just prove the depth and intensity of their love, their targets will awaken to their "true feelings" and reciprocate that love. Using rationalization, obsessive lovers can reduce a target's rejection to a temporary aberration.

MINIMIZING THROUGH SELECTIVE FOCUS

If you say to an obsessor, "It's over. I don't want to see you anymore, and I don't want you to try to contact me. You're a terrific person, but it's just not working," the obsessor will typically only hear, "You're a terrific person." By extracting the one positive phrase of a clearly rejecting statement, the obsessor drastically minimizes the negative overall meaning of the message. I call this kind of minimizing "selective focusing." Obsessors resort to it all the time.

Don

After two and a half years, she finally *did* leave her husband. I thought, "This is it, she'll move in with me." But she didn't. In fact, she seemed to want to see me less. I just couldn't understand it. She'd make excuses for not coming over: she was tired or she had some problem at work. It was driving me crazy that she hadn't divorced him, she had only separated. What if she went back to him? What if she found somebody else? I'd grovel in these thoughts for a day or two and then I'd think, "She just needs time to adjust. She's just scared. She just needs time." On Monday I'd be ready to throw myself off a cliff, then on Tuesday I'd convince myself that if I just stood back and waited patiently, she would come to me. After all, she'd never met a man who offered her as much as me—those were her own words.

Cynthia's words became a lifeline for Don. He hung on to her bits and pieces of encouragement for dear life in order to minimize the conflicting messages of her inconsistent behavior.

Cynthia moved back in with her husband two weeks after she had moved out. Don was devastated. But then she started to heat up the relationship with Don once again. His hope for a future with her was renewed, buoyed by his denial of the significance of her return to her husband. Don carried on his affair with Cynthia for another two years, during which time he continued to bounce back and forth between denial and despair. When he was in despair, he saw Cynthia's marriage as an insurmountable obstacle. When he was in denial, he minimized this obstacle as a temporary inconvenience.

Margaret took this sort of tunnel vision to an extreme.

Margaret

Phil started staying out late a couple times a week, and then one day, he just up and moved out. I couldn't believe it. He had a friend come over with a truck and they just threw all his stuff in the back and he was gone. Just as easily as he moved in, he moved out. He said he just needed some space, and that really hurt me because . . . what did he need space from? Me. But at least he kept coming over to spend the night once or twice a week, so I knew he still cared.

Margaret minimized the fact that sex had become the sum total of her relationship. Phil was clearly losing interest in her, but she just focused on the one aspect of the relationship that still worked.

In their crusade to hold on to their One Magic Person, obsessors spotlight any fragment of hope that their lover still cares about them. At the same time, they push into the shadowy background any evidence to the contrary. They are masters of denial.

Obsessive lovers have enormous magical expectations for how their target will fill up their lives. These expectations are often fortified by fantastic sex and intense initial passion. Obsessors become so invested in their relationship that when they experience rejection, they truly believe they will never be loved again, they will never love again, they will never be happy, they will never be whole. Because of this, obsessors simply refuse to let go when their One Magic Person pulls away. They *cannot* let go. Holding on to or recapturing their rejecting lover is much more than a question of desire for obsessive lovers. It is a question of survival.

Two

Opening the Floodgates

I kept calling into the night, but she wouldn't answer the phone. So I just kept going at it on and on, over and over. Like a robot. Redialing and redialing and redialing and redialing. . . . I had to talk to her or it was the end of the world for me.

—*Robert*

Rejection can open floodgates of emotional pain for anyone—the pain of feeling unwanted, the pain of feeling humiliated, the pain of feeling inadequate, and the pain of reliving past rejections.

Pain—whether physical or emotional—is nature's way of telling us that something needs to be fixed. The natural reaction to pain is to "do something" about it. Healthy lovers do something *constructive* about the pain of rejection. Though the process may not be easy, they acknowledge their pain, recognize that they are in a no-win situation, and find ways to disconnect from their rejecting lover.

But most obsessive lovers cannot disconnect. Instead,

they try to "do something" about their pain by resorting to certain predictable, repetitive behaviors that are either self-punishing, oppressive to their target, or both. They try to escape from the pain they are *feeling* by becoming totally preoccupied with what they are *doing*. This translation of painful feelings into negative behavior is what, in my business, we call "acting out."

Acting Out
Through Self-Punishment

The image of obsessive lovers' behavior that we get from newspapers, films, and television involves intrusions on a target's life and threats or even harm to a target. But many obsessive lovers react to the pain of rejection by unconsciously turning against *themselves*, acting in ways that sabotage their own emotional and often physical well-being.

When Tom stopped calling Nora, for example, her pain was so great that it made her physically ill. And her self-punishing behavior only made matters worse.

Nora

I started hurting on the bottom of my stomach. The pain was unbelievable. It was like, Oh, God, why doesn't he call? I didn't go to work. I just sat home and got depressed and watched the phone. I'd just sit out there and drink wine cooler after wine cooler . . . eat junk, drink wine, eat more, ache more, eat more, drink more . . . all the time thinking about him.

Nora was on an obsessive treadmill. Her ruminations about Tom led to intense emotional pain that she tried to medicate with two favorite remedies of rejected lovers: food and alcohol. Self-punishing obsessors often resort to drinking excessively, overeating or eating poorly, taking drugs, gambling, becoming irritable or inattentive at work, sleeping too much or not enough, neglecting family and friends, and, in extreme cases, even suicide.

Nora's emotional stress probably gave her her stomachache. But that didn't stop her from consuming things that were bound to exacerbate the problem. Nora hoped that the alcohol would blot out the pain and that the pleasure of the junk food would lift her spirits. The effect on her system was hardly surprising, but for Nora, the stomachache was preferable to the heartache.

THE BOOMERANG EFFECT

When I pointed out to Nora how much she was punishing herself, she was confused. Hadn't *Tom* done all the hurting? Why would she want to compound her own misery? I told her that in addition to having to struggle with her *conscious* feelings of sadness and hurt, she was also going through a lot on an *unconscious* level.

Rejection is an insult, an emotional slap in the face. It is a blow to our self-esteem and to our dreams. It is only natural that we react to rejection not only with distress, but with anger. Considering how Nora had been jilted so suddenly and inexplicably, she couldn't help but be angry. Yet she wasn't aware of any anger. What was she doing with it?

I suggested to Nora that she was taking her anger against Tom and turning it inward against herself. And the enormous emotional effort of keeping it suppressed was pulling her into a downward spiral of brooding and depression.

Nora's profound suffering is common for obsessive lovers. Most psychologists call this transformation of anger into depression "acting in." The term "acting" implies behavior, but this type of suffering is not so much behavioral as it is emotional. In fact, I sometimes refer to it as the "boomerang effect," because when we fail to express or work through angry feelings, those feelings boomerang back at us. The anger then burrows into our unconscious, where it camouflages itself like an emotional chameleon, transforming itself into a variety of symptoms, from headaches to exhaustion to depression.

SUFFERING: THE DESPERATE CONNECTION

Some obsessive lovers have a great deal of trouble expressing their anger. Though this is true for obsessors of both sexes, it is especially true for women, who have so often been socialized to believe that showing anger, even in direct and appropriate ways, is unattractive. Like Nora, many women have learned to contain their anger, to suffer it rather than to acknowledge it.

Suffering has a special role in the obsessive drama. For obsessive lovers—both men and women—suffering provides a last tenuous connection to a dead or dying relationship. Suffering allows obsessors to keep their target vividly present in their lives. A relationship may be physically over, but suffering can prevent it from coming to an emotional end. However, in maintaining this kind of connection, the obsessor gains nothing but pain and postpones the possibility of taking steps to move on.

In addition to a minimal connection to the target, suffering also offers obsessive lovers a curious emotional side effect. Nora found that in a strange way her suffering almost made her feel heroic.

Nora

Even when I was really touching bottom, at least I knew I was going through this for love. It made the

whole thing seem so *meaningful*. Like I was some
kind of martyr to the cause of love.

For Nora, as for so many obsessive lovers, the magnitude
of her suffering kept her in touch with the magnitude of
her love. Nora felt secure—almost proud—in the knowl-
edge that no one else could possibly suffer for Tom as
much as she could.

In the beginning of obsessive relationships, obsessors
are nourished by the power of their passion. When rejection deflates that passion, something has to fill the emotional vacuum. Suffering is one of the few states that
generate strong enough emotions to do so.

Though almost all obsessors act out through self-punishing
behaviors and act in through suffering, few obsessors stop
there. These self-defeating responses to rejection affect the
obsessor's life, but they are all too often only a prelude to
more aggressive acting-out behaviors—behaviors that affect the *target's* life. These are the behaviors of obsessive
pursuit.

Obsessive Pursuit

When rejection makes obsessors feel that their lives are
spinning out of control, they usually see only one course
of action: to prevent their relationship from ending or, if it
has ended, to revive it. The goal of obsessive pursuit is to
recapture the interest of the One Magic Person. And when
obsessors attempt to do this, they invariably cross a crucial
line between acting out against themselves and acting out
against someone else.

Pursuit, in and of itself, is not necessarily obsessive.
New lovers often withdraw temporarily, in some cases
because their initial flood of emotion makes them afraid of

getting hurt. In such cases, a little encouraging pursuit may allay their fears. However, this pursuit should be limited to a few attempts. If the person continues to withdraw, finds a new lover or returns to an old one, or otherwise resists efforts to revive the relationship, then it is time to let go, no matter how painful that may be.

But obsessors see letting go as tantamount to jumping off an emotional cliff. In the face of rejection, this leaves obsessive lovers with only one option: to pursue . . . and pursue . . . and pursue.

PURSUIT TACTICS

Obsessors try to salvage relationships by resorting to a variety of pursuit tactics—behaviors that are generally excessive, invasive, frightening, and sometimes dangerous. The most common of these are:

- sending unwelcome gifts, flowers, or letters to the target

- creating excuses to meet with the target

- phoning the target incessantly

- driving repeatedly by the target's home or work place

- showing up unannounced at the target's home or work place

- stalking the target

- threatening to harm themselves or the target

Some of these pursuit tactics may seem relatively benign, but in fact they are *all* exercises in power. Even Jim's seemingly romantic gift to Gloria of six dozen roses was a power trip. He thought he was being loving, but what he was really doing was fighting how powerless he felt against

Gloria's rejection by *forcing* her to think about him. He was muscling his way back into her life. She did not want any contact with him, she did not want any reminders. But he imposed them on her nonetheless. Obsessive lovers use pursuit tactics to assert power where they feel most powerless—in the loss of their One Magic Person.

CREATING EXCUSES

When Margaret's relationship with Phil dwindled to infrequent sexual encounters, she began trying to manipulate him into seeing her more. She resorted to a seemingly harmless pursuit tactic: creating excuses to make contact.

Margaret

I was going to bed at one and I was waking up at four. I had nightmares. I was losing weight. It was like a slow death when I wasn't with him. So I'd find all kinds of excuses to get him to see me. I'd get extra concert tickets, I'd break something in my house and then ask him to fix it, one night I even made up a prowler so he'd come over to check it out. I'd call him at the station, I'd call him at home, I'd try him at his brother's, I'd try him at this bar where he hangs out . . . wherever I thought he'd be. I'd make up some reason for him to come over. There was almost always some reason why he couldn't come, but that never stopped me from trying.

In manufacturing transparent excuses to see Phil, Margaret was single-handedly trying to keep their relationship alive. Though her tactics probably annoyed Phil, they were relatively harmless to him. But they were doing enormous harm to Margaret. She was being repeatedly humiliated and demeaned by her own behavior. She was doing all the initiating, all the chasing. She was doing all the giving, and he wasn't even giving her the satisfaction of taking. She obviously wanted to see him a lot more than he wanted to see her, yet no matter how often Phil turned her down, she kept jockeying for more contact. By creating excuses to see him, she could fight her feelings of powerlessness over a situation that continued to slip away from her.

THE TELEPHONIC LIFELINE

One of the obsessor's most common tools for gaining some contact with an unwilling target is the telephone. I'm not referring to an occasional phone call, but to repetitive, relentless phoning. The telephone is often the only means obsessors have left to hear their target's voice.

Obsessors also use phone calls to prevent the target from ignoring them, to satisfy their need to know the target's whereabouts, and to determine whether the target is with someone else.

Robert, who is thirty-nine years old, is the cousin of a friend of mine. When his cousin told him I was working on this book, he called me for a consultation. Robert was becoming frightened by how much anger he felt toward a woman who had recently broken up with him and refused to see him anymore (for good reason, as it turned out).

Robert is a blond, freckle-faced, all-American-looking man who works as a stereo salesman. Twice divorced, Robert had a history of stormy relationships, none of which lasted more than a few years. From the way he described his past relationships, I suspected that Robert had become obsessive in virtually all of them.

When he came to see me, Robert was in love with a former customer, a medical secretary named Sarah. After an extremely volatile two-year relationship, Sarah had tired of his jealousy and told him she didn't love him anymore. He hadn't believed her. For a month, he'd called her, stopped by her house, and sent letters. To no avail.

Although Sarah continued to refuse to see him, Robert wouldn't give up. He believed there was something he could do to make Sarah realize what a mistake she was making by rejecting him. The telephone became his lifeline.

Robert

I remember it was my birthday. I stopped by her house, just thinking I would surprise her. But the surprise was on me because there was someone else there. It just broke my heart. I could see that she felt very uncomfortable about it. I got back to my apartment and started calling and I wouldn't stop. I had to talk to her, to fix it, to convince her she needed to see me. It was my birthday and she needed to be with me. Whether she wanted to or not wasn't really important at the time.

Repetitive callers like Robert have surprisingly little concern for how their invasive behavior affects their target. They may be extremely empathetic people in other relationships or areas of their lives, but once obsession takes over, the intensity of their feelings toward their target overshadows all other considerations.

Robert was convinced that if he could get Sarah on the phone, he could persuade her that their relationship was not over. The fact that his repetitive calling (among other behaviors) was upsetting Sarah, invading her privacy, and harassing her was of little consequence to him. He was oblivious to the fact that she had a right to her own feelings and her own life. He had convinced himself that it was in *her* best interests to be with him, and he was treating her as if she existed in the world only to serve *his* needs.

THE ELOQUENT HANG-UP

Nora, who became obsessed with Tom after only four dates, developed a pattern of repetitive calling that was quite different from Robert's. Instead of trying to force Tom into speaking to her, she would hang up whenever he answered the phone.

Nora

I called him last weekend and he finally answered the phone, but when he said "hello," I panicked and hung up. I mean, what do you say? I knew he didn't want to talk to me. Then I thought maybe I'd try again, so I called him right back but I got his machine. I figured the only reason he'd put it on is if he had a woman over there, so I kept calling and hanging up on his machine. I must have done it twenty, thirty times. I've called him every night since. I don't say anything, I just need to. . . . I don't even know what I need, I just keep doing it. Maybe I just need to know if he's home. I just call and hang up on him. It's really terrible. I know he knows it's me but . . . I don't know, maybe that's the point.

That was exactly the point: that Tom knew it was her. No matter whether Tom or his machine answered the phone, Nora was ensuring that he would feel her presence, that he would not forget about her, that he would not be able to enjoy the company of another woman without Nora's intrusion.

I call Nora's repetitive calling a pursuit tactic, even

though her "acting out" behavior would seem more likely to drive Tom away than to attract him back. In forcing Tom to pay attention to her, she was pursuing the only slim connection she had.

Obsessors have an overriding need for contact with their target, no matter how indirect, just to prove that some kind of relationship still exists, even if that relationship is based on continued rejection. To an objective observer, it may not make sense for obsessors to anger and harass their One Magic Person when what they want is to resurrect their relationship. But obsessive love has a logic all its own.

DRIVE-BYS

Repetitive phoning is rarely the culmination of obsessive pursuit; it is more often the beginning. Most obsessive lovers soon find the electronic connection wanting and develop a need for closer proximity to their targets.

After a week of repetitive phoning, Nora's slim sense of contact with Tom began to wane. She felt compelled to step up her pursuit.

Nora

I started driving over and sitting in front of his house. I just had to know if he was alone, but I didn't want him to see me because I felt like such a turkey spying on his house in the middle of the night. So I rented different cars to make sure he wouldn't know it was me. I'd get up at two or three in the morning and drive by to see if there was someone parked where I used to park my car when I stayed over. He has a boat in the garage, so whoever comes over has to park outside. So I'd go over and if I saw a car parked behind his car, I knew it was another girlfriend. And each time I saw one, the pain

just got worse. But every night, I'd have to drive by
again. I knew it was stupid, but I just had to go over
there.

The fact that Nora went to the trouble and expense of
renting cars to conceal her identity indicated how embarrassed she was by her behavior. But this expense, trouble,
and embarrassment did nothing to stop her.

At first, Nora's need was to know whether Tom had
rejected her for another woman, and indeed, she found
proof. But instead of using her evidence of his disinterest
to help her begin disconnecting from Tom, she continued
her drive-bys. Now she was no longer just gathering information. The drive-bys had become an additional source of
suffering for her, keeping her obsession very much alive.

Drive-bys may appear to be mislabeled as pursuit, because there is no direct contact with the target. In most
cases the target may even be unaware of the drive-bys. But
they *are* pursuit tactics just the same because they are
motivated either by the desire to have some sort of contact
with the target or by the desire to gain a strategic advantage by getting information on the target's whereabouts,
habits, and companions.

"I COULDN'T STOP MYSELF"

Drive-bys—like other pursuit behaviors—have a nasty habit
of taking on a life of their own. Obsessors are frequently
surprised and confused to find themselves driving by their
lover's house or office, as if their behavior were being
orchestrated by forces outside themselves. Obsessors often
feel unable to stop, even though they know that what they
are doing is pointless and demeaning.

This happened to Don when Cynthia briefly moved out
of her husband's house. Don was extremely disappointed

when, instead of moving in with him, she moved in with a girlfriend. He began to torture himself with the fear that she was trying to avoid him.

Don

I thought, "Well, if she could lie, cheat, and deceive her husband, why couldn't she do the same to me?" When I'd call her at work she would always be out "running errands." I got very, very suspicious. I'd drive by to see if her car was there. And in the evenings something would make me get in my car and drive by her husband's house to see if she was there. Not once did I ever find her there, but I couldn't stop myself from driving by.

By this point in his relationship with Cynthia, Don was a practicing attorney, yet his well-trained legal mind didn't help him. Don didn't think he *could* curb his behavior. When he said he couldn't stop himself he was echoing a belief I've heard from almost every obsessive lover I've ever worked with:

My behavior is out of my control.

By subscribing to this belief, Don was effectively eliminating all other behavioral options. In surrendering his free will, he allowed his panic to dictate his behavior.

"I JUST HAVE TO BE NEAR HIM"

For Margaret, drive-bys were sparked by longing, not suspicion or jealousy. Margaret felt the need to be with Phil every day, and he wouldn't allow that. So she resorted to drive-bys, to at least feel his presence.

Margaret

If I couldn't be with him, I had to be near him. Or
else I'd just sit home and ache. So I'd drive by his
house. I'd lie to my son about having to go to the
store or something and tell him to call our neighbor
in case of an emergency and leave him home alone.
What the hell was I doing? I felt like a high school
kid with a crush except I'm in my thirties. But I
needed to see his car or the lights on inside. Once or
twice I even saw him through the window. It just
made me feel good to know he was there, to know I
was near him. But I always felt lousy afterward. It
was never enough.

From the heights of a passionate romance, Margaret found
herself reduced to sitting alone in her car, staring at the
outside of the house that contained her fading dream,
feeling awful.

Adding to Margaret's misery was the growing guilt over
what obsession was doing to her most precious relationship—
with her son. Not only was she becoming increasingly
short-tempered with him, but she was being dishonest with
him and leaving him home alone. Obsessive lovers who
are parents are frequently dismayed to realize they have
relegated their children to the backseat as their need to
pursue eats away at their time and energy.

UNANNOUNCED VISITS

Phoning and drive-bys leave obsessors starved for direct
contact. As a result, they become exceedingly anxious to
see their lovers, often coming up with creative excuses to
visit unannounced. They claim to have "just been in the
neighborhood," to have baked extra cookies, to have left a
sweater at the target's home, to be returning a borrowed

book, to need the target's opinion on a new article of clothing, to have been worried because the phone appeared to be out of order, to need advice about a major life decision, or to want to take the target for a spur-of-the-moment meal at a new restaurant. In the context of a loving relationship, none of these excuses would be particularly upsetting. But to the target of an obsessive lover, they feel like blatant manipulations. The target usually responds with anger and further rejection.

In addition to her other tactics, Margaret began to "drop in" on Phil a few times a week, at the end of his shift, hoping to persuade him to have a drink with her. Once or twice she even stopped by his house at night, claiming to have just been "driving by." Phil was generally civil on these occasions, until Margaret showed up unexpectedly at the wrong time.

Margaret

One Saturday night he had a bachelor party but he said maybe he'd call after it was over. I was excited because I thought at least we could spend the night together, but he never called. Around three in the morning I finally gave up and went to sleep. So the next morning I called his house and the line was busy. I checked with the operator and she said it was off the hook. Something just took over and I got dressed and drove down to his house. All the way over there, I rehearsed what I was going to say to him. I knew he wouldn't be too thrilled when I showed up out of the blue again, but I figured once he let me in, I'd make him breakfast and he'd feel better about it. But when he answered the door in his robe, the color drained out of his face, and I knew I'd made a big mistake. "There's somebody here," he said. "I got drunk last night and she came home

with me.'' Well, I was devastated. I know he hasn't
exactly been Mr. Attentive lately, but I thought if I
just give him enough time . . . I mean, I thought I
was with someone who, deep down, really loved
me. And now . . . I mean he just crushed me.

Margaret should have known that her relationship was a
dead-end street long before she found another woman in
Phil's house. He may not have told her in so many words,
but his withdrawal from their relationship was pretty clear.

Unfortunately, she hadn't read the signs. Obsessors like
Margaret have their own way of processing information.
They don't allow evidence of their lover's disinterest to
filter through their denial. If obsessors show up unannounced five times and are met with a closed door, they
are likely to try a sixth time. Instead of learning from
experience, they remain convinced that sooner or later
their target's resistance will break down.

Even when armed with all the facts they need to see the
naked truth about their target's feelings, obsessors will
almost always turn their back on that truth in exchange for
an opportunity to spend time with their target, if only a
few moments. When it comes down to a conflict between
facts and obsessive love, obsessors invariably embrace the
outlook of one of literature's great deniers of reality, Don
Quixote, who put it quite succinctly: ''Facts are the enemy
of truth.''

''HOW COULD SHE DO THIS TO ME?''

Margaret's hopes were at least pinned to a tenuous reality.
If nothing else, she and Phil still had a sexual relationship.
Jim, on the other hand, had ample evidence that Gloria did
not want to have any contact with him. Gloria had told
him to stop calling, had refused to see him under any

circumstances, had returned all his letters unopened, had discarded his roses, and had even threatened to call the police on him.

Jim

A few weeks after she blew up at me on the street, I decided to go and just try to talk to her. I figured there'd be people around so she'd be less likely to make a scene. She can get so hysterical sometimes. So I slipped past the guard, took the elevator up, and headed through the newsroom. I was shaking I was so nervous. When I got to her door, I wanted to just walk in but I knew she'd be mad if she was in a meeting or something, so I knocked. When she opened the door I thought my heart was going to pound through my chest, then she slammed the door in my face and locked it. I don't know what she was so upset about, I just wanted to talk to her, but I suddenly felt like shit. All these people were staring at me. I begged her not to be unreasonable, but she just told me to go away or she'd call the police. I felt really humiliated with all these people staring. How could she do this to me? I just wanted to talk. And then these security guards showed up and that just snapped me. I don't remember much about what I did after that, except that the guards had to drag me away because I was screaming and kicking and pounding on her door. It was the first time I ever felt really out of control, and it scared the hell out of me.

The truth was Jim had been out of control long before he had to be dragged out of Gloria's office by security guards. He just hadn't *felt* out of control. For months his unannounced visits had frightened and oppressed Gloria to the point of panic, yet Jim thought he was just making innocent attempts to talk to his former lover. When Gloria was finally driven to call the authorities on Jim, he felt unfairly mistreated. The rage and frustration he had been repressing since she rejected him finally boiled to the surface. Jim, like many obsessors, felt that he was being victimized, even though it was he who was turning his target's life into a nightmare.

In the last chapter, we saw obsessors use selective focus to minimize their *target's* rejecting behavior, but during pursuit, selective focus plays just as big a role in helping obsessors minimize their *own* behavior. Jim was a wizard at selective focusing. Never mind that he was frightening and infuriating Gloria by showing up unannounced virtually everywhere she went—his emotional tunnel vision pushed this behavior into the blurry background. Jim simply couldn't understand why Gloria was "so upset." In focusing on his goal of recapturing Gloria, he failed to see that the tactics he was using to achieve that goal were making her life miserable.

Jim believed he had no alternative but to pursue Gloria. He was merely doing what any man with such a profound love would do: fight to overcome Gloria's "unreasonable" resistance. After all, *he* was the innocent victim here—he just wanted to talk to her. What was the big deal? Why was she being so inflexible?

Jim refused to see that it was the oppressiveness of his own behavior that had forced Gloria to become resolute in her decision not to speak to him. He had backed her into a corner, and she was protecting herself in the only way she could. If anyone was victimizing Jim, it was himself. By continuing to impose himself on Gloria, Jim was orchestrating his own disaster.

STALKING

Just as the trapper stealthily shadows his quarry without alerting it to his presence, many obsessive lovers covertly stalk their targets. Stalkers often copy the furtive cloak-and-dagger techniques they've seen in movies or on television. They follow their target from place to place; spy on their target in restaurants, bars, or other public places; or stake out their target's home or office.

Hal—the dentist we met in the last chapter—stalked his own wife. When Fran resumed her career after their daughter entered high school, Hal began to suspect her of harboring sexual desires for other men. To defend against his fear that she would leave him for someone else, he became increasingly possessive. If she talked to a man at a party, he would accuse her of flirting. He grew sullen when she got calls at home from male co-workers. And he constantly interrogated her about her day's activities.

Fran became increasingly resentful of Hal's distrust and began to withdraw from him. Hal saw this withdrawal as further evidence that his suspicions were valid and stepped up his behavior. Fran's resentment turned to anger. He was wearing her out emotionally, which turned her off sexually. Because of his oppressive behavior, Hal's fear of rejection was becoming a self-fulfilling prophecy.

When their daughter went away to college, Fran finally allowed herself to consider the possibility of leaving Hal. She still cared about him, but the situation had become intolerable for her. When she confronted him about it, he panicked. He swore that he'd do whatever she asked, if only she'd give him another chance. She told him that she wanted a trial separation and that she wouldn't even consider reconciling with him until he got professional help.

Though it was at Fran's insistence that he came to see

me, Hal recognized that his behavior had been extreme and out of control, and he was anxious to do something about it. In our first session, he was reluctant to talk about how he had been acting. He was embarrassed about it. But I finally got him to open up and tell me how his behavior had escalated over the last several months.

Hal talked about his "crazy accusations," his "Spanish Inquisitions," and his hourly phone calls to Fran at work. These tactics had done little to alleviate his suspicions as they all depended on his believing Fran's word. In the grip of obsessive jealousy, Hal was simply not prepared to do that.

Hal

About a month ago I started spying on her. I called her at work to invite her to lunch, and she said she couldn't because she had a lunch meeting. Something didn't sound right, so I canceled my appointments for the rest of the day and drove over to her office. I parked around the corner so she wouldn't see my car and waited for her to leave. Around 12:30 I saw her. She walked out with her boss, and they seemed to be talking very intimately. It sure didn't look like they were talking business to me. I followed them down the street to a pretty fancy restaurant and kind of found a corner of the bar where they wouldn't see me but I could see them. I was totally convinced that they were out for a lovey-dovey lunch. But then they were joined by a couple of businessmen. It hit me that I was weaving this whole thing in my mind. It was like I was looking at myself for the first time, and I felt really creepy, really disgusting. That should have been a real eye-opener for me, but then a couple weeks later . . . I did the same thing again.

Hal knew that Fran was withdrawing from him. Loving her as much as he did, he couldn't believe that *he* was doing anything to drive her away. There *must* be someone else. It never occurred to him that her rejection could be a response to his behavior. As a result, his life was being taken over by a quest to find a phantom rival.

Stalkers justify their behavior with an irrational logic. Hal reasoned that his stalking, despite the shame and self-reproach it caused him, would somehow put his suspicions to rest and give him some peace from the relentlessness of his obsessive jealousy. But his suspicions could not rest because no matter how often he found Fran innocent, he would have no guarantees against doubts in the future.

OBSESSIVE JEALOUSY

The persistence and depth of Hal's unfounded jealousy and suspicion suggested the possibility of what mental health professionals call a "paranoid personality disorder." A paranoid personality describes someone who is *frequently* envious, suspicious, oversensitive, and often hostile (not to be confused with "paranoia," a severe mental illness involving highly systematized delusions of persecution or grandeur).

When an obsessor has a paranoid personality, or even tendencies in that direction, I am always concerned about the potential for violence. If Hal had not been separated from Fran, I would have insisted that he do so as a condition of treatment, even though he had no history of violent behavior or of drug or alcohol abuse. Because extreme jealousy and suspicion are so often precursors to violent behavior, I always suggest that clients who fit this personality pattern separate from their lovers or spouses for at least three months while beginning to deal in therapy with the underlying psychological issues.

In fact, Hal's love for Fran made him highly motivated
to change. As Hal looked more deeply into himself in the
course of his therapy, both his suspicions and his obsessive
behavior began to abate.

SUICIDE THREATS

When all other pursuit tactics fail, some obsessive lovers
resort to the desperate tactic of suicide threats. While these
suicide threats are extreme reactions to deep emotional
pain, and often do lead to actual suicide attempts, they can
still be considered tactics of pursuit. Obsessors who make
suicide threats usually do so to try to evoke strong feelings
of apprehension and guilt in their target, hoping to manipulate their target into coming back. My client Anne resorted to this tactic in a particularly dramatic fashion.

Anne, a striking thirty-eight-year-old woman with a long
mane of blond hair, is co-owner of a large beauty salon.
She had married her high school sweetheart six months
after graduation. The marriage had ended two years later
when he was arrested for possession of cocaine—a habit
he had been hiding from her. After her divorce, she had a
series of short relationships, but none of the men seemed
interested in a commitment. She had been in and out of
therapy several times but had never discovered why she
seemed unable to find a stable relationship. Now that
she had only a few more childbearing years before her, she
was growing increasingly anxious to find a man with
whom she could fall in love and raise a family.

One night Anne was invited to the fortieth birthday
party of one of her clients, a television actress. To her
delight, the most attractive man in the room seemed attracted to her. Before the night was over, he asked her out
to dinner the following Saturday night. Anne couldn't
believe this was happening to her. John was a successful

producer. He had a sensitive look and manner, he was cultured, he was funny, and he was wealthy. In short, he was everything she was hoping for, and he seemed to like her as well. They began to see each other more and more often; within three months, they were inseparable.

Anne

It was bright lights and big city. He took me everywhere, flew me everywhere, did everything for me. . . . We both kept our own separate places but we were "either/or," his place or mine. I became very dependent on him. I wanted to marry him. I wanted to be with him the rest of my life. All the time.

Six or seven months into the relationship, things began to turn sour. John started spending less time with Anne, telling her that their relationship was getting too intense for him. He knew Anne wanted to get married, but for him it was too early in the relationship to consider such a commitment. The more he pulled away, the harder she clung to him. He finally told her he was feeling smothered, that he wanted to take some time off from her.

Anne tried to figure out where she had gone wrong. She was convinced that his decision was due to some shortcoming of hers. Perhaps he didn't find her intellectually stimulating enough. Perhaps she wasn't well enough educated. She determined to make herself over into what she thought he wanted. She enrolled in French and art history classes at her local community college. She also began going to a voice coach to improve her diction. She got little pleasure out of these classes and lessons, but she thought they were well worth the effort if they could make her more appealing to John.

Anne

All that time, my heart was broken. I'd call him
every couple days and ask if he was ready to go out
again, but he never was. He tried to let me down
easy, but the more he wasn't available, the crazier I
got. I just couldn't understand why he was doing this
to me, why he wouldn't want to be with me. He said
he loved me so much and he did so much for me and
he was so supportive but then he just cut off all
avenues. It destroyed me. I didn't know where to go
with those feelings. I didn't know what to do with
the pain. I started driving by his place, doing everything and anything to get his attention, but nothing
worked. I was becoming really crazy. I thought
about suicide. If I died, he'd have to look at my
grave and feel guilty. It'd say on the gravestone,
"She died of a broken heart and it's John's fault."

Anne's phoning and drive-bys had now escalated to thoughts
of suicide. The possibility promised to accomplish two
goals: ending her pain and punishing John for causing that
pain.

"IF YOU LEAVE ME, I'LL KILL MYSELF"

One night, in a fit of depression, Anne called John and
told him she had to see him. He refused and they argued.
In desperation, Anne finally expressed her suicidal thoughts
out loud for the first time, threatening to kill herself if he
didn't come over.

Anne

I couldn't believe I was saying anything like this. I
was drinking gin that night, which was just revolting
to me, but I was just throwing it down and thinking

"I'll show him." I remember feeling like I was throwing a tantrum, kicking my feet and screaming over the phone. He finally said, "All right, I'm coming over but I'm not staying." And I thought, "Great! If I get him to come over, he'll stay."

Anne used a suicide threat to try to make John feel responsible for keeping her alive. In essence she was telling him that her death would be on his conscience if he didn't come see her. It was an extremely manipulative ultimatum. And indeed, it worked. John did come over. But his visit hardly fulfilled her expectations. He stayed for only a few minutes to calm her down, then he told her that he wanted to make their trial separation permanent. He had come to the realization that there was no future for their relationship. He claimed that he still cared about her but that he just didn't love her anymore.

Anne

He started to leave and I told him I'd really kill myself if he walked out now. He just said, "Look, I really hope you don't do anything that foolish, but I have to go," and he started to go down the stairs to my front door. I had to do something to make him take me seriously, so I started breaking my apartment up, throwing things left and right. I broke every light, every dish, anything I could find . . . anything that would make noise or get attention. I could hear a neighbor shouting, "Call the police, Harry," but I just kept breaking things. And then John came back up. At this point I'd smashed all the lights so it was pitch-black. He lit a candle and we sat there in the dark—with about an inch of glass all over the carpet—until the cops came. This was now three or four in the morning. I just sat there while

John convinced them that everything was okay and they finally left. Then John left and I sat there alone just hating myself for being such an ass.

Getting John to come over was a hollow triumph for Anne. She knew he had withdrawn from their relationship because of the oppression of her obsessive love. Now, in threatening suicide, she had only made matters worse by geometrically increasing the weight of that oppression. Her hysterical out-of-control behavior only served to further alienate John, to reinforce his decision to pull away. Sitting there in her darkened apartment, surrounded by shattered glass, Anne hated herself for having acted so foolishly.

Although obsessors feel powerless to do anything about the "acting in" and "acting out" that makes them feel so degraded, they still believe that they *should* be able to control themselves. As much as they blame their lover for their torture, they also blame themselves. Painful self-reproach infuses the aftermath of almost any obsessive behavior. And for a few obsessive lovers, the ultimate expression of that self-reproach may be to destroy the hated self through suicide.

Two weeks after Anne threatened suicide and destroyed her apartment, she actually attempted suicide (as we'll see in Chapter Ten). It was this brush with death that finally brought her in to see me.

Suicide threats are never successful in recapturing a lost lover. Even if an obsessive lover's target should come back temporarily, he or she has returned out of fear and pity, not choice—hardly the basis for a successful relationship.

(NOTE: If you have considered suicide, have recurring suicidal fantasies, or have threatened suicide as a result of your lover's rejection, it is *essential* that you get professional help. There is nothing romantic about dying for love.)

THE FUTILITY OF PURSUIT

Whether they're phoning, driving by, dropping in unannounced, stalking, or threatening suicide, obsessive lovers are convinced that everything they do is in the service of a powerful, glorious, epic love. In the light of such love, issues of personal oppression, invasion of privacy, or harassment inevitably pale.

As Anne put it:

Anne

I think about the night I trashed my apartment and, it's funny, in some ways I'm really ashamed, but in other ways I feel like I didn't do enough. You have to understand, when you want somebody that bad, there's no such thing as too much, no matter how crazy you're making them. You do whatever you have to do to get them back.

Anne, without realizing it, had bought into one of the grand fallacies of obsessive pursuit:

The end justifies the means.

The "end" of course almost never works out as obsessors hope. They cannot force their target to love them.

And the "means" of obsessive pursuit create a punishing, self-perpetuating cycle that makes obsessors feel increasingly desperate and debased. The more obsessors act out, the more they alienate their target; the more they alienate their target, the worse they feel; and the worse they feel, the more they are driven to try and escape the pain by acting out more. This is how obsessive pursuit feeds on itself.

•   •   •

Once rejection has opened the floodgates of obsession, obsessive behavior becomes inevitable. But whether obsession is acted in through self-punishment or acted out through pursuit, obsessive behavior is always self-defeating. Sooner or later, all obsessive lovers are forced to confront the negative effects of their behavior, and when they do, the resultant frustration and humiliation often turn to rage.

For all too many obsessive lovers, this rage sets the stage for revenge.

THREE

From Pursuit to Revenge

I started thinking about making him feel some of the
pain that he'd made me feel. I was becoming really
crazy. I thought about slashing his tires, I thought
about breaking his windows, and then, at some
point . . . I started to fantasize about burning his
house down.

—*Anne*

Most obsessive lovers eventually reach a flash point—a
point beyond which their frustration over the failure of
their pursuit can no longer be contained. As denial breaks
down, their optimistic fantasy about reviving their relationship is replaced by a bleak conviction that their target is
deliberately ruining their life. They became enraged at
their One Magic Person for betraying them, for purpose-
fully depriving them of the love they need so badly.
Obsessive love might seem doomed in the wake of this
fury, but instead, rage stokes the fires of obsessive passion, turning the heat up even higher.

71

When Rage and Love Go Hand in Hand

Rage and love would seem to be diametrically opposed emotions, and yet within obsession, they coexist. Rage never completely consumes obsessive love; instead, the two battle for dominance inside the obsessor. Margaret bounced between her rage and her love like a Ping-Pong ball.

Even after Margaret found Phil with another woman, she continued to see him for another six months. Then she learned that the other woman had actually moved in with Phil.

Margaret

I'd never felt this kind of pain. I can't even describe it. He must have seen what he was doing to me. He must have seen how he was killing me, but he still did it. I couldn't figure out why he was doing this to me. I was so furious I just wanted to smash his fucking face in. Some days I couldn't think of anything else. But then I'd think about the good times we had together, how good he made me feel. He was very charming in his way, very sexy, you know? But then there were times when I really wanted to hurt him. I really wanted him to hurt. I hoped his dick would fall off. I don't think he'll ever completely understand how devastated the relationship made me. I really hope I never see him again because if I do . . . I'm afraid I might go back to him.

I don't know why Phil rejected Margaret. He might have been a terrific guy who just wasn't interested in a serious relationship at that time. He might have been a hit-and-run lover. He might have become alienated by her clinging, demanding behavior. He might have found another lover. Or he simply might have lost interest in her. But no matter what Phil's reasons were, Margaret was convinced that his rejection was a deliberate attempt to hurt her, to pull the emotional rug out from under her. She was enraged at him for making her feel so abandoned, betrayed, and deeply wounded. Yet her negative feelings did nothing to dampen her desire for him.

Margaret could not disconnect from Phil because her rage kept her thoughts and feelings for him boiling even after he had cooled off. Like obsessive suffering, obsessive rage is a hook. It keeps the lover alive as a presence in an obsessor's life. It allows obsessors to continue to feel passionately connected to a former lover, even when all other connections have been severed.

Revenge Fantasies

When obsessive rage grows too strong to be denied, most obsessors at least *fantasize* about seeking revenge. There's nothing wrong with that. Everyone entertains a malicious fantasy now and then. But, for obsessive lovers, revenge fantasies often fall into an endless loop, replaying over and over in their minds, taking yet another toll on their emotional well-being.

When John rejected Anne, she became as obsessed with fantasies of revenge as she had previously been with fantasies of love. A few days after he left her crying in her darkened, trashed apartment, she began to think about ways of getting back at him for the pain he had caused her. She latched onto the notion of burning down his beloved beach house—the house in which they had spent many romantic evenings together.

Anne

I'd be back-combing a customer's hair and I'd be thinking about where I'd get the gasoline. Or how I'd pour it around. Or how I'd light it. At first I thought I wanted to burn it down with him in it, but then I decided I'd rather know he was alive to see it burn. I'd think about it for hours. I knew it was sick, but it was the one thing that took my mind off my pain.

When Anne said that her revenge fantasies distracted her from her pain, she was unknowingly describing a common defense against depression. The rage that underlies revenge fantasies makes people feel powerful and energized. Depression, on the other hand, does just the opposite. Depression makes people feel powerless, exhausted, and hopeless. Because of this, people rarely experience rage and depression *at the same time*, though they *can coexist* in the same person.

Rage and depression are actually opposite poles of the same force: anger. Rage is usually anger turned outward toward someone else, while depression is usually anger turned inward against the self.

By turning her anger into revenge fantasies against John, Anne was able to relieve some of her feelings of powerlessness. But the relief was short-lived.

Anne

It was very melodramatic, like something out of a bad movie. I knew I wasn't about to actually burn his house down but I couldn't stop thinking about it. It made me feel like *I* was calling the shots. I was going to hurt *him* for a change. For a couple of days I even felt better, but the more I thought about it the more I realized how stupid it was.

As Anne's revenge scenario developed in her mind, she could begin to feel in control. She was no longer a helpless victim of John's rejection. In her fantasies, *she* was making the next move. For a brief period of time, she was finally playing the lead in her own life's drama.

HOMICIDAL FANTASIES

Anne's fantasies centered on destroying something that was meaningful to John. Robert's fantasies, on the other hand, were more lethal.

Robert was the stereo salesman who came to see me because he was afraid of his own anger when his lover, Sarah, moved out. When Sarah began living with another man, Robert's anger turned to disturbingly violent revenge fantasies.

Robert

If I couldn't have her, he wasn't going to have her. This guy just wanted to mess with my life and I wasn't about to let him. I had it all worked out. I'd go to some bar and find some guy who could break both his legs. I figured it would cost about ten thousand dollars, but I didn't care. I just wanted to hurt him pretty bad. There were a number of times when I seriously considered doing it.

Robert's revenge fantasies were initially directed toward the man he was convinced had stolen Sarah away from him. But the longer Sarah continued to reject him, the more his fantasies expanded to include her as well.

Robert

He had no money, he had no class, he was balding. . . . "How could she pick him over me?" kept running through my head all the time. I wanted to kill them both, like "If I can't have her, she shouldn't exist." I wanted to just blow them away. I kept thinking of the guy in the tower in Texas. And the guy in McDonald's. You can just push somebody to a certain point where there's no telling what they'll do, and I felt like they were pushing me to that point.

Robert's rage was so great that his fantasies had become homicidal. He thought that by eliminating Sarah and her lover, he would eliminate his ever-increasing pain. And the more he dwelled on that thought, the closer he moved toward that dangerous dividing line between fantasy and action.

Acts of Revenge

Revenge is the end of the road for obsessors. It is the point at which they finally give up the crusade to recapture their One Magic Person and devote themselves to a new goal: punishing the person who has caused them such pain. When obsessors turn to revenge, the struggle for dominance between love and rage is finally over—rage has won.

"I'VE BEEN HAVING AN AFFAIR WITH YOUR WIFE"

When Don's married lover Cynthia finally rejected him after five years of their on-again-off-again affair, his passionate love was overwhelmed by equally passionate rage.

Don

I'll never forget how it ended. She called me up and said, "I can't take the pressure anymore. I want to make my marriage work. I need to have peace in my life. I love you, but it can never work. We're too different." I couldn't believe it. I said, "Why is it you're always so willing to leave me, but you won't leave him? Why is it so easy for you to walk out on this relationship but you won't walk out on that one? I know I'm a better man. I know that I can offer you more. It doesn't make any sense to me that you would want him more." But she just said something like "it's not negotiable." How could that bitch just walk away from five years of love with one lousy phone call? It was like I was just a joke to her, just a clown. I was going to make sure she regretted it.

Don was devastated. He managed to continue working but when he got home every night he would just lie on his bed, drink, and brood about getting even.

Don

About a week later, after a half bottle of wine, I finally decided to do something. I knew she left me to try to make her marriage work, so I decided to really screw her. I called up her husband and said, "Hi, you don't know my name but it really doesn't matter. I've been having an affair with your wife for five years. She told me she loved me; she told me she was extremely unhappy in her marriage and she wanted to leave but didn't know how." Through this whole thing he says nothing, just silence on the other end of the phone. I half expected him to hang up or yell but he says nothing. So I said, "She told me she had several previous affairs, too. I don't know if this is the right thing for me to do, but you need to know what kind of a woman you're married to." There was a long silence and then he hung up, and it's weird, but that was the first time I empathized with him and it really made me feel like shit. In a funny way I had aligned myself with him. She had cheated and betrayed both of us and it was like we were comrades in arms.

Although Cynthia had ended her relationship with Don in order to commit herself to saving her marriage, Don's phone call was too destructive for her to overcome. Her husband divorced her soon after. Incredibly, this gave Don renewed hope for his relationship with Cynthia. From his self-centered perspective he thought he still had a chance to revive his relationship, even though his impulsive phone call had painfully disrupted Cynthia's life. As it turned out, she was so embittered by the phone call that she never spoke to him again.

Revealing an affair to a spouse or other lover is a common act of revenge for obsessive lovers. By revealing their affair, obsessive lovers strike two birds with one stone: their target and their rival. And, as we saw with Don, when obsessors destroy a rival relationship, the love that still lies beneath their rage often leaks through to fuel their faint hope for reconciliation.

EMOTIONAL VIOLENCE

Even though Don did not assault anyone or anything, his act of revenge was still an act of violence—*emotional* violence. Emotional violence can be just as destructive to a target's psychological well-being as can physical violence, because it creates the same feelings of violation, fear, helplessness, frustration, and rage.

Many victims of emotional violence are doubly frustrated because there are no laws to protect them. Victims of physical violence can call the police. Victims of emotional violence have no recourse. Don may have destroyed Cynthia's marriage but he broke no laws.

While revealing an affair is perhaps the most common act of revenge, other tactics are just as emotionally violent. I've known obsessive lovers, driven by desperation and anguish, to sabotage their ex-lover's career by making scenes at important business-related social events or in their ex-lover's office. I've known obsessive lovers to disrupt their ex-lover's social life by maligning him or her to mutual friends and associates. I've known obsessive lovers to undermine their ex-lover's finances by running up excessive charges on joint credit cards. I even had a client who posed as her ex-lover's wife and had his house reroofed, while he was on vacation, even though the old roof was in excellent shape. Though this may sound more like the plot of a TV sitcom than a malicious act, the ex-lover returned home to be confronted with a $7,000 roofing bill. He spent a year under tremendous stress because of the legal and financial complications that followed.

Emotional violence can be extremely damaging to a target's life, but for some obsessors, that is not enough. These obsessors need a physical outlet for their rage.

Violence Against Property

A target's possessions often become symbolic representations of the target to obsessive lovers. Obsessive lovers who believe themselves incapable of physical violence against another person are often shocked at how explosive they can become when they focus their vengeful rage against their target's property.

When obsessors fixate on a possession that symbolizes their target, it is generally something that is part of the target's daily life, that the target is particularly attached to, or that had meaning in the relationship. Houses, cars, clothing, furniture, appliances, pottery, glassware, jewelry, art, gardens—virtually anything may be fair game for the obsessor's rage.

"I JUST WENT NUTS"

When Robert's fantasies could no longer relieve the pressure of his rage, he lashed out at a symbol of his relationship with Sarah that was easily accessible.

Robert

Throughout this time she's still making contact and giving me hints. Maybe I'd meet another girl and I'd have a date or two, but then Sarah would call and talk about wanting to leave Danny and there I'd be again, thinking this was the chance, this was it. And then she'd have lunch with me, but that would be it. She'd go back with him. She'd come and hook me in and then break it off again. One time she even slept with me, and when she left, I just went nuts. I drove by his place wanting to kill somebody . . . and then I saw her car. Jesus, I'd cosigned the loan on that car. I'd helped her pick it out. How could she park it in *his* driveway? It was almost *our* car. I was so mad I had to do something. And there it was. So I took a hammer and just beat the shit out of it. I smashed the windshield, the lights, the hood, the fenders. I really believe that if I hadn't have smashed that car . . . I don't know what I might have done.

Sarah's car was more than a convenient outlet for Robert's rage. It was a symbol of his bond with her and of his dreams for their relationship. He also knew how much the car meant to her. It was her only valuable possession. It was something she had spent two years saving for. When Robert wrecked her car, he was striking out both at their relationship and at Sarah herself.

Sarah repeatedly tantalized Robert with indications that she might leave her new lover, Danny. Her double messages kept Robert in a state of intense anxiety. When Sarah slept with Robert, he felt she had finally made the commitment to leave Danny. But then, just as suddenly as she had come back to Robert, she was gone again, crushing his dreams. I don't mean to imply that Sarah's provocation in any way *justified* Robert's attack, but for obsessive lovers, shattered hope *is* often a powerful catalyst for violence.

"WHY SHOULD I BE THE ONLY ONE WHO'S HURTING?"

Vengeful acts merely express inner conflict; they never resolve it. Kay found this out the hard way. She came to see me because of the unrelenting anguish and guilt she was feeling after having turned a revenge fantasy into a reality.

Kay was a fifty-two-year-old divorced housewife with three grown sons. Her dark hair was lightly peppered with gray, and laugh lines were just beginning to appear on her still youthful face. Her brown eyes were swollen and red; she'd obviously been crying on her way to my office.

She told me she had been married for twenty-six years to a successful building contractor named Lewis. Toward the end of their marriage Lewis had become more distant, but Kay felt it was just a reflection of their aging together.

Then, when the last of their sons got married and moved out, Lewis told Kay that he'd been unhappy for several years and that he wanted a divorce. Kay felt betrayed, abandoned, and terrified.

Kay

I felt like I'd been run over by a tank. My whole life had been built around my family. Then my kids left. And now he was going off for no good reason. That's what I get after giving him half my life? What the hell did he expect me to do? I was so depressed.

Lewis was generous in the divorce settlement. Knowing that Kay had no marketable skills, he ensured that she had enough money to live comfortably. He remained supportive and friendly, hoping to soften the blow he knew he had dealt her. They still went out to dinner once or twice a month, and he sent her flowers on Mother's Day and gifts on her birthday.

Unfortunately, Kay interpreted Lewis's support as proof that he still loved her. For three years she clung to the hope that he would realize his mistake and return to her. When friends tried to introduce her to other men, she declined, saying that she and Lewis were trying to reconcile. Even though she knew he was dating other women, she believed he was "just going through a mid-life crisis."

Though Kay tried to throw herself into volunteer work and improving her tennis game, she was really just biding her time until Lewis "came to his senses."

During this period, Kay persuaded Lewis's sister and mother to try to pressure him into giving her another chance. She constantly urged her children to talk to their father about not breaking up the family. She even called up his business partner and wept on the phone, pleading with him to put in a word on her behalf. She continued to send Lewis romantic gifts and cards, even after he told her they made him uncomfortable. She called him every day "just to chat," but always seemed to let slip how miserable her life had become without him.

And then the unthinkable happened. Lewis called to tell her that he was engaged to be married.

Kay

I felt like my heart was going to stop dead, right there and then. I couldn't believe it. All this time I was so sure he would come back. I was so sure he still loved me. I was totally stunned. I couldn't even face my friends, I felt so pitiful. They seemed embarrassed for me, like they couldn't think of anything to say around me because they didn't want to touch a nerve. Then the big day came and he went off on his honeymoon and the idea of them sleeping together in some tropical paradise was just too much. Why should I be the only one who's hurting? *He's* the one who made me feel this way. I was going out of my mind.

No longer able to hide behind a wall of denial, Kay was tortured by visions of Lewis and his new wife. And every image of their happiness felt like another slap in the face.

"I'D NEVER DONE A VIOLENT THING IN MY LIFE"

Kay was understandably devastated. But instead of grieving her loss and starting a new life, she grew increasingly bitter. Her thoughts turned to revenge.

Kay

I kept seeing them come home from their honeymoon swooning with love and him carrying her across
the threshold and throwing her on the bed like he did
to me when we got married, and I couldn't stand it. I
kept thinking I had to ruin that moment. Their happiness was like this stabbing pain in my heart. I don't
even remember driving over there, I was on automatic pilot. But I knew exactly what I would do
when I got there. I'd been thinking about it for a
week. I went around to the back and broke a window
to get in and once I was inside I just started ripping
things up. His suits, his shirts, her dresses, the
sheets—that was a big one, the sheets—the couch,
the curtains, anything that would tear. I just wanted
to knock them off cloud nine, I just had to destroy
that moment, to make them hurt and to make sure
they knew how much I hurt.

As Kay drove home from Lewis's house, she began to
shake. She had never done a violent thing in her life, and
now she was overcome with feelings of shame and disbelief. When Lewis returned from his honeymoon a few days
later, her guilt over what she had done compelled her to
call him and apologize. He told her he would refrain from
pressing criminal charges against her if she would seek
counseling.

Kay

My first reaction was to accuse him of being arro-
gant, trying to tell me that I need help after what
he'd done to me. But then he just broke down and
started crying. He went through a list of all the
things I'd done to drive him crazy over the last three
years and then *I* started to cry. It was like he was

describing another person, but it was me. I thought about myself raising three wonderful sons, running a big house, being active in a lot of charities . . . and then I saw myself in their bedroom with a scissors in my hand, ripping up their sheets, and I . . . I knew he was right. I did need help.

Lewis's litany of Kay's obsessive behavior was so clearly at odds with her self-image that it got through to her. Her defenses came tumbling down, and for the first time she recognized that she was not the only one who had suffered. This acknowledgment was her first step toward recovering from the blow of Lewis's rejection.

"I DON'T KNOW HOW FAR I MIGHT GO"

Some obsessive lovers believe that by attacking objects they prevent themselves from attacking their target personally, as if attacks against property were somehow justified because of the greater crime they derail. But, while destroying property *may* provide a brief respite from the pressures of accumulated rage, those pressures are not released. And because the rage remains, attacks against property provide no guarantee against personal assaults.

Robert

If Sarah had come out of the house while I was bashing her car, I don't know . . . I mean, I've never hit a woman in my life, but at that moment I wasn't myself. It was like somebody else swinging that hammer, somebody I had no control over. It scares me just thinking about what might have happened.

Robert's fears were well-founded. When obsessive lovers open the floodgates of rage, there is no telling where the flooding will stop. Even obsessors who have never been violent before are highly susceptible to having their violence against a target's possessions unexpectedly escalate into violence against their target.

Physical Violence

In the heat of obsession, people lose their sense of self, lose their predictability, and do things they never dreamed themselves capable of. Physical violence against other people is the most extreme example of this.

Obsessive lovers who resort to physical assaults are so consumed by rage that it often interferes with their ability to function in their lives. For these obsessors, vengeful assault is an attempt to regain control by exorcising their rage. But physical assault is a futile catharsis. Obsessors who try to cause pain to others are unconsciously trying to hand off their own pain. But this sort of transfer inevitably fails because the rejection that created the pain in the first place is not eliminated, it is exacerbated.

Some obsessors lose control and assault their target only once. Other obsessors, with severe character disorders, are chronic batterers. The tragic reality is that it only takes one uncontrollable outburst to end a victim's life. (We will explore obsessive assaults in greater depth in Chapter Seven.)

Revenge Isn't Sweet

If you find yourself preoccupied with revenge fantasies, I strongly recommend that you seek professional help to ensure that your fantasies don't escalate into realities. If you have already crossed the line into some sort of destructive "acting out" behavior against property, it is essential that you seek help before you hurt someone.

If you have already exploded into physical assault—even if only once—*you must get help*. The impulses that are driving you are outside of your conscious control. It is foolish to imagine that you can regain control over your behavior by yourself. Treatment is more than essential for you—it could mean the difference between life and death.

Revenge, in any form, is always self-defeating. It both perpetuates the pain of rejection and further alienates the target. Whatever momentary satisfaction it may bring, in the end revenge is never sweet.

FOUR

The Savior Complex

Everybody's got problems. But his just seemed to be so overwhelming. It really broke my heart. I had to help him. I knew that if I could just pull him through this, things would be great. What a moron I was.

—*Natalie*

Some obsessive lovers are magnetically drawn to targets who have perpetual life problems of enormous proportions. The partner may be unable to hold a job, or an alcoholic who is usually drunk or hung over, or a drug addict whose life revolves around the next fix, or a con artist. The partner may be struggling with severe or chronic sexual problems or, in extreme cases, may even be a physical abuser or habitual criminal.

But no matter what the problem, the obsessors who are attracted to these lovers believe that they have the power to fix it. They believe that if they can just love enough, give enough, do enough, or care enough, they can save their lover from the jaws of personal demons, freeing him or her for the idyllic relationship they so desperately want. I call this potent group of beliefs the ''Savior complex'' and the obsessors who live by them ''Saviors.''

The word *Savior* has a religious meaning to many people. To others, it conjures images of knights slaying dragons, cavalry riding to the rescue, or superheros saving the world. The word *Savior* connotes power, nobility, virtue, and compassion. Of all the many roles we play in our lives, the Savior role is one of the most romantic and enticing.

A Different Kind of Pursuit

In every obsessive relationship we've seen so far, rejection was a major element. Either the target withdrew over time, cut off the relationship, or found another partner. Saviors are different because they are almost always deeply involved in a relationship with their target. Many Saviors live with or are married to their target. This physical proximity would seem to eliminate the Saviors' need for pursuit, but Saviors engage in their own circuitous style of pursuit that is just as consuming as that of other obsessive lovers.

Saviors' lives are taken over not so much by active pursuit as by the pursuit of solutions to their lover's overriding problems. Saviors believe that once those problems are solved, there will be no more obstacles to their fantasy relationship and their lover will gratefully become their One Magic Person.

The Need to Be Needed

The Savior role taps strongly into our desires to be giving, to be needed, to be seen as good, compassionate people.

This is especially true for women, who tend to be caretakers both by nature and by socialization, but almost anyone can derive a sense of satisfaction and validation from helping other people deal with problems. For Saviors, the salvation of a troubled lover is the cornerstone of their self-worth and very identity; it's their reason for existence. Saviors' lives are dominated by their need to be needed.

This intense need manifests itself in very specific ways for Saviors. When they shoulder some of the burden of their lover's problems, they feel noble. If they can fix or solve some of those problems, they feel needed. If their fixing becomes habitual and their lover becomes dependent on them, they feel indispensable. And once they believe their lover can't do without them, they can, for the time being, allay their greatest fear—the greatest fear of every obsessive lover—the fear of abandonment. No wonder so many obsessive lovers are drawn to the role of Savior.

The mythical Saviors of old heroically faced impossible odds without losing faith. They slew giants; they battled heathens; they defied death. Obsessive lovers who take up the cause of a deeply and consistently troubled partner also face impossible odds without losing faith. Their faith is sustained by their need to be needed. But this faith is never enough to overcome the very real problems that Saviors attempt to solve. Unlike the Saviors of old, these obsessive lovers never win.

Are You a Savior?

To help you determine if you are a Savior, I have devised the following checklist. In considering your responses to this checklist, remember that there is nothing wrong with trying to help your partner once in a while. We all need a helping hand now and then. But if your partner's problems have become the focus of your life, and if *all* the effort is coming from you, if your partner has regularly shown little or no interest in taking responsibility for his or her own life struggles, you are a Savior.

Please take your time and determine whether any of these statements describes you.

You think you can change your lover even though . . .

1. you repeatedly find yourself lying or covering up to protect your lover from the consequences of his or her behavior.

2. you repeatedly have to bail your lover out of financial difficulties.

3. your lover repeatedly borrows money from you and doesn't pay it back.

4. your lover repeatedly lies to you about family background, job history, or marital status.

5. your lover repeatedly cheats on you.

6. your lover abuses alcohol or drugs.

7. your lover is a compulsive gambler.

8. your lover is verbally, emotionally, or physically abusive.

9. your lover habitually gets into trouble with the law.

You are regularly preoccupied with . . .

1. trying to get your lover into therapy or a twelve-step program.

2. trying to get your lover to quit drinking, taking drugs, or gambling.

3. trying to get your lover a job.

4. helping your lover overcome sexual problems.

5. feeling guilty about not doing enough to help your lover.

6. trying to get your lover to see how wonderful things could be if he or she would change self-defeating behavior.

If even one of the statements in either list describes your situation, you are probably a Savior. You will undoubtedly find yourself taking responsibility for solving your lover's problems—whether financial, sexual, emotional, or addictive—even though these problems are not within your power to solve. A great deal of your time and energy will be used up tilting at these windmills, leaving you feeling drained and used and frustrated, just like Natalie, whose words opened this chapter.

Obsessed with a Lover Whose Life Is a Mess

Natalie, forty-three years old, is a brown-haired, brown-eyed historian who teaches civics and government in a Los Angeles public high school. She joined one of my therapy groups because she was in a relationship that was proving to be very costly to her, both emotionally and financially. Her calm, soft-spoken manner belied the inner turmoil she expressed on her first day in group.

Natalie
I just wish he'd leave. This is too toxic, too destructive, too crazy. I don't care if I never get a penny of my money back, I know I'd be better off without him. But I just can't kick him out. We're so bonded together. Our lives are so intertwined.

Natalie had left her husband two and a half years earlier
when she discovered his long-standing affair with his secretary. Since then she had had a two-year rebound relationship with a married colleague that ended disastrously when
his wife came home unexpectedly one afternoon and discovered them in bed together. About a month later, she
met Rick. He was behind her in line for an afternoon
movie, and they both happened to be there alone. They
started talking and decided to sit together. After the film,
they went out for coffee and really hit it off.

Natalie

I was probably at my neediest, my worst, my most
desperate alone time in my life. I really wanted to be
with somebody, and here was this gorgeous blond,
blue-eyed, thirty-five-year-old Pisces who kind of
attached himself to me as of day one. I mean here I
was, eight years older than him, and he didn't care.
It felt great. Before I knew it, he was all I could
think about. I wanted to be with him all the time.

Rick worked sporadically as a used car salesman. When
Natalie met him, he was rooming with a friend, as he
didn't have enough money to rent an apartment of his
own. He told her that he had been working for a car-
leasing company that had gone out of business without
paying him for his last month's work, forcing him to use
up his dwindling savings. He was waiting to hear about a
job at a Mercedes dealership in Beverly Hills. Within three
weeks, she offered to let Rick move into her spare bedroom, knowing that it would only be a matter of time
before he would get back on his feet. Unfortunately, money
wasn't Rick's only problem, as Natalie would soon discover.

THE BOTTOMLESS PIT OF PROBLEMS

Rick and Natalie's emotional relationship seemed to progress very quickly, but Rick never made a sexual move. This baffled Natalie.

Natalie

When we first started dating I just thought he was shy. He would never, ever approach me. A little kissing, maybe, but that was it. It was making me crazy. By the time he moved in, I could tell he wanted to get more intimate but there was this holding back . . . *that* only made me want him more.

Though hot passionate sex forms the core of most obsessive love relationships, Rick avoided sex. This both troubled and tantalized Natalie. She became increasingly preoccupied with Rick's lack of sexual interest. She was determined to find out what was wrong and to do something about it.

Natalie

It was really bizarre. He wouldn't talk about it and I didn't want to push him, but I was getting desperate. One night we rented *Body Heat* and were watching it on my bed and I was getting pretty steamed up so I started unbuttoning his shirt. He seemed really uncomfortable about it and I finally just out and asked him what was going on. He became really apologetic and said he was so depressed about money problems that he just couldn't get in the mood. He was having trouble making payments on a condo in Bakersfield he'd bought as an investment—his father had left him a little money—and it was really getting him down. He'd rented the place to a deadbeat who hadn't paid rent in six months, but he couldn't go up there to evict the guy because the transmission just went out in his car and he didn't have the eight hundred dollars to fix it . . . he was feeling very desperate about keeping his head above water. I couldn't stand to see him like that. I had to help him out.

The more Rick told her about his financial woes, the more sympathy Natalie felt for him. Driven by her compassion, she lent him the money to fix his car, barely giving a second thought to his inability to pay her back. To Natalie, Rick was an innocent victim of bad luck and worse people.

Natalie willingly accepted this notion of Rick as an unlucky victim because that meant he needed someone to change his luck. Like all Saviors, she was drawn to her target's helplessness. In appealing to her need to be needed, this man, whom she already found physically attractive, became irresistible to her. She saw in him the potential to become her One Magic Person, once she could turn his financial problems around—as well as his sexual ones.

THE SEXUAL SAVIOR

Natalie bought into Rick's story that his lack of sexual desire was a direct result of his financial pressures. Now, after lending him money, Natalie expected him to become more sexually responsive. But when their sexual relationship—or lack of one—didn't change, she decided to become more aggressive.

Natalie

I finally had to seduce him. What a disaster. He just lay there. I thought, "Well, he's never had a real woman, someone as experienced as I am . . . someone who's as giving and as good in bed. I'll be able to teach him, and what a life we'll have ahead of us when I can show him how good it can be.'' I tried everything—and I mean *everything*—but I just couldn't get him hard. Then I felt guilty because I was afraid I'd made him feel inadequate. It was awful. But I didn't give up. I figured next time I could make it better.

Natalie's reaction to Rick's sexual difficulties was identical to her reaction to his financial difficulties. She took on the responsibility of fixing his problems before she had any idea how deep or how serious those problems were. She saw Rick's need to be awakened sexually as a personal challenge, and that was all the motivation she needed to put up with an unsatisfying sexual relationship.

Natalie

He never wants to have sex, but every so often he gives in. And it consists of a lot of my stroking him and, you know, trying to excite him with my mouth. But he only touches me when we're actually . . . when I'm actually poised to get him in me. And before he can get hard, he has to grab my nipples and pinch them and twist them. Maybe he thinks it turns me on, I don't know. But then he comes without making a sound. I keep saying to myself, ''I have to let him do this because this is the only thing he wants to do and we've got to start from what feels good to him.'' Sometimes it even hurts, but as long as he's enjoying it, I can stand it. Whatever it takes.

Natalie was sacrificing herself on the altar of Rick's sexual salvation. To sexual Saviors, unfulfilling, degrading, or even painful sex seems trivial when compared to the anticipated bliss of rescuing their partner from sexual problems.

When Natalie first determined to save Rick sexually, his problem seemed relatively minor—many men experience temporary loss of sexual desire during periods of stress or depression. But with more sexual contact, the seriousness of his problem became evident. Natalie might have told Rick that what he was doing to her was unpleasant, but she was afraid to turn him off, not willing to risk losing ground in her crusade to save him.

When I asked Natalie why she didn't encourage Rick to go into therapy, she told me she was afraid he would resent her implication that there was something wrong with him. And besides, why would he need therapy when she was absolutely convinced that she could save him herself?

ALWAYS ON THE BRINK OF DISASTER

Natalie had about as much chance of saving Rick from his sexual and financial troubles as she did of sweeping back the ocean with a broom.

Natalie

Things just went from bad to worse for him, and the worse they got, the more depressed he got. When he finally went to Bakersfield to sell the condo, he found that his tenant had practically destroyed the place. It needed carpets, drapes, painting, a lot of repairs . . . it was a mess. He called me really upset. He couldn't sell it without fixing it up, but he couldn't fix it up because he was broke. I knew it was going to be expensive, but I told him to come on home and we'd work something out.

Natalie, like all Saviors, was being dragged by her lover
into a whirlpool of problems. Rick was a classic loser,
always on the brink of disaster. If it wasn't his transmission, it was his brakes. If it wasn't a repair for his condo,
it was a creditor breathing down his neck. If he managed
to get a job, he couldn't get along with his boss. He was
always out of money but, according to Rick, it was never
his fault. He just couldn't get a break.

Rick's solution was to borrow from Natalie to stave off
the succession of people who seemed bent on betraying
him, using him, or failing him. Overwhelmed by his never-
ending problems, Rick never even thought about the possibility that he might be betraying, using, or failing Natalie.

THERE BUT NOT THERE

It is hard to understand what Natalie was getting out of this
relationship.

Natalie
Sometimes I'd feel like he didn't even care if I was
alive. He'd go into the bedroom, flop back on the
bed, and just stare at the ceiling. And when I'd go in
to comfort him, he'd tell me he didn't want to talk
about it. It really hurt me because I wanted him to
know I was there for him, but he'd close me out.

Natalie's emotional needs inevitably went unheeded. Neither she nor Rick paid any attention to how *she* felt or
what *she* wanted because her feelings and desires seemed
so minuscule in the enormous shadow of his problems.

Natalie was suffering from a particularly painful form of
loneliness: being in a relationship with someone from whom
she was getting almost nothing in return. Like all Saviors,
she found herself feeling rejected even though her partner

was with her physically, because he was emotionally unavailable to be loving, supportive, or even appreciative.

An emotionally unavailable lover is every bit as rejecting as one who walks out the door. The give-and-take of feelings, ideas, dreams, and experiences is what constitutes emotional intimacy. In a healthy relationship, this give-and-take may fluctuate with the currents of daily stress—no one can be loving and giving twenty-four hours a day. But in a Savior's relationship, emotional unavailability is the rule rather than the exception.

NOTHING IS EVER ENOUGH

When Rick returned from Bakersfield, Natalie was unprepared for how much his latest crisis was going to cost her, both financially and emotionally.

Natalie

He needed seven thousand dollars to fix up the condo. I told him I didn't have that kind of money, and he just went to pieces. He started ranting about how everything in his life always turned to shit anyway. Why should he expect anything to change now? I was the one person in his life he thought was on his side and now he couldn't even depend on me anymore. The more he went on, the worse I felt until I just couldn't take it anymore. I found myself apologizing for letting him down and the next thing I knew I was going to my credit union and borrowing the money.

When Rick sensed that Natalie's sympathy and maternal feelings were not sufficient to induce her to make this enormous sacrifice for him, he pulled out the heavy artillery: guilt. He made Natalie feel like the villain. Now his misery was *her* fault because she was abandoning him at the worst time in his life. Forget the fact that she had moved him into her house, had bailed him out of numerous financial jams, had comforted him when he was low, and had put up with his painful, unfulfilling sexual practices—nothing was ever enough.

To a committed Savior like Natalie, the guilt was unbearable. It threatened the very foundation of her self-worth by contradicting her belief that she was a giving, loving person. Once Rick persuaded Natalie she was being selfish, he had her in the palm of his hand. The only way she could live with herself was to go into debt for him.

The more deeply involved Natalie became with Rick, the more difficult it became for her to extricate herself. Her pattern of rescuing became a way of life for both of them, a way of life that depleted her financially, emotionally, and sexually.

Obsessed with a Deceitful Lover

Natalie's obsessive love and her need to be needed made her vulnerable to Rick's never-ending litany of troubles. These same factors make other Saviors—like Debra—vulnerable to pathological liars and con artists.

Debra is a longtime friend who works as an account executive for a mid-sized advertising firm. An attractive, vivacious, intelligent blonde, she is nobody's fool in business, but in her personal life she has a pattern of rushing headlong into relationships.

When Debra met Hal she was forty-seven, five years divorced, and with three grown children. She had joined an old college friend, Dave, for a bite at a marina restaurant, and while they were waiting for their table, Dave ran into Hal, an acquaintance. Hal wound up having dinner with them, and he and Debra really seemed to hit it off. After the meal, Hal asked Debra if she'd like to walk with him down to the water to see the boats.

Debra

I remember thinking he looked like a movie star. He was a real charmer, really got me talking. Every time I'd ask him something, he'd switch it around to me. And I remember thinking, "Isn't this interesting? Finally someone who wants to know about me." And the way he looked me in the eye . . . he really seemed like someone I could connect with. We walked all the way around the marina that night, just talking. . . . I remember my heels were killing me, but I'd be damned if I'd let on. When we got back to the parking lot, he played this little game and wouldn't tell me which car was his. Then he wouldn't tell me what he did for a living. He just said, "It's not important. It's how we feel about each other as people that's important." I was really turned on by him, so I gave him my number. As I drove home, I realized we'd been talking all night but I didn't even know where he lived, whether he was married, whether he had kids. . . . I didn't really know *anything* about him. He was like this man of mystery, and for some reason that really excited me.

Debra actually knew a lot more about Hal than she was willing to acknowledge. Caught up in the momentum of her strong physical attraction, Debra was overlooking important clues that, as it turned out, would have saved her not only a lot of grief, but a lot of money. Hal had been evasive about even the most basic information about himself, but instead of reading this as a warning, Debra allowed her infatuation to overcome her better judgment. When Hal gave Debra the runaround, she should have had serious doubts about his character, his honesty, and his life situation, but she chose to couch his secrecy in romantic terms like "mysterious" and "exciting." She was so taken by his charm and his appearance that she refused to allow any suspicions to color her view of him. Judgment is one of the earliest casualties of the Savior complex, or of any form of obsessive love.

AN ANSWER FOR EVERYTHING

Hal called the next day and invited Debra to the beach. When he came to pick her up, she was shocked to see him driving a fifteen-year-old Chevy with rusted hinges, mismatched dented fenders, and torn upholstery.

Debra

I was so stunned that he would drive such a horrible wreck of a car. . . . I mean, the way he talked and the way he dressed, he seemed so . . . successful. He must have read my mind because the first words out of his mouth were, "This is just a loaner. Someone rear-ended my Maserati, and it's been in the shop for a month." That seemed plausible to me, but on the way home he asked me to fish some Kleenex out of the glove compartment, and when I did, I saw that the car was registered in his name. I was a little upset that he'd felt he had to lie to me, but I knew it was because he was embarrassed, so I didn't say anything about it.

It's not unusual for people to exaggerate certain aspects of their lives or slightly color the truth to try to impress new or potential lovers. But Hal's deception about the car was an out-and-out lie that should have alerted Debra to serious questions about his honesty.

We all receive clues to our lover's personality and character early on in relationships. But once the Savior complex takes hold, the interpretation of those clues is biased to serve the obsessor's rescue mission—no matter what lies the deceitful lover tells.

Debra was so dazzled by Hal's looks and charm that, instead of letting him know how she felt about his lying to her, she made excuses for him. She was afraid to jeopardize any future possibilities with him. The relationship was barely off the ground, and she was already establishing a pattern of covering up for him.

As Debra and Hal saw more of each other, Hal began to drop by her office on weekdays, which caused her to wonder why he didn't have to be at work. When she asked him about it, Hal had an answer for that, too. He said he was a real estate investor with several deals in escrow; until one of them closed, he had plenty of free time.

Debra

He never spent any money. We'd always be at my house. I'd cook dinner, then we'd wind up making love. I'd get this incredible rush, just seeing him naked. He was amazing . . . he'd pour champagne over my body and lick it off really slow, or he'd bring these scented massage oils and spend hours just making me melt . . . it was heaven. But in the back of my mind I always wondered why we never went out, so one night I finally got him to tell me why. He was a little embarrassed about it, but he told me he had all his cash sunk into these multimillion-dollar real estate deals. But each one seemed to have some sort of temporary stumbling block that kept forcing delays or escrow extensions, and until one of them came together he was land rich but cash poor. At the same time, he said, he was paying over two thousand dollars a month in alimony and child support to his ex-wife, who was fighting to prevent him from seeing his son and was out to bleed him dry. This was the first time I'd even heard of any wife or son, but I felt like, "At least he's opening up to me."

Instead of seeing the blatant inconsistencies between Hal's self-description and his life-style, Debra chose to see his stories as personal revelations, welcoming them as signs of his budding trust in her. To not trust him in return would be to sabotage her own dream of a truly honest relationship. How could she not believe him?

Like all Saviors, Debra avoided looking at the holes in her lover's story. It was more important to her to establish a trusting relationship. She was afraid to paint herself as a suspicious cynic, fearing that he might find her less loving or less lovable. In her desire to cement a lasting relationship with Hal, she was predisposed to overlook his discrepancies.

As the relationship progressed, Debra caught Hal in a number of small deceptions. For example, she found that he had used her credit card without asking. He apologized, saying he had intended to tell her about it but "just plain forgot." On another occasion, she found a number of lengthy phone calls to Costa Rica on her bill. He denied making them, even though he had told her that he had a good buddy living there. Taken singly, any of these deceptions might have been explained away as a lapse in judgment, but taken as a group, they indicated an alarming pattern of dishonesty and exploitation. Still, Debra refused to lose faith in Hal and accepted all of his apologies.

"I'M NOT LIKE HER"

When Hal finally told Debra about his ex-wife, he depicted her as greedy, cruel, and abusive—and himself as her poor, helpless victim. He even confessed to having been afraid to trust a woman since he left his marriage. Buying his story lock, stock, and barrel, Debra felt compelled to save Hal from his emotional wounds by proving that not all women were as bad as his ex-wife.

Debra

When he'd apologize that he couldn't afford to take me out, I'd tell him that I could take *him* to a restaurant or a concert once in a while. What difference did it make who picked up the check as long as we were together? He really fought it. I had to *beg* him to let me take him out. When we finally started going places, it really seemed to lift his spirits, and that made me feel terrific. I really wanted to show him that I didn't care about money; I cared about him. I wasn't just some selfish, scheming bitch like his ex-wife.

To Debra, Hal was an injured soldier on the marital battlefield. She was determined to be his Florence Nightingale and heal his wounds. She would make him whole and then they could be happy together. By showing him that she was a giver, not a taker, she would teach him to trust again.

The restaurant tabs were just the beginning. A few months later, she moved him into her house so that he could save rent. A month after that, she insisted on helping him out of a legal and financial hole by lending him $6,000 to cover delinquent alimony and child support payments.

Debra

Then one of his deals ran into geological problems
that required an additional twenty thousand dollars
from each partner. He obviously didn't have it, so I
offered to put up the money in exchange for a piece
of his percentage. He seemed reluctant to take my
money, but since he thought it was a sure thing, he
decided it was okay. It wasn't a loan, it was an
investment. It felt good to be able to do it for him,
and besides, I stood to make money off the deal.

Even though Hal's problems were becoming increasingly
expensive for Debra, she didn't care because it was all part
of her campaign to rescue him. Hal didn't even have to ask
Debra for money. He merely had to complain about problems and she was there to volunteer her hard-earned savings.

SEE NO EVIL, HEAR NO EVIL

Debra wasn't worried about lending money to Hal. She
had no doubt that he would pay her back as soon as one of
his deals went through. She believed he had the potential
to be the most dynamic, successful, loving man. . . . She
believed it because her heart told her so. She knew once
she helped him through his temporary hard times, she
would have her One Magic Person.

And then the roof fell in.

Debra

I ran into Dave at the market. He seemed amused to
hear that I'd gotten together with Hal. We went out
for a cup of coffee and I asked him if he knew Hal's
ex-wife. He was surprised. He said, "What ex-wife?
He's never been married in his life." My first thought
was, "Dave's kidding." But he swore he wasn't.

Then I got so upset I thought I was going to have a heart attack. I started screaming about how it couldn't be true! "Hal's paying two thousand dollars a month in alimony and child support! You don't know what you're talking about! How can you play such a cruel joke on me. . . ." I even told him I never wanted to see him again. I ranted and raved and then stormed out. I'll never forget the total shock and confusion on his face.

Dave's bombshell threatened to destroy Debra's world. If she believed him she would have had to believe Hal was lying to her, and her One Magic Person couldn't lie. Like most other obsessive lovers, Saviors will tolerate no reality that threatens to erode their idealized image.

Debra's anger at Dave was her way of defending against the panic she felt at the possibility that her lover was deceiving her. If he were lying about his ex-wife, he could also be lying about his love for Debra, about needing her, about wanting her. He could also be lying about his financial deals, playing her for a sucker. The possibilities were too terrifying for her to even contemplate. To keep her world from falling apart, she turned her fury on Dave like an ancient monarch killing the messenger who bears bad tidings.

"IF YOU'LL JUST TELL ME THE TRUTH I CAN HELP YOU"

As much as Debra tried to hear and see no evil about Hal, she could not stop Dave's explosive words from threatening her defensive wall of denial. There was simply no escaping the possibility that Dave's allegation might be true. All of a sudden, Hal's "explanations" about his car, the credit card, and the long-distance calls came back to haunt her. Until now, she had easily dismissed them as isolated incidents, but now she worried that she might, after all, be the victim of a pattern of deceit.

Debra

By the time I got home I was going crazy. I had to know the truth. Hal was lying out by the pool, not a care in the world, drinking one of his piña coladas. I told him what Dave said and begged him to be straight with me. How could we have a relationship if we weren't honest with each other? He got really upset. He pleaded with me to forgive him. The truth was, there was no ex-wife, there was no child, there were no delinquent alimony payments. His kid brother had been arrested for a burglary, and he'd needed six thousand dollars to bail him out. He was afraid I wouldn't give him the money if I knew what it was really for, and he was scared of what would happen to his kid brother in jail. I told him I was really hurt that he hadn't trusted me enough to tell me the truth. I told him I loved him but we had to start fresh. No more lies, no more stories, no more bullshit.

When Debra confronted Hal, she thought she wanted the truth, but what she really wanted was for Hal to reinforce her crumbling trust in him. So she accepted his increasingly complicated and unlikely explanations. She needed him to make the pain and fear go away, to reassure her that the relationship was still viable. And once again, he obliged her.

Debra

He swore I would never hear another lie from him, and we both had a good cry. The idea of kicking him out didn't even cross my mind because I knew we were in this together for the long haul. That night we had the best sex we'd ever had. The next morning I woke up and he was gone.

Debra never saw Hal again. When she looked into her real estate "investment," she discovered that the papers he had given her referred to a nonexistent project. He had committed a well-planned, well-executed fraud. By the time she tallied up her financial losses, she was out almost $30,000, but that was a drop in the bucket compared with her emotional damages.

"HOW COULD I HAVE LET THIS HAPPEN TO ME?"

Debra told me this story over lunch, a week after Hal took off. At first I was astonished. She had always been open with me about her relationships in the past; yet during the course of this relationship, I had seen her a number of times and she had never even hinted at problems. But once the details were clear, Debra's secrecy was hardly surprising. Saviors routinely lie for their lovers, make excuses for them, cover up for them, and put on a brave front both for the rest of the world and for themselves.

Debra realized that, even at the last, she had overlooked absolute proof of Hal's continuing deceit. When he admitted to lying about having an ex-wife and child, he claimed it was to get $6,000 for his brother's bail. But Hal had made up the story about the alimony and child support money at least a month before his alleged brother was supposedly arrested. How could he have known a month in advance that his brother would need bail money?

As Debra got to this part of her story, her eyes filled with tears and she said, "My God, Susan, I'm an intelligent woman. How could I have let this happen to me?" I told her to stop beating up on herself. She wasn't the first intelligent person to be taken in like this, and she certainly wasn't going to be the last. Her Savior complex had set her up to be a perfect victim for a skilled con man.

The last time I saw Debra, she seemed to be doing much better. She could laughingly describe herself as "poorer but wiser" without any bitterness in her voice. She is still struggling to rebuild her nest egg, but emotionally, after an admittedly difficult year, she has come a long way toward rebuilding her life.

THE SEDUCTIVENESS OF THE SOCIOPATH

Hal moved in and out of Debra's life like a hurricane, leaving chaos and destruction in his wake. He ruthlessly exploited her obsessive love for him until she began to catch him in such enormous lies that he felt threatened by imminent exposure. Then he moved on, presumably to his next victim.

Unfortunately, the world is full of Hals—charming people who have little or no conscience and no ability to empathize or feel remorse for the harm they do to others. They skillfully manipulate their lovers in many ways, the most common of which is financial. The clinical term for people like this is "sociopath."

Sociopaths are bewildering, fascinating, frustrating, seductive, and persuasive. They exude an aura of high drama and excitement. They promise passion, adventure, and romance. When they speak, their words seem drenched in truth. Sociopaths dazzle on the outside but, like an elegant movie set, their promise of an equally dazzling interior gives way to the reality of an empty shell.

Sociopaths are users, chronic liars, and manipulators. They move through life creating suffering for anyone who trusts them, whether in a business or personal relationship.

Yet emotionally, they rarely suffer themselves, lacking the emotional mechanisms to feel what most people feel in normal human interaction. They lack the internal monitors of morality, ethics, and caring that cause most of us to feel guilt and anxiety when we hurt others.

Saviors often wind up in relationships with sociopaths because Saviors are givers, and givers are easy quarries for predatory takers. Sociopaths have the added advantage of often being extremely adept at the art of seduction. Unfortunately, the goal of that seduction is not love, but money.

Most sociopaths move so fast that their victims know little about them before becoming inextricably enmeshed. When Debra allowed Hal to move into her house, she had no idea where he lived previously, how he supported himself, or what his background was. She was swept away by passion before she had a chance to think about the dubious nature of his stories, and once she was committed to the relationship she didn't *want* to think about it.

If you, like Debra, find yourself continually rescuing your lover financially (or are tempted, *even once,* to hand a large sum of money to your lover, whether as a gift, loan, or investment), don't be afraid to consult a lawyer or a financial adviser to protect your interests. I don't mean to imply that if your lover asks you for money he or she is necessarily a sociopath, but in the real world, the only way to protect yourself from someone like Hal is to seek the advice of an objective third party whose perspective is not clouded by emotions. Third-party involvement may anger your lover or threaten the trust you believe exists in your relationship, but financial dealings should never be matters of the heart.

Sociopaths always seem to offer the moon at the outset of a relationship, but by the time they leave, that moon is invariably eclipsed by the shadow of betrayal.

Obsessed with
an Addicted Lover

Nowhere do Saviors confront more powerful demons than when attempting to rescue a partner who is addicted to drugs or alcohol. Physical addictions cannot be overcome by a lover's efforts, no matter how much that lover may care, understand, sympathize, nag, or plead. Without a strong personal commitment *on the part of the addict,* all of the rescuing in the world is not only doomed, but often contributes to the problem by softening the consequences of the addictive behavior. Obsessors who love addicted partners tend to have especially chaotic relationships. Kirk's story is a dramatic illustration.

Kirk is a thirty-eight-year-old recovering alcoholic who works as a programmer for a large computer company. He was referred to me by his AA sponsor, who shared Kirk's concern that his lover, Loretta, would drag Kirk back into his former life-style. Kirk was involved in an obsessive, tempestuous relationship with Loretta, who was heavily drug and alcohol addicted, and who showed no interest in changing her destructive life-style.

Loretta had lived with Kirk on and off for the last two years. She would move in for a month or two, then move out again without warning. He would not hear from her for another few months and then she would show up on his doorstep, usually in some sort of trouble. When Kirk came to me, Loretta had just moved back in a few weeks before and was already threatening to leave again.

Kirk

I'm hurting like hell right now. She told me she was moving out last Sunday, but here it is five days later and I don't know if she's moving, I don't know if

she's staying. I really want to know. I really want
her to stay. I really want her to get into recovery.
The woman makes me crazy. *I* make me crazy about
the woman.

Before meeting Loretta, Kirk had spent four years going
from brief affair to brief affair. He had been deeply hurt
when his wife of ten years left him because of his drinking
and took their four children with her cross-country to
Florida. Whenever he found himself getting interested in a
woman, that pain would come back, making him wary of
committing to new relationships.

All that changed when he met Loretta. She was a file
clerk working across the hall from his office.

Kirk

One day my car wouldn't start, and I knew she lived
nearby, so I asked her if she'd give me a lift home.
When we got there I invited her up for a drink and
she said sure. I felt really grungy so I said I had to
take a shower, and as soon as the words were out of
my mouth I had this feeling. So I asked her if she'd
like to join me. She said sure and we ended up
making love in the shower. After that we did some
speed and had some more extremely mad and passionate sex and I was in love. Everything was coming up roses. We spent the next ten days in bed, only
taking time out for food, work, booze, and dope.

Kirk's relationship with Loretta was born in the distorted
reality of alcohol, drugs, and lust. This already heightened
emotional atmosphere was tailor-made for obsession.

A DIFFERENT KIND OF IDEALIZATION

When most obsessors idealize, they use denial to sweep their lover's shortcomings under the rug. Saviors, however, are often well aware of their lover's inadequacies or destructive life patterns.

Kirk

Sure, she was a junky and a drunk, but so was I when we started. I mean, who was I to judge? Inside, I knew she was good, she was sensitive. I remember once I squashed a spider and she got really upset. I knew, deep down, she was the perfect girl for me, absolutely terrific. She looked great, she made me feel great, she really knew how to turn me on. We were totally obsessed. Then, at the conclusion of those ten days—the best I ever had—she disappeared. She just took all her stuff and split. I was a basket case.

Kirk was looking at Loretta as if he had emotional X-ray vision. He thought he could see a core of goodness and beauty through the overlay of her troubled exterior.

Kirk may have been unconcerned about Loretta's drug and alcohol abuse, but the way she disappeared should have warned him about her volatility. She left him without warning, showing no concern for his feelings. In addition, she stopped showing up at work. But her blatant irresponsibility did nothing to tarnish Kirk's belief in Loretta as his One Magic Person.

"STOP TELLING ME WHAT TO DO"

Instead of idealizing who Loretta *was*, Kirk was idealizing who she *could be*. This strengthened his determination to pursue her and to get her back.

Kirk

I got both her parents' addresses from personnel, then went to Hollywood to her mother's house, to Huntington Beach to her father's house. . . . All they said was, "She's not here. She's not here. She's not here." I hung around the Winchell's Donuts where I thought she might be. I couldn't find her. It drove me absolutely insane. I cried a lot and downed a lot of dope and Jack Daniel's. I started coming to work late or calling in sick, and pretty soon my boss figured out what was happening and told me to either go to AA or get a new job. That's when I got in the program.

Kirk really connected with Alcoholics Anonymous. He began going four times a week and seemed to have no trouble staying sober. Then, a few months later, Loretta came back into his life.

Kirk

She presented herself at my doorstep, totally loaded, and said, "I need a place to live." I asked her where she'd gone, and she told me if I was going to play cop, she'd go back and live in her car, so I said, "Fine. Come and live with me, but no drugs or alcohol." She said fine.

Loretta moved in that day and resumed her drinking that same night. While supporting Loretta over the next several months, Kirk tried to persuade her to go to AA meetings with him, but she refused, seeming resentful that he was trying to tell her what to do.

Kirk

I knew from AA that I couldn't help her unless she wanted to help herself, but that didn't stop me from trying. She had no self-esteem and no job, and was going nowhere. I kept trying to convince her to get work, but she never did anything about it. I started circling jobs in the newspaper and leaving it open on the bed, but that only made her furious. She'd scream and yell about how I was a miserable son of a bitch who just wanted to control her life. I didn't get it. I was doing everything for her, and she was screaming at me like I was some kind of monster.

Kirk thought that if he took care of Loretta, she would have to love him. He would make himself so indispensable to her that she would never leave him, as his wife had. But Loretta experienced his "help" as an encroachment on her freedom. Yes, she was dependent on him, but she resented that dependence deeply and struggled against it. Kirk's support only served to underscore how much of a failure she was.

Saviors often find themselves in love-hate relationships with troubled lovers. The more troubled lovers take from their Savior, the more dependent they feel, and the greater their dependence, the greater their rage over losing control over their own life.

Yet if Saviors hesitate to rescue—as Natalie did when Rick needed more money than she had in her savings— their troubled lover is equally enraged at being abandoned. Saviors are damned if they do and damned if they don't.

"HER SLOW DANCE OF DEATH"

Despite Loretta's fury, Kirk was convinced that by loving her, taking care of her, and wearing down her resistance, he could still persuade her to pull her life together.

Kirk

I just didn't know what else to do short of kicking her out, and I couldn't have done that in a million years. I was her only chance. She'd cook for me once in a while, and she was great in bed, but I paid all the rent, I bought all the cigarettes, gasoline, food, medical care. . . . I even gave her money to support her habits. I was afraid she'd leave if I didn't. I was madly in love, but I was working my butt off and she was just doing this slow dance of death, drinking more and more whiskey and smoking more and more dope.

Loretta was the prima ballerina in this "slow dance of death," but Kirk was setting the stage and playing the music. In his fervor to help her, he was simply making matters worse. Instead of setting limits on her substance abuse, he actually paid for it. Instead of insisting that she take responsibility for herself, he gave her the message that anything she did not do for herself, he would do for her. He allowed her to survive without having to take care of herself, and in so doing, he allowed her to continue her self-destructive life-style.

Kirk had two powerful rivals for Loretta's affections: drugs and alcohol. She was the focus of his life; getting high was the focus of hers. Kirk understood that he was not Loretta's primary interest, but he foolishly believed he could eliminate his rivals. Most Saviors labor under the delusion that the power of their love alone will eventually persuade their partner to stop drinking or taking drugs. But addiction is complex and tenacious. It demands a courageous commitment on the part of the addict to actively pursue his or her own rehabilitation. Without that commitment, *nothing* can make a difference.

"I RAN OUT OF LOVE"

Because of Loretta's addictions, both her life and Kirk's were in a shambles. Sooner or later, even the most devoted Saviors reach their limits. Kirk eventually burned out.

Kirk

I was sick and tired of paying the bills. I was sick and tired of hearing her complain. I ran out of money. I ran out of love. I ran out of compassion. We were just bitching and nagging at each other, and I'd had it. So I decided to invoke the golden rule, which is that he who has the gold makes the rules. I told her, "Look. I've been paying for everything. I can't afford to pay the price any longer. It's time for you to leave." The next day she packed up all her things and a couple of her doper friends came over, threw her stuff in a truck, and drove away. I expected to feel relieved, but instead, I felt sick.

Kirk didn't feel half as tough as he sounded. The lopsided nature of the relationship had ground him down. Saviors are typically used, exhausted, and drained by their lovers, so it is hardly surprising that many of them eventually give up. Unfortunately, this healthy decision is rarely permanent.

THE HIGH COST OF SALVATION

Kirk may have run out of love, but he was far from running out of obsession.

Kirk

That first night without her was horrible. I couldn't sleep. I had to go to the bathroom every five minutes. My stomach hurt, my palms perspired, my head ached with guilt for what might happen to her without me. I was kicking myself for letting her go. A couple of days later I went looking for her and I couldn't find her. My sponsor was on my back to let go, and I finally just told him to go fuck himself and fuck AA, too. By the time he found me I was unconscious from a couple bottles of Jack Daniel's. I woke up in a detox unit.

Kirk had hit rock bottom. In his mind, he had thrown Loretta to the wolves. He had abandoned his One Magic Person. He had been selfish, uncaring, and cruel. In finding the strength and the wisdom to cut his lover loose, he paid a high price in guilt and self-reproach. This is the Savior's dilemma:

The more you act in your own best interests, the worse you feel.

Though Kirk was doing the best thing possible for himself (and perhaps for Loretta) by trying to get her out of his life, he felt as if he had done just the opposite.

"I Thought We Were Finally Through"

After Kirk got back on his feet, he began to forge a new life without Loretta.

Kirk

The next few months I really cleaned up my act. I went back into AA with a passion, I was dating a few women from the program and we seemed to hit it off, I made up work that I'd let slip while I was with Loretta. . . . I couldn't stop thinking about her, but I was determined to forget her. I thought we were finally through. Then she showed up again. She told me she needed a hundred and fifty bucks for some drug dealer who was going to cut her if she didn't come up with it. I gave her the money but I told her I thought she was acting like a hooker. She got real upset at that. She admitted she'd spent some time up on Hollywood Boulevard but she said all she could attract were vice cops. She was in really bad shape. She was doing a lot of drugs and she looked really pathetic. She was scared about going back on the street, so I offered her the rescuing that I always do. The next thing I knew, she'd moved back in. Now I'm feeding her, I'm feeding her scumbag friends, I'm giving her money. . . . We're exactly back where we started except now I'm sober.

Kirk hadn't realized that, despite his attempts to cleanse his life of Loretta's toxic influence, he was still extremely vulnerable, both to his obsessive love for her and to his need to be needed. He falsely believed that time and distance alone would eradicate his feelings for her. Predictably, when Loretta returned, her appeal for help was all it took to shatter his commitment to live without her.

Many obsessive relationships, especially those between Saviors and troubled lovers, end not once, but many times. These relationships easily fall into a frustrating, repetitive pattern of breaking up and reuniting.

If you are a Savior and you have found the strength and

the insight to set limits on what you are willing to do for your lover or even extricate yourself from the relationship, it's important that you don't make the mistake of believing you are out of the woods. Even though their better judgment invariably tells them otherwise, most Saviors find it extremely difficult to resist taking a troubled lover back into their lives.

The Imbalance of Power

Troubled lovers play the guilt, pity, and compassion of their Saviors like the finely tuned strings of a violin. Loretta took full advantage of the fact that Kirk couldn't bear to see her out on the streets and would go to almost any lengths to save her. Hal used Debra's obsessive love to lure her into a web of lies and to expertly maneuver her into thinking she was volunteering to help him out. Rick came to rely on the fact that the more depressed he became over his financial problems, the more Natalie would open her heart and her checkbook.

The paradox of the Savior complex is that troubled lovers seem to be weak and helpless and yet they call the shots in their relationships. By the same token, Saviors seem to be in control and yet are totally manipulated and drained by their lover's neediness.

It is very hard for obsessive lovers to resist the impulse to save their target when the Savior complex pulls their emotional strings. But it *is* possible to escape this repetitive rescuing pattern. In the third part of this book, we will explore ways of renouncing the Savior role once and for all.

PART TWO

Targets
of
Obsessive
Lovers

FIVE

The Co-obsessive Target

It drives me crazy being in this relationship where
I'm loving all the attention I'm hating.

—*Karen*

It is fashionable to believe that both partners in a relationship are equally responsible for the problems that arise
between them. But for many targets of obsessive love, the
concept of shared responsibility simply doesn't hold true.
Some targets are not even aware that someone is obsessive
about them; others do nothing to encourage their obsessor
to pursue the relationship; and still others—who find that
their partner in a relationship has become obsessive—make
very clear, decisive efforts to get that lover out of their
lives. These targets don't invite the obsession, they don't
enjoy the obsession, they don't want the obsession.

But there *are* targets who are as deeply enmeshed with
their obsessive lover as their lover is with them. They
behave in ways that either encourage their lover's obsessive behavior or fail to discourage it. In fact, these targets

actually have some obsessive tendencies of their own. They often share the obsessor's need for intense passion and excitement; they share the obsessor's terror of rejection; and they share the obsessor's deep sense of inner emptiness. I call these targets "co-obsessors."

The Co-obsessive Relationship

In co-obsessive relationships, the line between obsessor and target begins to blur. Karen and Ray provide a classic example.

Karen, a doe-eyed, statuesque brunette, is a professional dancer in films and television. She first met Ray—a film camera operator—on a movie set. She was immediately attracted by his striking resemblance to Harrison Ford.

Karen and Ray had a lot in common: they were both thirty-two; they were both only children raised in Chicago; and they were both unattached. Both had been married—Ray for five years, Karen for seven—and both had been divorced for several years. Neither one of them had children.

Since his divorce, Ray had been unable to become involved with anyone for more than a few months. Karen, too, had not had a steady lover since her divorce, "because they always seem to get restless and leave." That was one problem she didn't have with Ray.

Karen and Ray's relationship was stormy from the start. They disagreed on just about everything except for their mutual attraction, and the heat of their arguments seemed to crank up the heat of their sex. For the next two years they lived in constant turmoil. Karen would periodically tire of the chaos and break up with Ray, but they had developed such strong emotional ties that he always managed to talk her into giving him another chance.

On one of these occasions, Karen insisted that Ray enter

therapy with her as a condition of their getting back together. She hoped that with professional help, they could finally get beyond their on-again-off-again relationship. When they came in to see me for a consultation, they both seemed highly motivated to find a way of building a lasting, healthy relationship from the wreckage of what they had.

Karen

I have a lot of inner conflict because I'm suffocated and pressured and I always resent it when he intrudes on me. But, by the same token, we really love each other and I know how hard that is to find. He fills this need in me and I can't let go of that.

Karen was expressing the inner strife that almost all co-obsessors feel. One minute she wanted in, the next minute she wanted out. Like most co-obsessors, she was torn between love and frustration, and her indecision was fueling Ray's fear of rejection, provoking him to become even more possessive.

Ray

Every time she tells me she wants to call it off, it kills me. She kicks me out and then in a couple of weeks she changes her mind. It drives me nuts. I love her so much . . . it's really painful. We get into these enormous fights and then we make up. Up and down, up and down. I keep fighting to get and she keeps withdrawing, fighting not to give. So I try even harder. And that's how we've related for most of the relationship. It's like her sickness plays off of mine.

Ray and Karen's pattern of repetitive breaking up and reuniting is common for co-obsessors. But even if co-obsessors never reach the point of actually trying to break up with their partner, they typically describe him or her as being impossible to live with and impossible to live without. This kind of relationship is bound to be turbulent, draining, and ultimately debilitating.

Are You a Co-obsessor?

To help you determine whether you are a co-obsessor, I have designed a checklist that describes the conflicting emotions that co-obsessors typically feel.

As the target of an obsessive lover . . .

1. Do you bounce back and forth between feelings of passion and oppression?

2. Do you love your partner one minute and resent him or her the next?

3. Do you feel both flattered and invaded by the intensity of your lover's attentions?

4. Do you feel turned on by the excitement and the unpredictability of your relationship?

5. Do you feel guilty when you stand up for your rights in your relationship?

If you have answered yes to *any* of these questions, you may very well be a co-obsessor. While riding the emotional roller coaster of a co-obsessive relationship, it is almost impossible to see the things you are doing—either actively or passively—that actually encourage your partner's obsessive behavior. But until you have a clear perspective on your own role in the relationship, any kind of change for the better will be difficult.

When Passion Turns Oppressive

Obsessive passion is a double-edged sword for co-obsessive targets, both attractive and alarming. On the one side, they find the intensity and the romance irresistibly flattering and exciting, while on the other, their lover's volatility makes them feel pressured and off balance.

Karen

I felt his desperation from the first phone call. He wanted to see me right away, all the time. There was a poem in my mailbox every day. There were phone calls from him several times a day. There were flowers. I was very drawn to him, it was great in bed, and I loved all the attention . . . that was a big part of it. I knew something didn't feel right about it—it was just too much, too intense—but I had come out of a marriage to an alcoholic who ignored me and was having a lot of affairs, so the fact that Ray was so hot to see me was an incredible lift for me.

Karen's self-worth had been devastated by a bad marriage and a long string of unsuccessful attempts to find a new relationship. She was hurting and needed reassurance about her desirability. Ray's hot and heavy pursuit was just what the doctor ordered. Ray tapped deeply into her need to once again feel good about herself as a woman, and his validation was far more important to her than her misgivings.

"I FEEL SO SMOTHERED"

From the very beginning of their relationship, Karen noticed certain aspects of Ray's personality that disturbed her. Even though she initially welcomed his romantic pursuit, it soon escalated into intense jealousy. This was a major source of conflict between them.

Karen

I had many male friends before I met him . . . friends of six years, seven years, ten years . . . platonic friends. And we would get together and have lunch or work out business arrangements or things like that. But when Ray came into my life he was immediately very, very jealous of all these men. If there was a phone call, he'd go, "Who's that? How many times has he called you? Why is he calling you? What's going on here?" He would not believe me that these men were just friends. He wanted to know what I was doing all day, who I was with, even if it was at work. I couldn't understand why he'd get so upset.

Ray

Almost everybody who knew her wanted a relationship with her. That really played on my insecurities. There was a lot of time I couldn't account for. I'd ask her, "How was your day?" And I wouldn't get an answer. Or I'd get an answer where there were about four hours that she wasn't telling me about. It drove me absolutely fucking nuts—excuse my language.

Karen

It was always like he was on top of me. I couldn't breathe. I had a lot of resentment, and I couldn't express it. I felt I had to make it okay for him all the time, so I'd answer questions and give details and hate every minute of it.

Ray's interrogations would have been inappropriate under any circumstances, but coming so early in the relationship, they were especially extreme. His jealous behavior was smothering Karen, creating negative feelings within her that percolated through the sexual and emotional passion that had initially drawn her into the relationship. Her way of handling this was to placate his feelings by responding to his inappropriate questions. Her acquiescence only confirmed his belief that he was justified in subjecting her to his inquisition.

INVADING PERSONAL BOUNDARIES

Karen felt violated by Ray's interrogations. He was invading her "boundaries"—the lines of demarcation that defined the personal territory made up of her feelings, thoughts, desires, needs, and rights. He was running roughshod over her freedom to be separate and independent, and that enraged her.

Karen

There's all this anger inside of me but it never comes out as anger. I feel overwhelmed and intruded upon like I have no individuality and no life. Like I'm not my own person anymore. I always had to be whoever he wants me to be. It infuriated me, but the only way I ever expressed it was by withdrawing. That was my way of expressing anger, kind of sideways. I started putting up walls. I'd bury myself in the paper every morning instead of talking to him. I'd stay late at work. I wouldn't hold his hand when we'd go for walks. It was the only way I could feel like my own individual person again.

Instead of openly resisting Ray's psychological trespassing, Karen withdrew. She built an emotional wall and hid behind it. Other co-obsessors deal with this sort of encroachment by resisting. They argue, they make scenes, they make accusations, or they walk out (invariably to be pulled back). They believe that through uproar they can reclaim their lost autonomy. But as soon as the dust settles, their relationship tends to slip back into the familiar patterns of suffocation and resentment.

By withdrawing, Karen thought she was regrouping and getting her feet back under her, and in a different kind of relationship, she might have done so. But one of the paradoxes of co-obsession is that the very withdrawal that many targets use to try to deal with their resentment only serves to incite more of the invasive behavior that angered them in the first place.

Ray

She'd go into the bathroom and close the door. That's all she'd do. But I'd go nuts. There was something about the closed door that meant rejection to me and that terrified me. It wasn't that I had to have the door open when she was going to the bathroom and doing private functions. What it was about was, when she'd get up in the morning and she'd be combing her hair or brushing her teeth, we used to share that time. All of a sudden, she wanted that bathroom time alone, and I hated that. I thought, "You're just brushing your hair. What the hell is that all about? That's insane to me."

Karen

I felt like "Goddammit! Stop doing this to me. I want you to give me my space!" The man has no sense of privacy. I can't have a life of my own around him. I can't even brush my teeth in peace. But I wouldn't say anything. . . . I'd just open the door. I mean, who wants to fight first thing in the morning?

Karen continued her patterns of placating Ray, allowing him to usurp her privacy in virtually every area of her life. Bit by bit, she surrendered her physical and emotional boundaries, and in doing so, she gave Ray tacit permission to continue, and even to escalate, his oppressive behavior.

The Quicksand of Co-obsession

Co-obsessors often see themselves as victims of their obsessive lover. After all, it is the obsessor who is acting crazy and jealous and irrational. And certainly, the obsessor is responsible and accountable for his or her own behavior. But co-obsessors are not entirely innocent bystanders. They make their own choice to stay in the relationship as it is, virtually guaranteeing that they will continue to feel victimized.

Co-obsessors are so deeply enmeshed with their obsessive lover, and with the drama and passion of the relationship, that they can't bring themselves to either leave their lover or set limits on what kind of behavior they are willing to accept—limits that might steer the relationship onto a healthier course. Co-obsessors become mired in a quicksand of confusion, ambivalence, self-reproach, guilt, and most of all, neediness.

CO-OBSESSIVE NEEDINESS

While there are some differences between obsessors and co-obsessors—primarily that obsessors tend to be dominating and aggressive while co-obsessors tend to be passive—the two invariably share one overriding character trait: an insatiable need to find a love that can fill their inner emotional emptiness.

Karen

All my friends keep telling me to get out of it, that Ray is a real sick person and this relationship is an unsafe place for me to be. But I have this big void inside of me, and I need to fill it and be with a person who fills it. He fills it better than anybody else in the world.

When Karen talked about her "void," she was describing an emotional vacuum that went far beyond the yearning for love and romance that most of us share. To obsessors and co-obsessors alike, nothing—not work, not family, not friends—can be fulfilling enough to overcome this deep sense of emptiness.

When Ray came into Karen's life, he filled this void for her. Unfortunately, he filled it with the chaos of obsession instead of the nourishment of healthy love. Karen failed to see the distinction. Her neediness was too great—a neediness she had been harboring since childhood.

Karen's parents had a very troubled marriage. She remembers her father shouting at both her and her mother whenever he was home. He would frequently spend the night away, and Karen's mother became increasingly preoccupied by the fear of losing him. As the marriage deteriorated, Karen's mother suffered from severe depressions, making her emotionally unavailable to Karen for a great deal of Karen's childhood.

Karen

Looking back, I don't think my father and I ever had more than ten minutes together unless he was yelling at me. And whenever my mother was there, she wasn't *there*. She was always sleeping or crying. . . . She didn't have much to say. So when Ray came along and wanted to be with me all the time and just make me his world . . . it satisfied that part of me that had been fatherless and motherless. He fed that hunger in me.

I was not surprised to discover that Karen had "toxic parents." Most co-obsessors—as well as most obsessors— do. "Toxic parents" is my term for parents whose emotional or physical abuse or neglect dramatically impairs their child's psychological development. Even though Karen's parents didn't overtly abuse her, they deprived her of the basic emotional attention and affection that would have enabled her to develop into an emotionally well-balanced adult.

As an adult, Karen tried to quench her great thirst for love and security through her relationships with men. Unfortunately, she had had such negative role models that she never learned what love was supposed to feel like. She never had the chance to learn by example about healthy relationships. Like many other children of toxic parents, she married an unloving and rejecting man, recreating the only kind of relationship she had ever known.

Karen emerged from the marriage badly wounded. Once again, a man had made her feel unloved and unlovable. The burden of the negative self-image she had developed so long ago was compounded. So was her neediness.

Then she met Ray. For the first time in her life, a man wanted to make her the center of his universe. She seized the attention like a drowning woman would a life preserver—and like that drowning woman, she'd be damned if she'd let go.

Karen

I'm afraid of the emptiness I used to feel. I'm afraid it'll come back. Just total emptiness. After somebody swarms in on you the way Ray does . . . I'd never be able to stand the quiet afterwards.

As Karen spoke, her terror was palpable. She saw her relationship with Ray as an either-or situation—either she put up with his turmoil or she returned to her emptiness. What a choice.

CONFUSING JEALOUSY WITH LOVE

From the beginning of their relationship, Ray was extremely jealous of Karen. She felt suffocated by his suspicions and accusations, and yet she put up with them because, like most co-obsessors—as well as most obsessors—she interpreted jealousy as an expression of love.

Karen

He gets upset if I leave a button unbuttoned on my blouse. He says I'm showing too much. Or if I wear a skirt with a split on it, he'll say he can see right up my dress, right up my crotch. I feel like he wants me to wrap myself up like one of those Persian women, so no one can even see my face. He wants all of me for himself . . . all of me . . . more than I have to give. I hate it, but I need it, too. When he gets jealous I can feel how much I mean to him, all that

love, all that fear . . . it's exciting and maddening at
the same time.

Karen realized that when Ray criticized the way she was
dressed, he was saying a lot more about himself than he
was about her. He was really expressing how threatened he
felt by her attractiveness, how afraid he was of being
replaced. So she saw his increasingly frightening jealousy
as an expression of how much he cared for her. How could
he get so upset unless she meant everything to him?
Ray, like Karen, romanticized his jealousy.

Ray

When we fight, I never hear what I need to hear to
alleviate my doubts. So I probe . . . and I know I
get verbally abusive . . . I come down heavier and
heavier, but it's never enough to satisfy me. So I
physically try to restrain her from going out of the
house. I'll grab her by the arm, or I'll block a
doorway. I know I'm doing some very outrageous,
crazy things, but it's just because I love her so
much.

Oppressive jealousy is anything but a sign of love. Repetitive patterns of interrogation, accusation, and suspicion are
actually signs of a lover's deep insecurities and emotional
instability. These patterns prevent the development of trust
and intimacy, and without trust and intimacy, a truly
loving relationship cannot exist.

THE CO-OBSESSOR'S AMBIVALENCE

When Karen withdrew from Ray to reestablish her emotional autonomy, he turned up the pressure. As a result,
her withdrawal gave her less and less of the breathing

space she sought. She began to bounce more and more
frenetically between wanting to stay in the relationship and
wanting to get out of it. She became as preoccupied with
her own indecision as Ray was with his need to possess
her. Instead of trying to resolve her conflicts, Karen became handcuffed by them. She was mired in the quicksand
of ambivalence.

Karen

I feel paralyzed. I want to break up and I don't want
to break up. I've ended it before and it never works.
He knows that with enough time and effort he can
always break me down. And I think I want to be
broken down. Because I start to miss him . . . that
hole opens up for me. I just don't know what to do,
so I don't do anything, and then I feel like an idiot
for being so wishy-washy.

As for almost all co-obsessors, Karen's ambivalence was
more than just a state of conflicting emotions. Ambivalence is an immobilizing, frustrating, infuriating state of
being, trapping co-obsessors between the terror of leaving
and the pain of staying.

Co-obsessors respond to this dilemma in one of two
ways. They either bottle up their ambivalent feelings,
putting up with an intolerable amount of internal conflict,
or they act out their ambivalence, repeatedly standing up
for themselves and then backing down.

One day Karen would resist Ray's demands, the next
day she'd give in. One week she'd break up with him, the
next she'd take him back.

In their ambivalence, most co-obsessors are so confused
about what it is that they really feel and what it is they
really want that they can't make the most basic decisions
about their relationships. They lose trust in their own

instincts and perceptions, which makes it even harder for them to be decisive. This paralysis makes them feel inadequate and weak, leading to an enormous amount of shame and self-reproach.

THE CO-OBSESSOR'S SELF-REPROACH

Self-reproach is an ongoing source of pain for co-obsessors. In addition to the self-reproach they feel because they can't make decisions, co-obsessors chastise themselves for acting weak in the face of their obsessive lover's demands and sometimes even for staying in what they know to be an unhealthy relationship.

Karen

When he's being a shit, I never stand up and say "Ray, that isn't any of your business" or "I don't want to answer that." And I feel ashamed of myself because I don't stand up to him. I feel "less than" because I stay in the relationship. I feel like I'm as sick as he is because of my own decision to stay.

Despite her insights, Karen was unable to change her capitulating ways. Instead, she fell into a frustrating cycle of giving in and blaming herself:

- The more she reproached herself, the less confidence she had.

- The less confidence she had, the more powerless she felt.

- The more powerless she felt, the more passive she became.

- The more passive she became, the more she tolerated his inappropriate behavior.

• The more she tolerated his inappropriate behavior, the more she reproached herself.

In small doses, self-reproach can be constructive. It often motivates us to make changes in our lives. But when self-reproach becomes a constant companion—as it did for Karen—it grows increasingly destructive, stepping up the erosion of the co-obsessor's self-confidence and autonomy.

THE CO-OBSESSOR'S GUILT

It is impossible for co-obsessors to meet the expectations and demands of their obsessive lover. The insatiable nature of obsession ensures that. Co-obsessors cannot help but fall short, and the obsessor—who depends totally on the co-obsessor for personal fulfillment—suffers tremendously. When an obsessive lover expresses this pain and disappointment, co-obsessors feel enormously guilty, as if they were responsible.

Karen

About a year after we started living together, I felt like I really needed to get some time by myself, so I told Ray I was going out of town for the weekend. He gave me a really hard time about it because he wanted to come too, but I really stood up for myself—I just had to get away for a while. So I went up the coast to visit my cousins in Ventura. It was such a relief to be with family and have this time, but an hour after I got there, he showed up. I couldn't believe it.

Ray

I figured she'd be pissed at first but I knew she'd be glad to see me. I mean, it's so romantic up there on the beach. How could she have a good time without me? And, as it turned out, she let me stay.

Karen

He begged me to let him stay, even though we'd had this big discussion about my getting away. I felt really resentful, but then he started crying and I felt guilty for feeling resentful. The elemental mom in me came up—he needs that and he needs this and I'm being such a shit. It was like he loved me more than I loved him and I was somehow bad because of it. So I finally said okay and he spent the whole weekend telling me what a good time I was having. It was horrible.

Karen reacted to Ray's suffering as if she had committed a crime, though she had done nothing cruel or malevolent. Once again she accommodated his feelings at the expense of her own, and she was miserable for the entire weekend. But Karen endured her suffering because it eased her undeserved feelings of guilt. Unfortunately, it did nothing to ease her anger.

The Turning Point

For Karen, Ray's violation of his promise to ''give'' her the weekend to herself turned out to be the last straw. It finally drove home the fact that she was paying too high a price.

Karen

I stewed in the car all the way to town. It just felt like the whole relationship was him getting his needs taken care of and him always coming first. But love is respecting another person's wishes, it's not having to come first all the time. I was fed up with his jealousy, fed up with his arguments, fed up with *him*. I was tired of waking up in the middle of the night with my stomach in knots. By the time I got home, I was really worked up. . . . He was there waiting for me, grinning. I was very, very angry and he didn't even notice. He just kept talking about what a great weekend it had been. Well, that was it for me. I really blew up and told him I wanted him out of my life.

Many co-obsessors never come to recognize the destructive nature of their relationships and continue to feed their lover's obsessive tendencies for years. But many others, like Karen, finally decide that the negatives in their relationship outweigh the positives. Along with Karen's decision came a discovery.

Karen

He was so shocked when I kicked him out that he just went. I was amazed. But then he came back a couple of hours later. He knocked on the back door. I didn't answer. He went to the front door. I didn't answer. He went to the window. I didn't answer. I was furious because he was making me feel like a prisoner in my own house. Then I had the most incredible realization—this tormenting kind of realization—that I had needed a person who was as sick as he was, and that's how sick I had been. I couldn't believe I had needed his neediness so much. So I swore that this time I wasn't going to back down. I finally had to threaten to call the police to get him to leave.

When Karen finally came to see just how unhealthy her relationship had been, she was flooded with shame and self-reproach. But this time, instead of allowing these feelings to paralyze her, she took control of her own life, determined to finally stand up for herself. That's when she insisted that she and Ray get professional help.

The line between co-obsession and obsession is thin because the drives and needs of both co-obsessors and obsessors are virtually identical. The primary difference between co-obsessors and obsessors lies in the extent to which they act out these drives and needs.

Co-obsession is a maddening emotional tug-of-war between oppression and passion. Co-obsessors tolerate an enormous amount of suffocating possessiveness in order to get the love they need to fill the inner emptiness they have in common with their obsessor. But by tolerating inappropriate behavior, co-obsessors inadvertently encourage their lover's obsessiveness. They become increasingly enmeshed in a chaotic and unhealthy relationship until they find the courage and determination to make some positive changes in their life.

SIX

Breaking Up Is Hard to Do

It takes two people to make a relationship, and it takes two people to break one. That's why it's never easy to break up with an obsessive lover. Obsessive lovers invariably refuse to let go, and targets often have conflicts of their own that complicate the process.

In the last chapter we met a target who was torn by conflicting feelings and unsure about whether to leave the relationship. In this chapter we will meet targets who are crystal clear about their desire to get out. Yet they still have a very hard time finding a way to do it.

It is normal, in any failing relationship, for the person who wants out to take some time coming to that decision and then more time putting it into action. There are usually stages to ending a relationship, just as there are to building one. But with an obsessive lover, the final stage—carrying out the decision—itself becomes a frustrating, drawn-out, emotionally draining process.

A fortunate few targets are assertive about wanting to end their relationship and do just that. Others find themselves locked in a struggle to leave an obsessor who will not accept the fact that the relationship is over. But many targets have trouble ending the relationship because they are handcuffed by their *own* feelings—feelings of compassion, guilt, and sexual desire.

When the Target's Feelings Get in the Way

No one with any conscience likes to be the cause of someone else's pain. But in the complex and often bewildering maze of human relationships, it is inevitable that lovers sometimes get hurt. Even if we have no unkind intentions, even if we commit no malicious acts, we are all still susceptible to feeling cruel when we hurt a lover by ending a relationship. In an obsessive relationship, these feelings are amplified by the enormity of the obsessor's suffering.

"I COULDN'T STAND IT WHEN SHE CRIED"

Elliot, thirty-five, is a husky, blond, bearded New York–based documentary film producer. While at a party, he met Lisa, a free-lance graphic designer. He had been seeing a woman named Hanna fairly regularly for about a year, though they both dated other people. When he started going out with Lisa, he was open about Hanna, and Lisa didn't appear to be bothered by it. She seemed to agree that because she and Elliot were just getting to know each other, it was premature to expect any emotional commitments. But it soon became apparent to Elliot that Lisa's acceptance of his other lover was a facade. In subtle ways, she began to let him know that deep down, she found his relationship with Hanna very upsetting. She became increasingly possessive.

It took only five weeks for Elliot to feel suffocated by Lisa. He realized that he didn't want to continue seeing her.

Elliot

I absolutely wanted out, no ifs, ands, or buts. But I got so hung up in trying to let her down gently that I wasn't letting her down at all. I really didn't want to see her anymore, but I couldn't bring myself to just say it. So I gave her a song and dance about needing a little breathing space. I didn't say we should stop seeing each other, just that we should see each other less often. I thought I was being pretty gentle, but she fell apart anyway. She started sobbing about how this couldn't be happening to us, things were going so well, we were so happy together. . . . I thought to myself, "Whose relationship is she talking about? This doesn't sound like ours." But she looked so pitiful and so hurt. . . . I felt incredibly guilty. Here was this grown-up, intelligent woman and I'd reduced her to a helpless, sobbing little girl. I had to do something to calm her down so I backed off. I made some lame excuse about being under a lot of pressure at work and told her maybe this wasn't a great time to be talking about this.

Elliot, unlike Karen, knew he wanted out. Unfortunately, he was no match for the one-two punch of compassion and guilt. His own emotions undercut his resolve, preventing him from making a clean break.

Elliot mistakenly thought he was being kind by "letting Lisa down easy." He was trying to act humanely in a difficult, unpleasant situation. But in the long run, he was merely delaying and possibly exacerbating Lisa's pain, the very pain he was trying to assuage.

"HOW CAN I HURT HIM
WHEN HE LOVES ME SO MUCH?"

If Elliot could feel so responsible for Lisa's feelings after only a month of nonexclusive dating, imagine how responsible Shelly felt when she decided to end her two-year marriage.

Shelly, a twenty-seven-year-old green-eyed brunette, works as a hygienist in my dentist's office. Shelly met Mark, a high school counselor, at a charity bazaar at the church in which they were both very active.

On their very first date Mark asked Shelly to stop seeing other men. She had serious misgivings but, intrigued by the intensity of his interest, she agreed. As their relationship progressed, she was initially drawn in by his growing adoration but eventually began to tire of his need for constant reassurance.

Six months later Mark asked her to marry him. With some trepidation she agreed, hoping that her "sacred vows" would relieve his fears. It didn't work. By the end of their first year of marriage Shelly was fed up with what had become a constant barrage of suspicious outbursts and accusations. She was convinced that she and Mark could never make the relationship work. But she couldn't bring herself to tell him. Shelly came to see me as a client a few weeks after their second anniversary.

Shelly

I don't even know if I was ever really in love with him, but he was so in love with me that I figured it was meant to be. The Lord must have had a plan and purpose to lead me into this relationship. There were a lot of things about him that bothered me—he has this horrific temper—but I figured once I made the commitment, I would open up to him and he would calm down. So we got married and I really tried to love him, but he gets so upset about the littlest things. I've talked to my minister about it and he suggested coming in together to try and save the marriage . . . but that's just not what I want. I want out. Period. I just want out. I just can't figure out how to tell him. He's so. . . . I mean, I don't know *what* he'll do. He's always saying, "I can't live without you . . . I love you so much it scares me . . . you're my whole life. . . ."

Shelly married Mark for all the wrong reasons. It was *his* love, not theirs, that led them to the altar. In addition, she made the mistake of underestimating—as most targets do— the insatiability of obsession. She believed that marriage would make him feel secure enough to "calm down," when, in fact, no commitment is reassuring enough to overcome the jealousy and volatility of obsessive love. Shelly's commitment was doomed from the start. And once she had made that commitment, she found herself locked into the relationship by her own misplaced sense of duty.

In telling Shelly things like "I can't live without you," Mark made it very clear that he considered her the guardian of his emotional well-being. It was as if he had packed up his happiness and handed it to her for safekeeping. This was a terrible burden for Shelly, one that she didn't take lightly. By accepting custodial responsibility for his happiness, she was setting herself up to feel guilty if she were to let him down.

Shelly's struggle to end her relationship was complicated by her religious belief that marriage was sacred and by the fact that she was ashamed that she had married a man she didn't really love. She found herself trapped between the same immobilizing feelings that had thwarted Elliot—compassion and guilt.

Shelly

He tells me, "You're so perfect. There's nothing about you I don't love," and I just want to AAAAGH! I can't go to the market without him going; I can't do my gardening without him hanging around; I can't write a letter without him wanting to read it; I don't see any of my friends anymore because none of them like him, but he won't let me go out without him. He loves me so much . . . and that only makes it worse. I've always seen myself as a nurturer and a giver. I mean, I've been doing church work since I could walk. And here I am wanting to devastate the man who wants nothing more out of life than to love and adore me every second of the day. What kind of a Christian does that make me? Aren't I supposed to give as well as receive?

Shelly was convinced that if she were to tell Mark how she really felt, she would be a bad person—both in her estimation and in God's. How could she inflict that kind of pain on a man who was so totally devoted to her? Even though she was miserable in the relationship, her beliefs about how a loving, moral person is supposed to act prevented her from doing anything about getting out.

THE TRAP OF GREAT SEX

The power of sexual pleasure can also make it difficult for a target to act decisively to end a relationship. While some obsessors are as insensitive to their target's sexual needs as they are to his or her emotional needs, many obsessive lovers are so preoccupied by their target that they become extremely responsive to sexual needs. These obsessors can make unusually satisfying lovers.

Even though Elliot had made the still-unspoken decision to stop seeing Lisa, he continued to want her sexually. This desire was initially more powerful than his resolve, but under the circumstances, sex led to increasing guilt. So a few weeks after his aborted attempt to cut back on seeing her, he told her he "just wanted to be friends."

Elliot

She agreed to do whatever I wanted as long as we could keep seeing each other. I cut back on seeing her to once a week, and we stopped sleeping together, but she kept trying to tempt me back into it with new massage techniques, sex toys, whatever. She'd model her new lingerie for me under the pretext that she had bought it for some other guy, then she'd wind up sitting in my lap half-naked, trying to seduce me. Then one night, after we'd had a bottle of wine, she was massaging my feet and she was . . . just the way she was rubbing my skin, it was really sensual . . . and then she started inching up my calves, up my thighs. . . . I was getting incredibly turned on. I thought to myself, "What am I doing?" Sex was the only thing I still enjoyed doing with her, and it was the only thing I was denying myself. And it wasn't like abstinence was making any difference to her—she was still calling me ten times a day. So I thought, "What the hell." Before I knew it we were back to seeing each other three times a week.

Surrendering to the tremendous sexual electricity between them, Elliot once again backed down. He could have said no. He could have resisted. But he didn't. He saw Lisa's seduction as something he had no power to resist, something that just happened to him. Once Lisa realized, whether consciously or unconsciously, that she could hold on to Elliot through sex, she had a great deal of power at her disposal.

Men hold no monopoly on surrendering to intense sexuality. Many women targets fall into the same trap.

Shelly

When I was growing up, sex was always the big carrot at the end of the stick. It was something to save yourself for. I've never slept with another man, so sleeping with Mark was a big thing for me. It was more than just being a dutiful wife in the eyes of God—although that's important to me—it was something I really enjoyed. I still do. I'll hate to give that up when I finally leave him. It seems so hard to find a man out there, especially if you don't believe in premarital sex.

Shelly's sexual hook had a barb—the religious beliefs that she knew would prevent her from enjoying sex until she could remarry. The fear of sacrificing sexual pleasure is not limited to those who are strictly religious. Many single people in today's world are daunted by the dating scene and by the threat of sexually transmitted diseases, including AIDS. These fears are enough to cause many targets, both male and female, to have second thoughts about leaving obsessive relationships.

Double Messages

When targets delay acting on the decision to end a relationship, they invariably become dishonest, saying and doing things that contradict their true feelings. They send out a series of confusing messages, which only succeed in fanning the flames of their lover's obsessive behavior.

Most people mistakenly believe that we communicate our feelings primarily by talking about them. Psychological research indicates that as much as 75 percent of all communication is nonverbal. Body language, behavior, and attitude are often more expressive than words. When we are conflicted, or are trying to hide our real feelings, we often say one thing but *do* another, giving out what are commonly known as double messages.

SAYING ONE THING, DOING ANOTHER

Despite grave misgivings, Elliot continued his sexual relationship with Lisa. He also continued to see Hanna, which increasingly frustrated Lisa. One night she finally exploded. But this time, instead of backing down, Elliot got angry and told her this just wasn't working for him and he didn't want to see her anymore. Then he stormed out, leaving her in tears.

Elliot didn't hear from Lisa for two weeks, leading him to believe it was finally over. Then she showed up unexpectedly at his apartment.

Elliot

I opened the door and there she was, all smiles and sweetness as if nothing had happened. She was wearing this fancy coat and these sexy spike heels, and I remember wondering what she was dressed up for. Then she opened her coat and she was naked underneath. My first thought was, "Oh, no. Not again." I tried not to hurt her feelings, but I told her to go home, this was a bad idea. I might as well have been speaking Swahili. She just walked right in. I kept thinking, "Don't be an idiot. She's too crazy. You'll just start the whole thing all over again." But she looked so good, and she was *so* sexy. . . . I mean, a naked woman showing up at your door—this was like a lifelong fantasy come true. I kept saying, "no, no, no," but there was no way I could get any conviction in my voice. She sure had my number, boy.

Elliot gave Lisa a classic double message. His words said, "I don't want you," but his nonverbal message—which culminated in his sleeping with her—was just the opposite. He might as well have saved his breath.

When Lisa opened her coat she was exposing herself not only physically, but emotionally. Elliot's difficulty in resisting Lisa was clearly based on sexual desire, compounded by reluctance to humiliate her, especially when she had made herself so vulnerable. Torn between his desire and compassion on the one hand and his determination to get out on the other, Elliot found himself unable to give Lisa a clear, unambiguous message about his feelings. Instead, she got the message that there was still a place in his life for her if she just kept up her pursuit. No wonder Lisa refused to give up—once again he had let her back in, both literally and figuratively.

THE TRUTH WILL COME OUT

Lisa may not have taken Elliot seriously when he told her he wanted to end their relationship, but at least he had spoken the words. Shelly, however, couldn't bring herself to tell Mark that she wanted out. Instead, she used words to try to hide what she really wanted.

Shelly
It's come to the point where I really don't want to be with him. I really think I made a big mistake, and I

feel awful about it, but I'm not ready to tell him how I feel. So I put on a front. Stuff still leaks through, though, you know? Like when we're at church, he always has to be touching me. He's always got to be messing with my hair or touching my shoulder or holding my hand. He makes me feel really claustrophobic, like I'm being squashed, and I feel myself shrugging or pushing his hand away. Then he says, "Are you all right?" And I go, "Yeah, I'm fine." But he doesn't buy it and for the rest of the day he's all over me, trying to make me "feel better." I just want to scream, "Let me breathe!"

When Shelly pushed Mark's hand away, she didn't have to *tell* him she didn't want him to touch her, she was speaking with her *behavior*. And in questioning her, he was making it clear that he got her message. Though she hoped that by not expressing her feelings out loud she could somehow hide them from Mark, he still sensed that she was slipping away from him. But her reassuring words reinforced his conviction that there was something he could do to woo her back. So he acted increasingly clingy and solicitous, irritating her all the more.

When a target wants to end a relationship, there is no way of keeping the negative feelings secret—there are just too many ways for true feelings to escape. And when obsessive lovers sense negative feelings, their possessive behavior invariably escalates, making any kind of breakup that much harder.

It is natural for targets to slip into a pattern of double messages, but they invariably pay an emotional price when they do. As we've seen, when targets say one thing and do another, they rarely feel good about themselves. Instead, they feel weak, anxious, and above all, deceptive, adding to the guilt that already compounds their difficulties in ending the relationship.

If you are the target of an obsessive lover and have come to the decision to end your relationship, you need to recognize that double messages only add confusion to an already chaotic situation. In the end, you are only prolonging your unhappiness and delaying the inevitable.

Many targets fail to recognize their own role in perpetuating a failing relationship because they are so focused on how the obsessor is behaving or might behave. I don't mean to imply that once you stop giving double messages your obsessive lover will simply pack up and go away quietly. But your partner is not the only one preventing a clean break. Until you deal with your own conflicts and ambiguous behavior, you can't even begin to deal assertively and effectively with your lover. And until you become assertive with an obsessive lover, there is no chance that he or she will leave you alone.

The Assertive Target

In ordinary usage being assertive means communicating wants and needs frankly, honestly, and directly without becoming belligerent. But when I use the term in the context of an obsessive relationship, it goes a critical step further. Assertive targets must not only express their decision to end the relationship, they must take whatever actions are necessary to enforce that decision.

Breaking up with an obsessive lover is ultimately a power struggle. The target wants to leave and the obsessor wants to prevent that. Targets who hope to win this struggle must begin by digging their defensive trenches, which means knowing what they want and communicating it clearly and repeatedly without backing down.

"I WASN'T RAISED TO DO THIS"

Shelly knew she had to be assertive, but she had no idea where to start. Her upbringing had not prepared her for this.

Shelly

Every other day I screw up my courage and plan to tell Mark how I feel, but when he comes in, my palms start to sweat and I get all shaky inside and I just can't do it. When I grew up, we didn't talk back. If we didn't like it we had to lump it. That's the way it was. And that's how I feel with Mark. I know it's stupid . . . I mean I've got my own career and I believe women should be independent and everything . . . but when it gets down to the nitty-gritty . . . that's just how I feel. I've got all these ideas about how I want it to be, but inside is this little girl who never learned to stick up for herself.

Shelly grew up in a relatively normal family. Her parents were loving, but—like many parents—they believed that children should be seen and not heard. Shelly was not allowed to talk back or to argue with her parents. If she became upset, she was told to go to her room until she could "put on a happy face." She was constantly admonished not to say anything at all if she didn't have anything nice to say.

Shelly's mother (and role model) also lived by these homilies, rarely expressing a negative thought in front of her children. Shelly never saw her parents argue and, as a result, came to see domestic conflict as something unnatural, to be avoided at all costs. She never learned that personal confrontation was a normal part of human relationships and a necessary tool for resolving conflicts.

As an adult, Shelly had no personal experience to draw from when she wanted to express her dissatisfaction to Mark. She knew that what she had to say would upset Mark, and she felt much more comfortable hiding her feelings than she did precipitating an argument. That was how she had avoided conflict all her life. The very thought of expressing negative feelings filled her with anxiety. It would have been uncharacteristic of her to confront Mark and, like the rest of us, she was extremely resistant to anything that went against her nature.

Few of us grow up in a household where the open expression of our negative feelings is encouraged. This is as true for men as it is for women. Though some people overcome this upbringing and manage to develop assertive communication skills on their own, many never do. People with undeveloped assertiveness skills have neither the vocabulary nor the confidence to hold their own in a relationship with an overbearing lover. And obsessive lovers are almost always overbearing.

I didn't think Shelly needed intensive psychotherapy to deal with her relationship with Mark. Instead, she needed to learn how to stop giving double messages and start getting her real message across to Mark. I suggested some short-term crisis resolution work that included assertiveness training. After a few months Shelly was finally ready to tell Mark, honestly and decisively, that she wanted to end their marriage. He was extremely upset, but when she refused to back down after he made an eloquent, teary, and lengthy plea, he finally accepted what she had to say.

Most obsessive lovers are not so accommodating.

MAKING ASSERTIVE STATEMENTS

If you haven't been as successful as Shelly in persuading an obsessive lover that your relationship is over, here are some assertive statements that might get him or her to take you seriously.

Though these statements may seem harsh, there is no room for subtlety or uncertainty when trying to communicate with someone who doesn't want to hear what you're saying. The key to all of these statements is not to let your lover back you into a defensive position.

- It's over. This is not negotiable. I won't discuss it anymore.

- I'm going to hang up now, and if you call back I'll hang up again without speaking to you.

- I want you to leave now, and I don't want you coming back. If you do, I won't let you in.

- Don't call, don't write, don't show up, don't contact me in any way.

- If you continue to harass me, I will have no choice but to get a court order against you.

Remember that obsessors believe they know your true feelings better than you do, so you won't accomplish anything by letting yourself get drawn into an explanation of your position. Instead, make clear, unequivocal statements about what you want and what you will do if they don't leave you alone. Explanations may make you feel less cruel, but they only muddy the waters, giving the obsessor hope that you can be persuaded to reconsider. An obsessor will never give up as long as you're still willing to talk.

"I NEVER THOUGHT I COULD BE SO CRUEL"

Assertive messages can have a significant impact on an obsessor, and they should certainly be the first step for any targets who want to end their relationship. However, many obsessive lovers are infuriatingly deaf to even the most articulate, emphatic, unambiguous, and decisive statements.

Elliot

When I first tried to break up with Lisa, it was like "I don't think we should see each other anymore" but then I went to bed with her. Obviously, that was a mistake, so I tried, "Let's not sleep together anymore. We can still be friends, but that's it." When that didn't work, it became, "You're really terrific, but we're just not compatible, and I think the feelings between us are too confusing for us to have any kind of a relationship, even a platonic one." When that message didn't compute, I was forced to get into, "I don't want to see you, I don't want you calling me, I don't want to have anything to do with you." And when even that didn't work I had to finally start hanging up the minute I heard her voice and slamming the door in her face.

Elliot learned the hard way that nothing short of being cold and blunt would get through to Lisa. When he tried to let her down easy, Lisa misread his attempts to be kind and supportive as proof that he cared about her. It didn't matter what he said. She wasn't listening, she was just looking for an opening. Her unwillingness to take no for an answer left Elliot with little choice but to act in ways that he hated.

Elliot

I'd always thought of myself as a pretty sensitive, honest guy. But she really brought out the worst in me. I mean, she forced me to be an asshole. I believe in communicating with people, that's how you solve problems. I'd never just slammed the phone down on anybody in my life. It really made me feel shitty about myself.

Elliot had strong feelings of self-reproach. He'd acted in ways that contradicted his self-image. Instead of feeling assertive, he felt brutal. But Lisa's behavior had backed him into a corner. In the end, his only alternative to being "cruel" would have been to stay in a relationship that had become unbearable.

"I THOUGHT IT WAS FINALLY OVER"

To Elliot's relief, his relationship with Lisa finally seemed over. He hadn't heard from her in almost two months. But then she called.

Elliot
She said she'd been in therapy and she'd learned that a lot of the conflicts she had with her parents she had been taking out on me. She wanted to get together with me, just for lunch, just to clear the air between us. She said she couldn't stand the idea of having anyone running around thinking she was crazy. She really sounded different, and she made a lot of sense. After all, the end had been pretty ugly . . . and it was just one lunch. . . . If it would help to get it all behind us, I figured why not?

Under the circumstances, most of us might have said "why not." The thought of retroactively turning a bad ending into an amicable one is very tempting. And Elliot had good reason to believe that Lisa had finally accepted the reality of their separation. After all, two months had gone by without her attempting to make any contact. Her description of the insights she had gained through therapy sounded plausible. And she was only asking for one lunch—how much harm could there be in that?

Elliot

The second I saw her, I knew I'd made a mistake. She was wearing a very sexy dress and she greeted me with a big hug "for old times' sake." We had hardly ordered our food before she started trying to rope me into another date. Things like, she was taking a Chinese cooking class and wondered if I'd be willing to be the guinea pig for her class project. Or the wedding of a mutual friend that she wanted to carpool to because she always got lost when she drove herself to this person's house. I kept saying no, until she finally asked me point-blank why I was turning her down on all these things, since they were all so innocent. I told her I just didn't trust her. So she went into this very calm, lucid argument about how she'd changed in the last two months and how unfair it was of me to judge her now on the basis of a very troubled time in her life. By the time she finished, I was drowning in my own guilt again. I came *this* close to agreeing to see her again. But I didn't. I just knew if I gave her the inch, she'd take the mile.

When Elliot agreed to have lunch with Lisa, he was, in effect, giving her a few crumbs of hope. But from crumbs, obsessive lovers make loaves. Elliot should have known that Lisa wasn't about to give up easily. What appeared to be a harmless meeting quickly turned into another seduction. Only this time, instead of using sexuality, she used reason. She knew that he feared her volatility and emotionality, so she managed to keep those parts of her personality in check. She presented herself as a changed woman. But Elliot sensed that she had changed only her style, not her goal.

Obsessors take the slightest indication of friendship or even curiosity to mean that the target is still ambivalent and can perhaps be won back. In some cases it may be possible to maintain some friendly contact with a former lover, but because there is no way of predicting how an obsessor will interpret or experience a brief act of openness, it is safer to err on the side of caution. The harsh reality for many targets is that once they make the decision and manage to extricate themselves from an obsessive relationship, it is risky to let their former lover back into their lives in any way.

After his lunch with Lisa, Elliot decided—again—to cut off all future contact with her, no matter how persuasive her approach might be. He simply wasn't willing to make himself vulnerable to her manipulations anymore. Still, she continued to call every few months for the next two years, each time with a different clever story. She kept it up even after Elliot married Hanna. But her calls came less and less often as time wore on. It has now been a year since Elliot last heard from Lisa.

TAKING ASSERTIVE ACTION

Sometimes assertive words—even cruel ones—are insufficient. Gloria found that no matter what she said, her former lover Jim just wouldn't believe she didn't want to see him. She finally resorted to assertive *action*, when she called the security guards to remove Jim from her office.

Gloria

I heard him shouting and pounding on the door, and I thought, "The hell with him, I'm tired of having him walk all over my life. It's *my* life.'' The first time I told him I didn't want to see him anymore, I felt a lot of ambivalence about it, but after six months of his full-court press, I was totally fed up. I was tired of being a victim. When I watched Security drag him out, I expected to feel guilty, but I didn't. I just felt proud of myself for finally taking charge.

Unlike Elliot who was racked with guilt, Gloria found a new sense of confidence, strength, and relief in her assertive action. Many targets find that assertive action frees them from the sense of helplessness they had been experiencing in the face of their obsessive lover's refusal to let go.

But even when assertive action is emotionally gratifying, it is rarely easy. Assertive action often causes considerable inconvenience in the target's life. Here are some examples of assertive action:

- Hanging up on phone calls or even changing your phone number

- Returning letters unopened

- Returning unsolicited gifts

- Telling mutual friends that you don't want them inviting you and your former lover to the same party

- Refusing to open the door to your former lover when he or she makes unexpected visits

- Calling security guards or the police

- Getting a restraining order

You don't need a therapist to teach you these behaviors— you simply need to become determined enough to put them into practice. This is always tough at first, but if your obsessive lover refuses to stop pursuing you, I promise you that assertive action will get easier with practice. And sooner or later, in the face of truly assertive and unambiguous action, most obsessive lovers *do* give up.

I know some of you will feel guilty over the lengths to which you are forced to go, but guilt under these circumstances is *not* an indication that you are doing something wrong. Instead, it is an indication that you are doing something you are not used to doing. In order to become truly free of an obsessive lover, and to regain control of your own life, you need to tolerate that guilt. The guilt will go away, but if you don't act assertively, your obsessive lover probably won't.

WHEN THERE'S
MORE TO LOSE THAN A LOVER

Sometimes assertive action is complicated not only by emotional factors, but by practical considerations. Some obsessors take advantage of positions of power to pursue their targets. Whether it's the clergyman who pursues a member of his congregation, the psychologist who pursues one of her interns, the physician who pursues his receptionist, or the college professor who pursues one of her students, obsessors in positions of authority make it infinitely more complicated for a target to end the relationship.

Rhonda is an associate professor of literature at a large university in southern California. She is a very delicately featured brunette, whose oversized tortoise-shell glasses give her a whimsical, almost owlish look. Rhonda came up to me after a speaking engagement, during which I had mentioned that I was working on this book, and she offered me her story.

Rhonda was competing for a tenured position in her

department, a position that would ultimately be awarded according to the recommendation of the powerful department chairperson, a slightly older woman named Lynn. In the academic world, tenure is often a matter of survival, since without it there is no job security. Now forty, Rhonda was ready for some security in her life. In fact, she had been pursuing this position for five years.

A year earlier, Rhonda had broken up with a woman with whom she had been in a long-term lesbian relationship. At that time, Lynn had been very kind and supportive, helping Rhonda deal with the pain of the breakup. Rhonda was aware that Lynn was attracted to her, but Rhonda was not physically drawn to Lynn. Still, as their personal relationship deepened, Rhonda found Lynn's intelligence, sensitivity, and warmth increasingly attractive. Lynn took her time developing her relationship with Rhonda, and by the time she finally made a sexual advance, Rhonda had become receptive.

Rhonda

I knew it was dangerous to get involved with her—she held my whole future in her hands—but she assured me that she could keep our personal relationship separate from our professional one. I knew it wasn't that simple, but she told me I was really talented, that I was a natural, that I was the most gifted associate she'd ever seen, so I figured I had the job anyway. And I really needed someone in my life right then . . . she was so supportive, so full of ideas, so full of life, so full of love. She was like a magnet for me. She just drew me in.

Rhonda believed she was attracted to Lynn's personal qualities but, as Henry Kissinger once said, power is the ultimate aphrodisiac. Rhonda's attraction was undoubtedly influenced by the seductive trappings of the power of Lynn's position.

Rhonda knew her relationship with Lynn was complicated by the imbalance of power between them, but it wasn't until Lynn's obsessive nature began to emerge that Rhonda realized just how great that complication really was. As Lynn and Rhonda settled into their sexual relationship, Lynn began to have jealous fantasies about Rhonda. She became increasingly possessive. When Rhonda went to San Francisco for a two-week seminar, Lynn flew up to see her three times. Lynn also called Rhonda four or five times a day and interrogated her about whether she was having sex with anyone else. Then, when Rhonda returned, Lynn began showing Rhonda off to her friends, as if they were engaged to be married.

Rhonda

I began to feel like a piece of property. I knew I had to end it, but I was afraid that I couldn't get out. Not only would she go nuts, but I was sure I could kiss my tenure good-bye. Five years of my life down the drain. She really had me over a barrel.

Rhonda had gotten herself trapped in a situation that had no easy exit. In past relationships, she had generally tried to express her emotions clearly and assertively, but if she were to do that with Lynn, she would be risking serious consequences to her career. On the other hand, if she stayed in a relationship solely for the sake of her job, she would be selling out her emotional well-being.

Rhonda

Then one night we were having dinner with her sister and Lynn started rambling about all these plans for the future that I'd never heard of before . . . and how I was the woman she was going to spend the rest of her life with. I realized I couldn't put it off anymore. It wasn't fair to her; it wasn't fair to me. No matter what it cost me professionally, I had to get out. When we got back to my house that night, I told her.

Lynn was deeply hurt by Rhonda's rejection. She became enraged and, as Rhonda had feared, Lynn acted out her anger at work.

Rhonda

We had a department meeting about three days later, and she really tore into me about some minor curriculum changes I wanted to make. She got incredibly critical about what I thought were very good ideas and went out of her way to humiliate me in front of the whole department. I didn't say anything, hoping she'd get over it, but she didn't. For the next couple of weeks she never missed an opportunity to take a potshot at me. It seemed pretty obvious that she was going to stand in the way of my getting tenure, so I decided to play hardball. I accused her of letting her personal feelings intrude on my career, and I warned her that if she didn't lay off I was going to report her to the administration for sexual harassment. That finally got her to stop sniping, but there's still a lot of tension between us. It makes my work harder, and sometimes we clash, but it looks like I *will* get tenure next year.

Rhonda might have changed jobs to escape her obsessive superior, as many targets do, but this choice is not always possible or practical. In Rhonda's case, another tenured position would have been extremely difficult for her to find, and even if she had, she might have had to spend another five years on a "tenure track" before that position opened up for her. So Rhonda chose to be assertive with Lynn, despite the professional risk, and in so doing, made the best of a very difficult situation. Granted, her working environment remained sometimes tense and uncomfortable, but for Rhonda, that was the lesser of two evils.

It is always dangerous to get involved with a lover who is in a position of power. This is especially true if your lover is obsessive, because obsessors have a tendency to become punitive and retaliatory when they are rejected. It is hard enough to break up with an obsessive lover without having to worry about your job as well.

The Ultimate Emotional Blackmail

It is not unusual for obsessive lovers, in a desperate attempt to prevent a target from leaving, to threaten suicide (as we saw with Anne in Chapter Two). When obsessors declare that their life now lies in the hands of their target, they place an enormous amount of pressure on their target to stay in the relationship. This happened to Gloria the first time she told Jim she wanted to leave him.

Gloria
I decided it wasn't working about a month after we started going together, but it took me another couple months to actually do something about it. When I told him I was leaving him, he started sobbing about how he was just going to go drive off a cliff. Without me, he had nothing to live for. I mean, he was really melodramatic about it, but he's so damned unpredictable . . . I was terrified that he might actu-

ally do it. So I calmed him down and told him I'd give him one more chance but he had to stop acting so possessive. He swore up and down that he'd change . . . of course, he never did.

To assuage her understandable fears, that he would follow through and that she would feel guilty, Gloria submitted to Jim's emotional blackmail and backed down on her intention to leave him. In capitulating, Gloria was virtually guaranteeing that he would repeat this threat whenever he felt fearful that she might leave him.

Gloria

Within two weeks I was climbing the walls again. It got to the point where I felt like it was him or me. So I decided I was just going to have to tough out the breakup and pray that he didn't mean what he said. I begged him to get professional help, but that was as far as I could go. After I left he called me and more or less threatened to kill himself a couple more times, but he never actually tried anything.

Gloria had no way of knowing whether Jim's threats were serious. No one ever knows. Some people who threaten suicide never actually attempt it. Many others do. The bottom line is: *suicide is ultimately a personal choice*.

If you, like Gloria, are the target of an obsessive lover who has threatened to commit suicide because you want to leave the relationship, you must take that threat seriously. But that doesn't mean that you have to assume responsibility for your lover's life. The most constructive thing you can do is to encourage your lover to make use of one of the many professional resources available to help people in crisis. If your lover has sympathetic family members or friends, you might also alert them to the suicide threat, and to the fact that you are firm in your decision to end the relationship. But beyond that, your lover's life must be his or her own responsibility.

I know this may be very hard for you to accept, but you have no moral obligation to sacrifice your own emotional well-being if your obsessive lover threatens to act irrationally in response to your decision to leave—a decision you have every right to make.

Breaking up with an obsessive lover can be a very painful, complicated, anxiety-ridden process. Once you come to the decision to end an obsessive relationship, you must be prepared to confront significant obstacles, not only from your obsessive lover, but from yourself as well. If you have decided there is no way to make the relationship work, breaking up may be hard to do, but it is far better than the alternative.

to the fact that you are .... relationship and the
relation .... be like

SEVEN

When Obsession Turns to Violence

We're about to explore a dark realm—the chaos inflicted on the lives of targets whose rejected obsessive lovers become violent. This is a tough chapter for me to write because I know how shocking some of these stories can be to read. The last thing I want is to dissuade anyone from entering into a new relationship, or to frighten anyone out of ending a bad one. But there are important lessons to be learned from the sometimes tragic mistakes made by the women and men you are about to meet.

Violence is an ugly reality for some targets of obsessive love, and you can't change that reality by pretending that it doesn't exist. We've all heard the highly publicized stories of celebrities who have fallen victim to an obsessive lover's violence, from actresses Dominique Dunne and Dorothy Stratton to Scarsdale Diet doctor Herman Tarnower. But this sort of violence is hardly limited to the rich and famous—the papers are full of stories of rejected obsessors who assault or even murder their former partners.

If you are planning to end an obsessive relationship or have already ended one, it's important that you don't underestimate the primal, powerful rage that rejection can ignite in an obsessive lover. If you are—or fear you might become—the target of a potentially violent obsessor, there *are* steps you can take to protect yourself. These steps are not fail-safe, but the better prepared you are, the better your chances of not becoming a victim or, at the very least, of not becoming a repeat victim.

Vandalism: Prelude to Assault?

Walter, fifty-seven years old, is a broad-shouldered, balding, blue-eyed mechanic who owns a small auto repair shop where I spend much more time than I'd like to. Fortunately, he is amiable and he likes to chat, so my visits are as pleasant as can be expected. I've gotten to know Walter pretty well over the years, so when I told him I was working on this book, he willingly offered his own disturbing experience with an obsessive lover.

Walter's first wife died four years ago after a long and draining battle against cancer. It took him a long time to get back on his emotional feet, but he had the help of several good friends, two loving children, and three adorable grandchildren. About two years after his wife's death, after considerable urging from his family, Walter began to date. A few months later, he met Nan.

Nan, forty-eight, was working as a hostess in a coffee shop when Walter met her. They were attracted to each other immediately, and he invited her out for a drink that same night. They saw each other twice more that week. On their fourth date, they went to bed. Nan was the first woman since his wife's death with whom Walter felt close enough to become sexual.

Nan was a passionate lover, and when Walter was with

her, he felt more excited and alive than he had in years. But Nan became increasingly demanding and possessive. After four or five months, she began pressuring him to marry her. Walter told her he was not ready to remarry, but she became increasingly insistent and agitated about it. Finally, he told her he wanted to end their relationship.

Nan didn't believe that Walter really meant it. She began calling several times a day, dropping by the shop, dropping by his apartment, and sending letters, hoping to get him to change his mind. When Walter refused to respond to her attempts, she became hysterical. On one occasion, she threw a coffee cup at Walter in his kitchen. On another, she threw a wrench through his shop window. Walter was increasingly annoyed and frustrated by her refusal to give up despite his blunt rejections, but he had no idea how to get her to stop. He just hoped that she would finally run out of steam and leave him alone.

About a month after he broke up with Nan, Walter met Betty, an insurance agent. They began dating and quickly fell in love.

Walter

When me and Betty got engaged I figured this was the straw that would get Nan off my back. The next time she came into the shop, I told her. She turned into an ice queen. She just shut down. I remember she muttered something about making sure I'd never forget her, then she just split. I figured that was that and went back to work.

Walter, like many targets, was lulled into a false sense of relief by the fact that Nan seemed to take the news of his engagement calmly. He had expected an explosion, and when it didn't happen on the spot, he assumed he was home free. But obsessive rage, as we have seen throughout this book, rarely remains contained. It may erupt against an innocent third party; it may erupt inwardly causing the obsessor to become self-destructive; but usually, it erupts against the target, too often in the form of violence.

Nan gave Walter a pretty blatant clue that he would be seeing more of her, but he failed to pick up on it. If he had paid closer attention he might have realized that when she "muttered something about making sure I'd never forget her," she was delivering a threat.

"I NEVER THOUGHT SHE'D GO THIS FAR"

When Walter got home that night, he found his front door wide open. His first thought was that he'd been robbed, but when he stepped inside he smelled smoke.

Walter

My adrenaline was pumping like a four-barrel carb. I walked into the bedroom and my clothes were every-where, like it was a twister come through. There were jockeys, socks, shirts, everything all over . . . except nothing big. No jackets, no pants, no closet stuff, you know? So I followed my nose into the bathroom and there was the rest of my stuff . . . in ashes. She took and torched my whole closet in the tub. The bath-room was smoked completely black, and the paint was burned off all the way up the wall. I called the police, but I couldn't prove she did it, so they couldn't do anything. But I knew it was her because the door was open and she was the only other one with a key. I guess it was stupid not to change the locks, but I never thought she'd do anything like that.

Like many targets of obsessive lovers—especially male targets—Walter had a tendency to be complacent about his safety. After all, he was so much larger and stronger than Nan; the thought of her being able to hurt him never even crossed his mind. But Walter knew that Nan had violent tendencies, because she had thrown objects during her tantrums. And he knew that she had easy access to his apartment, because during their affair, he had given her a key. A precaution as simple as new locks may not have prevented Nan from acting out against Walter; on the other hand, it may have. Even a minor obstacle is sometimes enough to discourage an obsessor from acting on a momentary impulse.

Walter

It was just dumb luck that she didn't burn the whole building down. And I gotta tell you, that's all I could think about for the next two months. I mean, what was to stop her from coming back, burning the place down while we're sleeping? I fought in Korea—I can take care of myself. But I was scared. I was real scared. I'm still scared. I heard she took an overdose and wound up in a hospital somewhere, but I still worry she'll come back. It's been two years, but I still think about it.

Walter, who started out without even a thought that he might be in danger, was still scared two years later. Even though Nan's violent outburst was directed only against his possessions, she had graphically demonstrated her capacity for violent revenge. He was justifiably concerned that the next time she might escalate into an assault against him or his new wife. Walter found no comfort in the fact that she never came back—instead, he became preoccupied with the fear that she might. When obsessive lovers transform violent feelings into violent actions, there is no way of telling how long they will continue or how far they will go. Even if they never escalate beyond attacks against property, the fear they engender can hang like a sword over the target's head.

Sexual Assault

Janey is an exceptionally beautiful twenty-year-old red-head, the daughter of dear friends. I've known Janey since she was born. Two years ago, when she was a freshman at an Ivy League college, she met Victor, who was twenty-four years old and a graduate student in business administration. She was not romantically interested in Victor, but they shared a love for classic films and on the weekends would often go to the movies, though always with a group of other friends. Janey became increasingly aware that Victor was very attracted to her, but she took care never to go out with him alone, and she went out of her way not to encourage his attentions. Then, one night, he showed up at her dorm room and professed his love.

Janey

He stood there in the hall with this hangdog look and just waited for me to tell him I loved him too. I told him he was a very nice guy but I wasn't interested in getting involved with him. He said, "Let's not make any decisions now, let's just wait and see." There was something really weird about the whole thing, but I've had a lot of guys say they love me, and it's usually just talk, so I tried to just forget about it. Well, he wouldn't let me. He started showing up everywhere I went. He'd wait outside my classes. He'd jump in line behind me in the caf, then sit with me even if I told him no—so I stopped eating in the caf. Even when I didn't see him I always had this feeling like he was watching me, especially if I was out with somebody else—it felt so slimy. Then I broke a couple of dates so I wouldn't have to deal with it, and a friend got on my case to do something, so I went to Campus Security. They had a long talk with him and he promised to lay off, but he didn't. So I just stayed in my room more. It was easier than being out there feeling like some jerk was spying on me.

Even though they did not have an intimate relationship, Victor's obsession was narrowing Janey's world. She found herself in a frustrating limbo state, common to many targets, where she could take no legal action against her obsessor because he had neither made any overt threats nor broken any laws. When she complained about Victor a second time, one college security officer told her, "If we arrested every guy on campus who got the hots for a girl, we'd have to call in the National Guard."

Janey

One night I was leaving the library and I realized he was following me, so I confronted him . . . told him to leave me alone. His response was, "I love you so much it's killing me. Just give me one kiss." I said, "You've got to be kidding," and it turned into this kind of power struggle where he tried to kiss me and I tried to fight him off, and all the time he's telling me how much he loves me, and the next thing I know he's got this knife and we're in the bushes and he's threatening to kill me if he can't have me. And then he rapes me.

After the rape, Janey became depressed and isolated, dropped out of school, and moved back home. She told her parents she wanted to take some time to get over the trauma, but she refused to talk about the rape, she refused to get counseling, and she refused to press charges. Like many rape victims, Janey was unwilling to face the ordeal of a trial, despite a haunting fear that Victor might find her and repeat his crime.

This went on for almost a year. Janey's parents were increasingly concerned. Although she seemed to be functioning on a day-to-day basis, they were aware of how much she had changed since the rape: she was making no moves toward returning to school, she was working in a dead-end job, and she wasn't dating. She saw old friends only occasionally, and when they asked her about her moodiness, she insisted that she was all right and that she would soon start thinking about getting on with her life.

"I'M TIRED OF FEELING THIS WAY"

Since the day she came home, I had been pushing Janey to let me help her find a therapist who could work with her to get over the emotional hurdle of her trauma, but she had steadfastly refused. Like so many victims of violent crime, once Janey's physical wounds had healed, she was so anxious to forget about what had happened that she chose to ignore, rather than face, her emotional wounds.

I felt incredibly frustrated at being unable to do anything about Janey's suffering—or about her denial. One moment of power for Victor had become months of torment and anguish for her. It infuriated me, as it always does, that the life of an innocent young woman could be so easily devastated by the impulsive violence of a vicious obsessor.

Then one evening, to my delight, Janey called and asked me to have lunch with her. We got together the next day, and I was delighted to find that, for the first time since the rape, she seemed anxious to talk.

Janey

I was watching this really corny love story on TV and all of a sudden I found myself sitting there sobbing. I kept thinking how I'm never going to feel normal enough to fall in love again. Susan, I'm so tired of feeling this way. Please help me.

Though asking for help may seem like a simple step, it required a great deal of courage and honesty for Janey. I referred her to a colleague who specializes in working with victims of sexual assault, and as Janey got stronger in therapy, she decided to stand up for herself by finally filing charges against Victor.

Her case was significantly weakened by the passage of a year, and she would have to travel to another state to testify, but these obstacles were ultimately unimportant to her. She needed to take this affirmative step to devictimize herself. Even if the case never comes to trial, she knows that she has the self-esteem to fight back, and that, more than any jury verdict, is helping Janey regain the self-confidence she once had.

FIGHTING BACK

We tend to associate rape with assaults by strangers, but the incidence of women being raped by someone they know is alarmingly high. Any rape trial is an ordeal for the victim, but when the rapist is someone the victim knows and once liked, or even loved, it is often harder for the victim to find the emotional strength to press charges. If the assailant was a husband or boyfriend, it can be especially difficult for a victim to defend her credibility against the accusations of implied consent that are so often part of cross-examination. But despite the difficulties of a trial, I always advise rape victims to act assertively by pressing charges. It is a way of combatting pain and fear rather than living with them.

When a rapist is an obsessor, his victim has additional fears. Unlike many rapes, this type of rape is not a random act. The victim has been *singled out* as the target. And the rapist is much more likely to try again.

If for no other reason than this, women who are sexually assaulted by obsessive lovers must press charges and be prepared to go the full legal route to get their rapist behind bars. Even if the trial does not result in a prison sentence, the target is sending a strong, clear message to the obsessor that she will not remain a victim. This *does* deter some obsessors from attempting further contact with their victims.

Janey was forced to uproot from the friends and teachers she had come to know because Victor remains a student at the university she had been attending, but she has begun applying to new colleges. She is less afraid to go out alone at night, she is empowering herself physically by taking a self-defense class, and she now carries Mace. She is also empowering herself psychologically by going to a rape victims' group once a week and volunteering on a rape crisis hotline twice a month. Janey has been plagued by nightmares since the rape, but they are becoming less and less frequent, and through therapy, she is beginning to reclaim her capacity for enjoying life.

Physical Violence

Violence is a very real threat in intimate relationships—at least one out of every ten American women is beaten by a husband or lover. For targets of obsessive love, the danger continues even after the relationship ends. Obsessive lovers who think they're losing their One Magic Person may be driven either by a need to regain power over their former lover or by a desire for revenge.

Though men can be the targets of violent obsessive lovers, the majority of reported victims are women. A violent ex-lover or husband can terrorize every corner of a target's world, making it impossible for her to live a normal life. Every memory is a fearsome reminder that he's out there. Every knock on the door, every footstep, every shadow raises the specter of an obsessed assailant poised to attack. While the majority of obsessive lovers *don't* become physically violent when their relationship ends, this is of little comfort to those targets whose lovers *do*.

"I Never Dreamed He Would Hit Me"

Samantha, twenty-seven, a tall, extremely thin ash-blonde with porcelain skin, worked as a teller at a large savings and loan. She was married for two-and-a-half years to Harry, thirty-one, a resident in cardiology at Los Angeles County Hospital. Harry's obsessive nature emerged early in their marriage. He would throw tantrums if she wasn't there when he got home from the hospital. He needed constant reassurance about her faithfulness and devotion.

At first, Samantha, like many targets, put up with Harry's insecurities because she thought they would recede as their relationship deepened. But after a year of marriage, she began to see a physical side of Harry's anger, a side she had never seen before. On one occasion he put his fist through a cabinet; on another he threw a beer bottle into a mirrored wall. These outbursts scared Samantha, but she downplayed their importance by attributing them to temporary stresses at work. She never imagined he would actually hit *her*.

Soon after their second anniversary, Samantha got pregnant. This seemed to provoke even more jealousy in Harry— it's not uncommon for obsessive lovers to feel threatened by the prospect of having to share their partner with the baby. Two months later, when Samantha came home late from a visit with a cousin, Harry exploded. Accusing her of having been with another man, he hit her across the face hard enough to knock her down.

Samantha

I was more stunned emotionally than physically. I was so sure that I knew him. I was so sure that he'd never do anything to hurt me. At that moment, something inside of me just died. For the first time he looked ugly to me. I knew I couldn't live with him anymore. It was just over.

That night she moved in with her mother. A few days later she filed for divorce. To prevent Harry from having an opportunity to repeat his assault, Samantha's lawyer went to court to obtain a restraining order. Harry was prohibited from contacting Samantha directly or from coming within 300 yards of her.

GRIEVING THE END
OF A VIOLENT RELATIONSHIP

Samantha had put up with Harry's outbursts and tantrums for two years, but she was not willing to put up with being hit. The moment he crossed that line, she knew she had to leave him, and she did so quickly and decisively. Yet, her decision was anything but easy.

Samantha

I got really depressed for a while. After all, I was still carrying his baby, and we had had some great

times. I had always thought I was going to be with
him for the rest of my life, then all of a sudden . . .
that's a hard thing to give up.

Many targets, like Samantha, believe that because they are
doing something healthy for themselves by ending their
violent relationship they will come away emotionally un-
scathed. But Samantha's shock and horror over Harry's
violence did not prevent her from suffering grief over the
death of their relationship and over the failure of her
expectations for the future.

It is difficult for most people to understand how a target
can grieve the loss of a violent relationship. But no matter
how bad a relationship has become, when it comes to an
end, most targets feel some sense of loss for the good
times, for the security of being connected to another person, and for "what might have been."

RATIONALIZING VIOLENCE

Samantha's natural grief softened her feelings toward Harry,
taking the edge off her well-justified fear of him. She
began a process, familiar to many victims of violent
obsessors, of rationalizing Harry's emotional and physical
abuse.

Samantha

I knew I didn't want to be in a relationship with a
guy who could hit a woman, but I still kept replaying that night in my head . . . maybe it was partly
my fault . . . I should have called to tell him I was
going to be late, I knew how crazy he'd get if he
didn't know where I was. Maybe it was just a one-
time thing, I mean, he'd never hit me before . . .
and he seemed as surprised as I was . . . he seemed

so apologetic. . . . I mean, he's not a monster. I
wouldn't have married him if he was.

Samantha didn't waver in her decision to divorce Harry,
but she was still playing some dangerous head games. By
assuming some of the responsibility for Harry's violence
against her she was letting her defenses down. Many
victims do this to help themselves feel that they weren't
fools to choose their partner in the first place and that the
time and energy they put into the relationship were not
wasted.

WHEN THE TARGET DROPS HER GUARD

Samantha's contradictory feelings about Harry were compounded by the fact that she was carrying their child. So
she was understandably conflicted when, a month after
she'd left him, he called and asked to see her.

Samantha

I told him he shouldn't be calling because of the
restraining order and everything, but he said it really
hurt him that I thought I needed to go that far, that I
thought he could ever hurt me again. And it made
me feel guilty. He said he just wanted to get some
stuff off his chest. He knew it was over, but he
wanted to apologize and at least make things civil
between us, if only for the sake of our baby. He
sounded so calm and so sweet and so sorry . . . I
just couldn't say no. So I told him he could come
over to see me for ten minutes, that's it, and then
he'd have to leave. He said okay.

When Samantha agreed to talk to Harry despite the restraining order, she gave him the message that she really

didn't care about the order. She was virtually giving him permission to resume his pursuit. It is always hard to remain firm in the face of a contrite, hurting former lover, but no matter how apologetic Harry may have sounded, Samantha never should have lost sight of the essential fact that he was still the same man who had hit her—nothing had changed.

Samantha was being careless by agreeing to talk to Harry, but once she had made that decision, she should never have agreed to meet him in private, alone at her mother's, where she was vulnerable and unprotected.

Samantha

We started talking and he seemed fine. He told me how bad he felt about what had happened and how sorry he was and he wanted me to come back to him. He wanted us to have our baby together and be a family. I tried to be gentle, but I told him it was too late, that I could never trust him again. I could never feel safe. He tried to persuade me that I could, and when it didn't work he became more and more frustrated until he started screaming at me. At that point I was getting pretty scared, so I told him his ten minutes were up and he should leave like he promised. But when I opened the door he refused to go, so I pushed him out. And when I tried to close the door, he went nuts and dragged me into the hall. Then I started to scream and he just heaved me down the stairs. The next thing I knew I was in an ambulance with this incredible pain all over. Later that night I lost the baby. I'll never forgive myself for being so stupid.

In an instant, Samantha's life had turned into a nightmare. In addition to her miscarriage, she suffered a concussion, two cracked ribs, and internal bleeding that almost cost her her own life. She also went into a deep depression, blaming herself for her baby's death.

In retrospect, Samantha realized that she had had ample evidence that Harry might repeat his violent behavior. If he could explode over something as minor as her coming home late, she might have anticipated the volcanic rage that could erupt when he was faced with the painful finality of divorce. But Harry was not a chronic wife-beater, and partly because of this, Samantha had let her guard down. That was just a brief lapse in judgment, but it exacted a terrible price.

Harry was eventually convicted of assault on Samantha and of involuntary manslaughter for the death of their unborn child. He is currently in a state penitentiary. Samantha has healed physically and is dealing with her emotional trauma in therapy. She is planning to move to another state before Harry comes up for parole in five years.

Targets need to be aware that if obsessive lovers act out their rage and frustration through physical violence, they are demonstrating a dangerous inability to control themselves. When they become enraged, men (and women) like this usually lose the ability to temper their emotions with rational thought or to care about the consequences of their behavior. Using explosive acts to relieve explosive emotions becomes a habit. Very few people act violently only once.

When Obsession Leads to Murder

Unless they come out of a relationship where they have already been physically assaulted, targets of obsessive lovers rarely take the possibility of violence seriously enough, even if they are actually threatened.

Ellie, thirty-three, came to see me shortly after the tragic death of her sister. She was on the verge of tears from the moment she walked in. Her petite, slender frame seemed especially fragile. She told me she had been having trouble sleeping and had lost a great deal of weight since her sister's funeral. Compounding her grief were strong feelings of responsibility for the death.

Ellie told me that her sister, Rachel, had been living with a handsome, extremely intelligent architect named Grant for a little more than a year when she had decided to end the relationship. All Rachel told Ellie was that she had gotten tired of Grant's "moodiness." But Grant had not been willing to give up. The day Rachel had moved out, Grant mounted a campaign to win her back. Every day he had sent her flowers, or candy, or a passionate love letter. He had left notes on her car—even when she was not at one of her usual haunts, which indicated that he was following her. Rachel had responded to his pursuit by ignoring him and throwing away his gifts. She had found it extremely annoying, but she believed that he would eventually tire of being rejected and give up. She had seen no reason to be afraid of him.

Ellie

Then one day he showed up at *my* house and begged me to help him. He seemed so sad and so in love . . . and I'd always thought he was a nice guy, certainly a lot nicer than some of the other jerks Rachel had gone out with . . . and all he wanted was a chance to talk to her. I told her she was really pissed off by the fact that he wouldn't leave her alone, and he swore to me that if I could get her to talk to him just one more time, if it didn't work out he'd go away and never bother her again. I figured, what harm could it do? So I invited her over for dinner and didn't tell her he was going to be there.

If Ellie had known the full extent of Grant's obsessive behavior patterns, she would never have agreed to set up the rendezvous. But Rachel had never told anyone in her family what Grant was really like.

Many targets are reluctant to disclose the full extent of a lover's obsessive behavior to relatives or friends. Some targets come from families that are not likely to give them much support or encouragement if they were to confide their personal feelings and experiences. Others, like Rachel, are afraid of looking foolish for putting up with behavior they know to be inappropriate. They may be embarrassed by their relationship and uncomfortable about defending it. In Rachel's case, her reluctance to be open with her sister turned out to be a fatal mistake.

"If I Can't Have You Nobody Will"

After Rachel's death, her best friend—and only confidante—told Ellie that though Grant had never been physically abusive to Rachel, he had certainly been emotionally abusive. He would often go into rages if he thought she wasn't giving him a hundred percent of his attention, and then he'd stop speaking to her for days at a time. On a few occasions he had hidden her car keys to prevent her from going out with friends. He had once thrown out an expensive new dress that he thought was too "revealing" for her to wear in public.

When Rachel told Grant she was leaving him, he became furious and *told her if she left him he'd kill her*. But she didn't take his threat seriously. When her friend suggested that she call the police, Rachel pooh-poohed the idea, insisting that Grant was just being his usual melodramatic self. After all, he had never hit her.

Ellie

If she had only told me what he had said, or even some of the things he'd done while they were living together, I *never* would have agreed to help him. But she'd always told me such wonderful things about him. . . . So she showed for dinner and there he was. I expected her to be annoyed, but she was furious. She wouldn't even come in. She told me I had no right to do this, and she left. That was the last time I saw her alive.

At this point in her story, Ellie began to sob. She didn't have to tell me the rest—I'd read it in the newspaper. Grant followed Rachel out into the street, they had a brief argument, he pulled a gun and shot her three times. She died instantly.

Ellie suffered terrible guilt over her role in setting up the events that led to her sister's death. But Ellie had been easily manipulated by Grant because she had no way of knowing how obsessive he was.

THE DANGER OF DOING NOTHING

Like Rachel, most of us have a powerful need to believe that we could never fall in love with someone capable of hurting us. We resist facing the possibility that we've misjudged a lover, that we've been duped in a romantic relationship. We like to believe that our judgment is sound, that we really know the people we're close to.

In addition, to some of us violence is so foreign to our nature that we can't conceive of anyone we've been intimate with actually assaulting us. Rachel made that mistaken assumption with Grant, rationalizing that he was just being his "usual melodramatic self."

There is no telling whether Rachel could have done anything to prevent Grant from making good on his threat, but she might have reduced his chances by taking his threat seriously. She should have reported it to the police. She should have told her family and friends about his threat and his behavior, and asked them to help her avoid him. This is not to say that Rachel was to blame for her own murder. Even if she had taken more assertive action to protect herself, she wouldn't have been able to *guarantee* her safety. But in underestimating the rage of her rejected obsessive lover, she made a very human mistake that made her more vulnerable—and slight differences can sometimes tip the scales between life and death.

Forewarned Is Forearmed

I wish I had a crystal ball to help you predict whether you have anything to fear from your obsessive lover, but no one can predict with absolute certainty how people will behave. There are, however, certain personality traits, behaviors, and backgrounds that can increase the likelihood that a rejected lover will become physically violent.

History of violence:

History usually repeats itself, and personal history is no exception. Obsessors who hit their targets during the relationship are, upon being rejected, extremely likely to use assault as a tactic to regain control or to exact revenge. But even if obsessors have never hit their target, they may have expressed their anger violently in other ways. They may have a history of getting into fights, of breaking or throwing objects, or of punching walls. These obsessors have a pattern of resorting to violence when they're upset and, under the extreme stress of rejection, they are especially likely to lose all control and assault their target.

Drugs or alcohol:

Substance abuse and violence often go hand in hand. The debate continues over whether drug and alcohol abuse is a physical or psychological illness, but regardless of the cause, the tendency to abuse drugs and alcohol indicates an inability to control destructive impulses and to appreciate consequences.

In addition, alcohol and drugs distort an abuser's judgment and perception. When this distortion heightens an abuser's feelings of anger or reduces fear of consequences, violence often results. Certain drugs—especially stimulants like amphetamines, cocaine, and cocaine derivatives—often actually increase violent impulses either by diminishing restraint or by intensifying irrational jealousies and suspicions.

Drug or alcohol abusers tend to sink deeper into their addiction when they're hurting. Violence is a tragically common result.

Threats of violence:

A lot of people make empty threats. But as we've seen in this chapter, obsessors who make violent threats often carry them out. Threats of violence should always be taken seriously.

Violent family background:

There are two kinds of family violence—spouse abuse and child abuse. Both teach a child that violence is an effective way to gain power and control. Though many people come out of violent family backgrounds determined never to repeat the pattern, others come away knowing no other way to deal with frustration. Obsessors who grow up with violence often resort to violence.

I want to emphasize that these are indicators, not forecasts. But if your obsessive lover has any of these characteristics, the risk is much greater that he or she may use violence against you in response to rejection. The more awareness you have of the risk, the greater your ability to take steps to protect yourself.

Protecting Yourself

We live in a world of uncertainties. There is no way to defend against every conceivable danger, but you *can* reduce your chances of becoming a victim of a violent obsessor by taking advantage of whatever protective measures are available to you.

Having worked with victims of violent crimes for many years, I am all too aware of the shortcomings and frustrations of our legal and law enforcement systems. They can only respond after a law has been broken, and too often, that is too late. I call this the "if-he-kills-you-give-us-a-call syndrome." However, these institutions and agencies are becoming increasingly sensitive to the needs of people who believe they are in danger but have not actually been attacked. If you fear for your personal safety, I can't emphasize strongly enough how important it is for you to contact your local police department.

Local battered women's shelters, your personal attorney, and legal aid offices are important resources for anyone concerned about a violent ex-lover. They may be able to help you obtain a restraining order against your obsessive lover or even have him or her arrested—in some states it is now a crime simply to *threaten* someone with physical harm.

In extreme situations, I have known clients to change jobs, homes, and even cities to escape an obsessive lover. These sorts of steps are wrenching personal choices that only you can make for yourself. But I have also seen the tragic consequences to men and women who avoided taking such steps, or avoided enlisting the legal system to help them, simply because they were afraid of overreacting or seeming melodramatic. Please don't be embarrassed to express your fears to family, friends, or legal authorities. When dealing with threatening or violent obsessive lovers, it is always better to be safe than sorry.

IT WASN'T YOUR FAULT

Fortunately, most obsessive lovers do not turn to violence. But if you are one of the unlucky minority of targets who wind up with a violent obsessor, do not blame yourself. Even though you may have fed the obsession by giving double messages or may have ignored warning signs, this does not make you in any way responsible for your obsessive lover's violence.

The responsibility for violence belongs to the assailant.

Please don't compound the damage to your well-being by blaming yourself for someone else's criminal and cowardly act.

If you have been the target of a violent obsessor, the trauma may have serious repercussions in other areas of your life. It will certainly have an effect on your ability to be open to subsequent relationships. If you have been the victim of violence, I strongly urge you to find a therapist who can help you restore some of your damaged trust.

Targets need to be freed from obsession just as surely as obsessors do.

PART THREE

Freeing Yourself from Obsession

EIGHT

Connection Compulsion: The Root of Obsessive Love

What do you mean it's not love that's making me do this! If it's not love, what the hell is it?

—*Robert*

What mysterious power propels obsessive lovers to feel, think, and act in ways that are so contrary to emotional balance, common sense, and loving behavior?

Why are obsessors so needy? Why are obsessors so angry? Why are obsessors so scared? Why are obsessors so confused?

To answer these questions we must begin at the beginning, where obsessive behavior is learned.

The Blissful Connection

As newborns we are purely emotional beings. When our basic needs are not met—when we are hungry, or tired, or cold, or uncomfortable, or in pain—we become miserable and angry. But when we are held securely in our mother's arms and find our hunger satisfied by warm milk, we experience pure bliss, a state of perfect connectedness with mother, a state of complete safety, warmth, and fulfillment. Our universe is a simple internal world of need and satisfaction, craving and bliss. We experience nothing outside of ourselves. Mother is a part of us. We and mother are one.

Regardless of our age or gender, there is an unconscious part of us that always yearns to recapture those comforting feelings, to return to that secure state of oneness. Of course, we can never return to that blissful connection, but the feelings it engendered remain deeply ingrained in us.

DISCONNECTING

As our awareness develops and we begin to sense that we are separate from mother, we begin to sense that the resource we have come to depend on to meet our needs is *outside* of us, not a part of us. Our sense of perfect oneness, of absolute connectedness is shattered. Everything we thought we could rely on proves unpredictable. Just as we are beginning to gain our emotional balance, the ground drops away. For the first time, we experience the fear that mother might not come when we need her—we feel the very primal terror of abandonment.

This is the first step in the ''separation process,'' and it is an agonizing step for all of us. You can't just cut the blissful connection, the way a doctor cuts an umbilical cord. And though succeeding steps may not be as traumatic, they don't necessarily get easier.

Separation from mother is a turbulent, stressful, on-again-off-again battle between our natural desire to become separate and our terror of losing the security of our blissful connection. As the process continues through childhood and adolescence, it is intermittently torturous for all of us. And for some, the painful process continues through-out adulthood.

Only if our parents for the most part meet our needs for respect, love, approval, and protection can we generally develop enough trust in ourselves and others to negotiate the stormy, uncharted waters of increasing separation.

WHEN SEPARATION GETS DERAILED

Parental love is the only love where the ultimate goal is separation. Good parents try to raise their children to become confident, self-reliant, and independent. But no matter how hard some of our parents may have tried, the realities of life may still have conspired to make our normal separation process especially difficult. An illness in the family, the birth of a sibling, unavoidable parental absences due to work schedules, the death of a parent— any of these events, even in the context of a caring family, can disrupt the journey from dependence to independence by making children feel abandoned. And if children feel abandoned, they usually lose the courage to separate, as if they had lost their safety net with their first step onto a tightrope.

If the separation process can be so easily disturbed in healthy families, imagine what happens if our parents frighten us, hurt us, abuse us, or neglect us on a regular basis. Such parents sabotage our separation by damaging the self-confidence, and confidence in others, that we need to continue on the path to independence. If we grow up in an unhealthy family, in an atmosphere where our needs for respect, love, approval, and protection are generally ig-nored or trampled, the disconnection process is more than interrupted, it is almost certainly derailed.

The Connection Compulsion

When we suffer a setback in the separation process, whatever the reason, we do a psychological about-face. Outwardly, we may appear to be increasingly independent, but inwardly, we feel frightened and we desperately try to reconnect with that now-unattainable original feeling of total fulfillment and safety. For obsessive lovers, the wish to recapture that blissful connection is more than a yearning, it is an overwhelming compulsion—what I call the "connection compulsion."

To get a better understanding of this compulsion, imagine a little child who leaves her happy cottage in the woods to see the world. Somewhere along the path, she comes upon a creature she's never seen before. Frightened, she runs back home. The child from a healthy family finds comfort and reassurance when she gets there. Her parents investigate, determine that the creature is harmless, and encourage her to venture out the next day to try again.

But the child from an unhealthy family finds herself locked out. She pounds frantically on her front door, begging for help as she imagines the monster approaching behind her. She sees a light beneath the door, a ray of hope encouraging her to pound harder, but no one comes to save her. The harder she pounds, the more desperate she becomes to get in.

Obsessive lovers are still pounding on the door, only this time, it's their target's door instead of their parents'. They are convinced that behind that door lies their only possible antidote to loneliness, despair, and abandonment. Though they may understand intellectually that their target is a new occupant in the cottage, the ray of hope they see beneath the door offers the same ecstatic emotional promise they had as children—of reconnecting with their original feelings of bliss.

When obsessors sense that their mystical, elusive feelings of pure connectedness are close at hand, everything else in the world becomes insignificant by comparison. They've finally located their Holy Grail and nothing can deter them from the struggle to reclaim it. The primal energy stirred up by these tremendous expectations can make obsessive lovers feel more alive than they have in years, compelling them even more to pursue their blissful connection.

Rejection: The Cornerstone of the Connection Compulsion

With emotional salvation within reach, rejection is the obsessor's worst nightmare. Rejection is that magical door slamming in their face. Whether they are rejected outright or simply frustrated because their needs are too insatiable to be satisfied, obsessive lovers are forced to relive the pain, fear, and desperation of childhood all over again.

The connection compulsion is invariably a reaction against these demoralizing childhood feelings. This is not to say that every child who experiences rejection will grow up to be an obsessive lover. Human behavior is not all that clear-cut. People are not simply jigsaw puzzles where all the pieces fit neatly into place. Our behavior in adult romantic relationships is affected by many other factors, the most important of which are:

• genetically determined personality traits

• biochemical imbalances that affect mood or temperament

• relationships with siblings

- relationships with childhood peers

- youthful romantic experiences

Any of these factors can be influential in shaping our approach to adult love. Recent research has shown that genetic makeup strongly influences our basic personality style. Imbalances in our body's chemistry can make us depressed or overly moody. Sibling or peer relationships can make us belligerent, jealous, or withdrawn. And failed youthful romances can scar us at a time when our self-image is extremely vulnerable.

But for most of us, our parents' behavior constitutes the primary classroom from which we eventually graduate into romantic relationships. From our parents we learn how men and women are supposed to interact. The way in which our parents treat each other is the model for how we usually come to treat our own partners in love relationships, and for how we expect to be treated by them in return. The way in which our parents treat us forms the basis for our understanding of love.

"NOBODY LOVED ME"

Nora's story exemplifies what most of us take the phrase "childhood rejection" to mean. Nora was the Beverly Hills dress shop manager who became obsessed with her lover Tom after only a few dates. Nora grew up in a small town in Mississippi. Her father was killed in a car accident when she was very young, and her mother soon remarried.

Nora

My mother always used to beat me with a razor strop and tell me how ashamed of me she was. She was ashamed of my Southern accent, she was ashamed of

my grades. . . . When I was thirteen, I started messing around with boys. When my mother found out,
she started freaking whenever I'd get near my stepfather. Nobody ever hugged in my house, so I never
touched him, but she'd still accuse me of trying to
turn him on when all I'd be doing was sitting around
in my gym clothes or asking him to help me put on a
necklace. When I got pregnant at fourteen, she called
me a whore and whipped me with an extension cord
so bad that I still have the scars. But I kept running
around because at least it was a little affection. All a
guy would have to do is walk me home from church
and I'd fall in love. When you don't get love at
home, you look for it anywhere you can.

There was nothing subtle about Nora's situation. Her experience of childhood and adolescence was dominated by
feelings of being unwanted and unloved. Her mother's
rejection was blatant and blunt. But many forms of rejection are less overt.

Nora

My daddy died when I was four. I remember thinking ''Why did he go away if he still loves me?'' I
didn't understand what it meant to die, I only knew
that he wasn't there for me.

Nora, like many children in her situation, reacted to the
death of her parent as if she had been rejected. Children
also often react that way to divorce or to unavoidable
parental absences. Parents need not overtly reject children
in order for children to experience rejection.

Even the most benign parent can make children *feel*
rejected at one time or another, merely by sending them to
their room to be disciplined or by being too busy to pay

attention to them. Rejection can be a highly subjective experience. The key to preventing this kind of subjective rejection from developing into a connection compulsion is to comfort and reassure children, to make it clear that they are loved and that no rejection is intended.

The majority of children who grow up to become obsessors come from families in which they *frequently* feel unloved, unwanted, ignored, or abandoned by their parents. Such continual feelings of rejection make children understandably desperate for love, but they know only one source to look to—their rejecting parent. The more they try to reconnect with parental love, the more they're rejected. The more they're rejected, the more desperate they become. And the more their desperate connection compulsion grows, the more likely it is to stay with them as they enter adulthood.

"I Would Have Done Anything to Get My Father Back"

Margaret's obsession with Phil was in many ways a replay of her childhood compulsion to connect with her father during and following his divorce from her mother. Margaret was the red-haired paralegal who showed up unannounced at her policeman lover Phil's house and found him with another woman.

Margaret

My father left my mother when I was seven. It turned out he left for some other woman, but at the time nobody would tell me that. I couldn't understand why he left me. I thought I must have done something to drive him away, but I couldn't figure out what it was. I just knew he didn't love me anymore. One minute he was there and the next minute he wasn't. He moved away, so I didn't see him for over a year, but I dreamed about him almost every night. He only called me once during that first year, on my birthday. I remember my mom got me a bike, but I still thought his call was the best present I got. I missed him so much. My mom tried hard to make it better, but no matter how much she loved me, she couldn't give me back the piece of my heart that he took. I would have done anything to get him back.

Margaret was yearning and grieving for a father whom she adored, but who demonstrated little love or interest in her after he left. If he had maintained some semblance of a relationship with Margaret, he might have been able to help her understand his decision to leave, so that she wouldn't have felt so rejected. He might have also been able to help her understand that she was not responsible for his leaving, a misconception common to many children of divorce. But when Margaret's father virtually cut her out of his life, he cut her off from the answers to questions that would haunt her for years to come.

Margaret's father left her feeling guilty, hurt, unloved, abandoned, and humiliated. In response to the pain he caused her, it was only natural for Margaret to become enraged at her father. But, like most rejected children, Margaret had no outlet for her anger. Afraid any "negative" emotions would drive her father even further away, Margaret buried her rage in her unconscious.

Margaret was convinced that only her father could make her pain go away. Despite how much she suffered over his disappearing act, she had an overwhelming need to reconnect with him. And that same need was reactivated with Phil, twenty-seven years later.

"I FELT INVISIBLE"

Margaret's feelings of rejection were the result of a literal childhood abandonment. But a child's feelings of rejection are by no means dependent on the actual loss of a parent. They can be every bit as intense if the child feels *emotionally* abandoned.

Anne, for example, had an intact family, but she grew up burdened by just as much unfinished emotional business as Margaret did. Anne is the hairdresser who threatened suicide and shattered all the glass in her apartment when her lover, John, tried to end their relationship. When she first came to see me she described her childhood as happy and loving. But when we started to explore her memories, she realized that her parents were so preoccupied with her older brother that they rarely had time for her.

Anne

My older brother was the golden boy. Everything he did was perfect. Everybody really loved him, including me. But when I was about eight or nine—he was seven years older—something happened and all of a sudden he was fighting with my parents a lot, and they were always taking him off to doctors, and he started having trouble at school and even with the police. It wasn't until later that I realized he'd gotten into drugs, but what it meant to me was that I felt like I didn't even exist and I couldn't figure out why. I was always going "Yoo hoo! I'm over here," but no one seemed to care. They just never had time for me anymore. I felt like they'd stopped loving me and just decided to ignore me. I hated it.

Anne's parents may have been loving and well-intentioned, but in their preoccupation, they emotionally shortchanged their daughter. The household turmoil brought on by her brother made Anne feel rejected because her needs for emotional support and encouragement were going largely unmet.

As a child, Anne couldn't understand that life events had taken her parents away from her; she only knew that she was being ignored, and it hurt. The humiliating message Anne got was that her parents found her unimportant, and she translated this to mean unwanted. She needed the love and attention that all children deserve, and when it was withdrawn without explanation, rejection dug a hole inside of her that she had no way to fill up.

Like Margaret, Anne was the victim of an overwhelming family crisis. Nobody left and nobody died, but the emotional abandonment she experienced was every bit as painful.

"NOTHING I DO IS EVER GOOD ENOUGH"

There is another form of rejection—sometimes overt, sometimes not—that I find in the family backgrounds of a surprising number of obsessive lovers. This rejection results from parents who withhold approval, who have such unrealistic expectations that their children never stand a chance to measure up. These parents are invariably domineering, highly critical perfectionists.

Robert's father was like this. Robert was the stereo salesman who became so enraged upon being rejected by his lover Sarah that he smashed her car. His father was an extremely demanding police lieutenant.

Robert

Nothing I did was ever good enough for him. *I* was never good enough for him. If I left a book out on my desk I'd get a lecture about being a slob. If I brought home anything less than straight A's, I'd get a lecture on how I wasn't working hard enough. If I dropped a pop fly, I'd get a lecture about how I wasn't trying hard enough. On those rare occasions when I did something right, he'd say "it's about time." I always felt like a big disappointment, like he didn't want me because I wasn't the son he thought he deserved.

Robert thought that the only reason he couldn't meet his father's standards was because of his own faults and weaknesses. He never dreamed that his father's standards might be unrealistic. He just kept trying and trying to meet them. And the harder he tried, the more humiliation he felt when he inevitably failed.

PEER REJECTION

Almost all children who have been rejected by their parents experience continuing, debilitating feelings of humiliation. Such feelings invariably distort a child's personality, affecting his or her ability to make friends. Robert was a prime example.

Robert

I had a really hard time at school. I was so shy and self-conscious that people used to call me Mouse. I hated that, but I never said anything. Every time I saw someone laughing, I thought they were laughing at me. Especially the girls. I just waited for each day to be over.

The rejection Robert felt from his peers added an additional load of rejection to the one he was already carrying, further damaging his sense of self-worth. As a result, he became shy and withdrawn.

It is all too common for children who are rejected at home to become victims of peer rejection at school or at play. Many become afraid to interact with other children because they anticipate being belittled or made the butt of cruel pranks. Others become so moody that they have trouble attracting friends and are often made fun of because they cry easily. Still others attempt to compensate for their feelings of inadequacy by becoming bullies or taking foolish risks to get attention.

Peer ridicule or ostracism adds insult to the injury of parental rejection, further fueling the child's compulsion to reconnect with the love his or her parent has been withholding.

Carrying on the Struggle: The Symbolic Parent

Children struggle against rejection in a number of ways. Since children are generally discouraged from verbally expressing their distress, their fears, or their anger, they usually express these painful feelings through their behavior.

Some children drive themselves mercilessly to overachieve in school, sports, cultural activities, or even household chores in the hopes of winning parental approval. Others, either as an expression of frustration or an attempt to gain attention, act out their pain of rejection by creating a great deal of uproar with drugs, alcohol, inappropriate sexual behavior, vandalism, or violence. No matter how they fight the battle, these children can't seem to win, but that only spurs them to try harder.

As adults, obsessive lovers experience a target's rejection as more than a here-and-now event: it reopens painful childhood wounds. Obsessive lovers find themselves renewing their old, familiar struggle, but now, as bigger, stronger, smarter, tougher adults, their odds seem significantly better. They can foresee the possibility of actually winning the battle after all these years. Their target is unknowingly offering them a heady, miraculous second chance, the opportunity of a lifetime. Gripped by an unrealistic, ill-fated optimism, obsessors take up the gauntlet against rejection once again.

In some relationships targets are rejecting from the beginning. But in relationships where targets are at least somewhat loving and accepting, obsessors have an unconscious need to find ways of precipitating rejection. The reenactment of childhood rejection in adult relationships is a basic need for all obsessive lovers. Without rejection, there is no struggle, and without a struggle, there is no chance for victory.

But obsessors face a dilemma: how to win an unresolved childhood struggle without facing the original object of that struggle—namely, the rejecting parent. Their only solution is to turn their lover into a "symbolic parent," a stand-in for the original.

When I suggest to obsessive clients that their lover has become their symbolic parent, they invariably react with disbelief or embarrassment, as if I were suggesting that they want to sleep with their father or mother. But I assure them that (despite Freud's Oedipal theory) I believe symbolic parents are *emotional* stand-ins, not sexual ones.

In turning a lover into a symbolic parent, obsessors are not recycling normal childhood romantic fantasies about mommy or daddy as much as they are resurrecting a childhood tragedy. Their relationship becomes a theater in which they mount an old, depressing play with a new, exciting actor. And the sole purpose of this new production is to give the old play a new ending—a happy one.

FAMILIAR EVENTS, FAMILIAR FEELINGS

When Margaret first told me the story about her father's abrupt departure, she resisted my suggestion that she was using Phil as a symbolic father. But then I pointed out the striking parallels between the two men:

- Her father left without warning.

- Phil left without warning.

- Her father left for another woman.

- Phil left for another woman.

- Her father's sporadic phone calls kept her hopes alive.

- Phil's sporadic sexual interest kept her hopes alive.

- Her father showed little interest in maintaining a close relationship after he left.

- Phil showed little interest in maintaining a close relationship after he left.

Phil was inadvertently pushing emotional buttons that switched on the same desperation and longing in Margaret that she felt when she'd been rejected by her father. She was terrified that Phil would abandon her just as her father had, and she was equally terrified of having to relive the same feelings. So she refused to accept Phil's rejection, just as she had refused to accept her father's.

As a little girl, there was nothing Margaret could do to pursue her father, but now, with Phil, she had an opportunity to overcome her earlier feelings of helplessness. Instead of being passive, as she was forced to be as a child, she actively struggled to defeat Phil's attempts to reject her. She unconsciously believed that if she could change

Phil, she would finally triumph over her father's rejection. As Margaret and I compared how she felt about her father with how she felt about Phil, the similarities became more and more obvious to her.

DIFFERENT EVENTS, FAMILIAR FEELINGS

For Ray, the parallels between his real parent and his symbolic parent were not as clear as they were for Margaret. Ray was the movie cameraman who was so possessive and insecure that he would panic when his co-obsessive lover Karen merely closed the bathroom door.

As a child, Ray felt constantly rejected by his alcoholic mother. As an adult, when Karen rejected him, his internal experiences were very much the same. But there were virtually no direct parallels between the external experiences of his relationship with Karen and the external experiences of his childhood.

Ray

My mother was always either screaming at me or passed out. It was like she wished I wasn't there, like I was some burden on her. My dad was always at work. I could hardly blame him for not wanting to be home with her the way she was, but that just left me and her. I tried to do things for her, to make her see how much I loved her, but I could never do anything good enough.

Ray's feelings of rejection stemmed from the emotional unavailability of both parents but especially from his mother's verbal and emotional abuse. His mother didn't physically abandon him or kick him out of the house, but she did turn him into a psychological orphan.

As an adult, Ray never found Karen drunk when he

arrived home. Karen didn't verbally abuse Ray, nor did she emotionally abuse him. In fact, she tried to be a loving partner. But even her minimal desire for privacy in the bathroom reactivated his childhood fears of abandonment and feelings of frustrated rage. Though the events of his childhood were not reflected in Karen's behavior, his emotional reaction was clearly a reenactment. Who but a toddler becomes terrified when a parent disappears behind a bathroom door? Who but a toddler becomes enraged when that parent doesn't open that door?

When Karen ultimately rejected Ray, she told him to leave—an experience that had no literal parallels in his childhood. Nonetheless, Karen's action made Ray experience, once again, the frustration and rage over being made to feel that he wasn't good enough, over being made to feel that no one loved him. He railed against the same deprivation and abandonment. He felt the same desperation to win Karen back that he had as a child to win his mother's approval.

Despite the difference between *events* in his relationships with his mother and with Karen, Ray was flooded with the same old childhood *feelings* of rejection. By turning Karen into his symbolic mother, he was back in the struggle.

HOW CAN A SHE BE A HE?

Just as parallel events are not required to turn a lover into a symbolic parent, neither are physical parallels. Though many of my clients object that their lovers don't look like, act like, talk like, or otherwise remind them of their parents, such external qualities are irrelevant.

Robert's case is a particularly poignant—though not unusual—example.

Robert

When I was about fourteen, my dad had an affair and ultimately left my mother. It was horrible. I just—the feeling that *he can't leave, he just can't leave, he just can't leave,* kept going over and over in my mind. *There has to be a way I can control this.* I really believed that our whole life was going to fall apart and there was no choice but for me to find a way to stop him. At one point I remember hiding in the back of his truck and jumping out to catch him with this woman. He was really furious but I just begged and begged him to come home. He kept yelling at me to shut up, but I just kept begging. So he just drove away and left me there.

More than twenty-five years later, when Sarah rejected Robert, the emotion that overshadowed all others and took control of him was—despite a multitude of intervening life experiences—that same pain he felt when his father abandoned him. His refusal to give up on Sarah felt just like his refusal to give up on his father. The fact that his symbolic father was a woman was immaterial. Emotionally, he was still in the back of that truck, determined to change the way things were going. And once again he was not good enough. Once again his emotional survival was threatened by a loss he could not accept. Once again he was humiliated. In the reenactment of his childhood drama, the feelings Sarah elicited in him were all the parallel he needed to cast her as his father.

Still, even though Sarah pushed the same emotional buttons in Robert that his father had, Robert understandably had a difficult time accepting the idea that in his mind a woman had come to symbolize his father.

Robert

Look, he's a he, she's a she, so how can I be confusing them? I mean, I may be screwed up, but I still know the difference between hes and shes.

The fact is, gender is irrelevant in the choice of a symbolic parent. Men can stand in for mothers; women can stand in for fathers. Some lovers can even stand in for *both* of an obsessor's parents.

While some obsessive lovers can turn any partner into a symbolic parent, others seem to respond to specific characteristics and resonances in their lover. These characteristics and resonances are extremely personal and subjective, often buried deep within the obsessor's unconscious. There's only one thing that all symbolic parents have in common: the mysterious ability to reawaken the powerful connection compulsion that lies deep inside their obsessive lover.

The Roots of the Savior Complex

Saviors are unique among obsessive lovers because of their need for a distinct type of target to play out their obsessive drama. Their need to rescue a deeply troubled lover is rooted, almost without exception, in a specific type of childhood struggle.

Saviors usually come from homes where at least one parent was either alcoholic, addicted to drugs, chronically ill, severely depressed, or physically or mentally incapacitated. Because of the enormity of their problems, these parents typically had very few resources available for meeting either their children's or their own emotional needs. As a result, their children had a chronic sense of deprivation, and as we've seen throughout this chapter, children invariably experience emotional deprivation as rejection.

The childhood rejection experiences of Saviors are compounded by the bewildering role reversal that often occurs. Children attempt to overcome their sense of rejection by taking on the responsibilities that the parent neglects, hoping to win their parent's approval. The children essentially assume the role of parent to their own parent.

Another, similar form of role reversal sometimes occurs in families broken apart by divorce, death, or abandonment where the remaining parent turns the child into a surrogate partner. The child becomes weighed down by the responsibility for making that parent happy, a heavy enough burden for an adult, let alone a vulnerable young child.

All these children become preoccupied with succeeding in their reversed roles, becoming caretakers both as a means of survival and as a way of struggling against rejection.

As adults, they reenact their struggle by trying to save their symbolic parents. They continue with their lover the caretaking behavior they learned as children in hopes of finally effecting a rescue and winning the approval they've always yearned for.

"THIS TIME I'M GOING TO GET IT RIGHT"

Natalie learned her role as rescuer early and well. She is the high school English teacher who went through her savings to bail her lover Rick out of his never-ending financial troubles.

Natalie

My father was an alcoholic. When he was sober he was funny and loving and terrific, but when he was drunk he'd just stare at the walls like a zombie. It was scary. Mom had to work two jobs because he couldn't even hold down one, so I had to come straight home from school every day to take care of the house and start dinner. I remember having to stand on a chair because I wasn't tall enough to reach into pots on the stove. In the morning I'd make him a sandwich for lunch when I made my own, praying that he might eat something during the day. It was so horrible when I'd get home and see that sandwich sitting untouched in the fridge and him sitting five feet away, clutching a bottle, just staring at nothing. I'd feel like I hadn't made the right thing. At night I'd put on these little plays, just to get him out of his stupor, but he'd always zone out about halfway through and I'd feel like I wasn't funny enough. I loved him so much I just wanted to make things better for him, so he could cheer up and stop drinking. That way he could get a job and Mom could stop working so hard. Then we could be happy and loving like the Cleavers. But nothing I did ever worked out. He never changed.

Natalie went above and beyond the call of duty to try to make her beloved father feel better, but no one was doing the same for her. Her mother's work kept her out late, so Natalie saw her only at breakfast and on weekends, and even then, her father's alcoholism absorbed most of her mother's emotional energy. Her father, of course, was in no shape to offer any emotional support.

Though Natalie felt important because of her responsibilities, she also felt lonely and unloved. The more deprived she felt, the harder she tried to overcome her feelings of rejection by making her father well. If she could make him better, life would be good for all of them and she knew he would love her for it.

Natalie was playing a game in which the cards were stacked against her. Not only was she taking on adult responsibilities at an age when she wasn't prepared to handle them, but she was attempting to do the impossible in trying to "fix" an adult who was unwilling to help himself. Natalie was destined to lose.

Natalie's inability to resolve her father's problems resulted in a deep sense of guilt over having failed. And, as is almost always the case, she carried this childhood guilt into her adult life.

Years later, when she ran out of money to help Rick and he accused her of not caring enough, he tapped into this rich vein of guilt. Rick's accusations felt like rejection to her, and she dealt with those feelings just as she had in her childhood, by trying harder, doing more, and making additional sacrifices.

"WHY DO I PICK LOVERS WITH SO MANY PROBLEMS?"

As I worked with Natalie, I learned that Rick was not the first troubled lover she had felt compelled to rescue. Her ex-husband had been an alcoholic. And a man she almost married in college had suffered from bouts of manic-depressive illness. As she thought about other past relationships, she began to recognize a pattern of being drawn to men who needed a lot of repair work.

Kirk was drawn to troubled lovers, too. Kirk is the recovering alcoholic whose substance-abusing lover, Loretta, repeatedly left him only to reappear when she needed money or a place to stay. His experience with Loretta reflected a pattern that ran through almost all of his relationships and, like Natalie, he discovered that this pattern was rooted in his childhood.

Kirk

Even as a little kid, I could tell my mother wasn't like anybody else. She talked to herself, she threw tantrums—and anything else that was close at hand— she accused people of stealing things. And she had all these "enemies." She was in and out of hospitals, but it was all a waste. She just kept going downhill. It was really hard to watch. I still flash on how when I was little she used to sing to me . . . and we used to laugh a lot. But by the time I was ten she was really in some other cosmos. Man, talk about heartache. I had to watch her slide to the point where she couldn't even take care of herself anymore. So my father hired some nurse during the week, and on the weekends it was my job. He'd go into his study to work or whatever, and I'd hang out with my mother and get her to eat. I used to hide her medicine in her food because she thought it was poison. Sometimes she'd throw her plate and I'd have to clean up. The hard part was keeping her calm. She'd get paranoid about enemies getting in and she'd make me check all the doors and windows about a million times. I'd promise her no one could get in, but ten minutes later she'd start panicking again. I'd try everything I could think of to calm her, but she'd just get more and more upset. It was so fucking frustrating.

In having to take care of his severely disturbed mother, Kirk not only learned to be a rescuer but also developed a high tolerance for chaotic, inappropriate behavior. His earliest experience of love came hand in hand with heavy doses of anxiety. He came to associate love with both external and internal turmoil.

Years later, when Loretta's self-destructive, impulsive

behavior turned Kirk's already unstable life into total chaos, she stirred up many of the old, familiar feelings that he unconsciously associated with love. This, combined with the fact that Loretta needed rescuing from a seemingly never-ending string of troubles, proved irresistible to Kirk. Through Loretta, he could attempt, once and for all, to finally win a symbolic victory over his mother's unintentional yet painful rejection.

Before Loretta, Kirk had fought this same battle in other relationships.

Kirk

Loretta was hardly the first. I had already gone through three women, or three women had gone through me, depending on how you want to look at it. It was always the same thing—total losers. I've managed to stay out of institutions and jails, and I haven't killed myself, and I've even cleaned up my act in the program. But I can't seem to stop repeating this idea of getting involved with women who choose to be completely self-destructive. And now it's Loretta. I know she's inappropriate to me, for me, and about me, but I can't just give up on her.

In his relationships, Kirk was symbolically trying to save his mother. He unconsciously believed that if he could overcome his partner's problems, he could overcome the sense of helplessness he felt as a child when he struggled to prevent his mother from slipping away.

Saviors, like Kirk and Natalie, come to believe as children that their parent's problems are standing between them and the love they need. As adults, in order to reenact their struggle to overcome their parent's personal problems, they become attracted to partners with personal problems. No other kind of lover can fulfill the requirements to be a Savior's symbolic parent.

But despite their singular way of replaying the struggle, Saviors are still motivated by the same pain of rejection that motivates all obsessive lovers. They are gripped by the same connection compulsion.

The Need for High Drama

Obsessive lovers who come from turbulent households—as so many do—learn to associate love with "high drama." When I use the term "high drama," I am referring to a confusing emotional climate in which stress, chaos, unpredictability, excitement, rage, and love become hopelessly mixed up. When obsessive lovers raised in such an atmosphere recreate their childhood struggles in adult relationships, they invariably recreate the familiar anxiety of high drama as well.

As Margaret put it:

Margaret
I look back on all the crazy stuff I did and I think it was very melodramatic. But this was how my mother was with my father. They were always fighting, it was very tense. So that was the image I had. It was always so dramatic. Lots of yelling and screaming and fighting and loving. She was the same way with me. And I was the same way with Phil. That's what kept the excitement going. The fact that he started seeing another woman really hurt, but even that pain was exciting, because it was all part of the passion I felt for him. When it was good, it was extremely good. When it went sour, it went extremely sour. But I'll tell you one thing, it was never boring.

In her continued pursuit of Phil, Margaret felt like she was living life on the edge, just as she had as a little girl. The furtive midnight drive-bys, the humiliating phone calls, the suspense of the unannounced visits, the pulsing heat of their sexual encounters, the agony of finding him with another woman—what a soap opera! This *had* to be true love; what else could be so explosive?

Without frenetic anxiety in their adult relationships, obsessors feel like the air has been let out of their emotional tires, as if their love has become passionless and flat.

Anxiety is the fountainhead of high drama. While anxiety may make many people uncomfortable, to obsessors it is like an electrical charge pulsing through their nerves, making their emotional peril as exciting as a roller coaster ride.

Why Only One Magic Person?

The power of the drive to reenact childhood struggles gives obsessive lovers psychological tunnel vision. Because their lover becomes a symbolic parent, and parents are not interchangeable, they cannot see any alternative to their choice of a partner.

Margaret was convinced that her emotional survival depended on reconnecting with Phil and only Phil. Even after the humiliating shock of finding him with another woman, Margaret could not bring herself to give him up.

Margaret

I felt like I was hanging on to a cliff by my fingernails. How could I let go? I either held on to Phil or
I fell.

When a member of Margaret's therapy group asked why she didn't try dating someone new, Margaret said she couldn't even consider the possibility. I wasn't surprised. After all, Phil had become her symbolic parent. Margaret could no more conceive of replacing Phil than she could have, twenty-seven years earlier, conceived of replacing her father.

If you have turned your target into a substitute for a rejecting parent, you are still waging a desperate campaign to overcome childhood rejection. Like that little girl in the woods, still pounding at her parents' door, your life has been dominated by your battle to recapture the one and only blissful, ideal love you've always so desperately craved. But in your efforts to fill your inner emptiness, you have become the prisoner of your own connection compulsion.

Let me assure you that you *can* free yourself. And in the chapters that follow, I'm going to show you how.

NINE

Setting Your Course

When I see obsessive clients, I am always struck by the sad irony that the feelings that are causing them so much unhappiness are feelings they call love. They tell me they feel like they're drowning, like they're falling apart. They tell me that they can't think straight, that they hate what they've turned into, that they feel lost. They're afraid of their own sudden outbursts of crying or rage. They think they're going crazy. They worry that they'll never feel normal again.

This is not how love makes you feel. This is how obsession makes you feel. These clients are not describing love, they are describing an ongoing emotional crisis.

But crisis can be a useful thing. The Chinese word for "crisis," *wei chi,* is a perfect illustration of what I mean. *Wei chi* is a combination of two characters that represent "danger" and "opportunity." There's a profound wisdom in this way of understanding crisis, a wisdom that puts obsessive love in a different light. Obsession poses a clear danger to your psychological (and sometimes physical) well-being. But that danger is often the only alarm that's loud enough to wake you to the need for change, and this awakening gives you an opportunity to take steps to free yourself.

A Healing Journey

Obsession *is* a treatable condition. It doesn't matter whether you can't stop mourning a relationship that has ended, you're still in active pursuit of a lover who doesn't want you, or you're trying to save a relationship that you now suspect is being ruined by your obsession. Though the healing path is not an easy one, I promise that if you are willing to follow it with me, your pain *will* recede and your life will begin to calm down.

We are about to embark on an important journey together, a journey to break old patterns and exorcise old ghosts. Along the way, I will guide you through a series of specific exercises and techniques to help you rid yourself of—or, at the very least, gain some control of—your obsession.

On the first leg of this journey we will isolate and identify your obsessive thoughts, feelings, and behaviors, so you can see how they interact. Then we can move on to work on actually controlling them. Once they are substantially under control, we will confront some of your childhood issues to begin to root out obsession at its source. And finally, we will explore new ways to live and love without obsession.

Of course, all this takes time, strength, courage, decisiveness, and *stick-to-it*iveness if you are to defeat the demons of obsessive love. But these exercises and techniques have worked for my clients. I know they can work for you, too.

BEFORE WE GET STARTED

I'm often asked whether the treatment sections in my books can be used without professional help. Certainly you can learn the behavioral and communication strategies on your own. For many of you, this can be enough to help you overcome your obsessive tendencies.

But if you are also struggling with problems like recurrent depression, severe anxiety attacks, suicidal impulses, eating or sleeping disorders, emotionally based physical disorders, or violent outbursts, then it is essential that you do the work in this book in conjunction with therapy and medical evaluation.

In addition, many obsessors tend to be compulsive in areas of their lives outside of their love relationships. If you are using drugs or alcohol to deaden your feelings, you must deal with those compulsions before attempting to do the work in this section. Alcohol and drugs impair your judgment and your perceptions, which seriously undermines your ability to deal effectively with your obsessive behavior and thoughts. If you are struggling with substance abuse, I urge you to lose no time in seeking out the unique support and help available from the many excellent twelve-step programs such as Alcoholics Anonymous.

You may find yourself resisting some of the things I'm going to ask you to do in the chapters in this section. Some of them may seem tedious or time-consuming to you. Some of them may bring up emotions that make you feel uncomfortable. But I can only assume that if you've read this far, you've come to the decision that you are ready to do something about your self-defeating behavior patterns. There are no guarantees that the work you're about to do will save your relationship, but it will go a long way toward saving *you*.

SHIFTING YOUR FOCUS

Most obsessive lovers I see in therapy come in hoping that I will help them find a way to recapture their lover. They want me to "fix" them so they will be more lovable and more desirable to their One Magic Person. Unfortunately, they're running toward the wrong end zone. The goal of this work must not be to get your lover back, but to *get yourself back*.

If you want to escape the torture of obsession, you must shift your focus from your lover to yourself.

Until now you've been putting your emotional well-being into your lover's hands. If your lover accepted you, you were in heaven; if he or she rejected you, you were in hell. This sort of misplaced responsibility is unfair to your lover and it's unfair to you. In focusing on yourself, you're going to begin to take responsibility for your psychological health back into your own hands where it belongs.

Don't worry that you will become too preoccupied with yourself. This is one time when it's going to pay to be obsessive. I want you to become obsessed with finding your misplaced dignity, your confidence, your self-worth, and your ability to love in a healthy, nourishing way.

Again, please don't go into these exercises under the misconception that you are doing them for the purpose of winning your lover back. If your lover comes back after you've made some changes in your own life, terrific. If not, the work you will have done will enable you to be at peace with yourself, either with a new lover in a very different way or without a lover at all. The most important victory for you is the rediscovery of yourself.

EASY DOES IT

For the first two weeks of your healing process I'm not going to ask you to stop seeing your lover or to even stop thinking about him or her. In fact, I'm not even going to ask you to stop acting in obsessive ways.

I know how frightening it may be for you to contemplate letting go of your obsession. You may be afraid that if you give up obsession, you will be giving up love itself. Obsession and love have become so intertwined in the minds of most obsessors that they cannot imagine one without the other. So we're going to avoid jumping into this work all at once. Instead, we're going to enter these waters slowly, carefully, and relatively painlessly.

Logging Your Obsession

Before you can begin the actual work of freeing yourself from the thoughts, feelings, and behaviors of obsessive love, you've got to become aware of exactly what they are and how they have been affecting you. The first step toward gaining this awareness is to keep a log of your obsessive patterns.

Ship's captains have always known the value of keeping a log in which they track tides, celestial sightings, compass readings, course changes, weather conditions, crew behavior—all the things that, should they wander off course, would help them determine where they went wrong.

To help you evaluate how your life went off course, I'm going to ask you to keep a log of your obsessive patterns for a few weeks. Armed with this written record, you will be able to uncover some of the ways in which your internal world has been driving you to sabotage yourself.

A log forces you to look at yourself with a much more

objective eye than you're used to. It makes you an observer of your own life and begins to distance you from your obsession. You can begin to step back from the chaos, and once you are no longer in its midst, you can sense that it doesn't *have* to consume you. There *is* life outside the storm.

HOW TO KEEP YOUR LOG

The format of your log is simple. Your obsessive behavior—whether or not it involves contacting your lover—is prompted by strong thoughts and feelings you have about him or her. Every time you become preoccupied with thoughts about your lover, or interact with him or her, I want you to make an entry.

If you have a passing thought about your lover, you don't necessarily have to enter it. But if the thought continues on, or if it causes you anxiety, it's important that you put it in your log.

Each entry will consist of the day and time and of answers to six questions:

1. WHAT CAUSED THE THOUGHTS?_____

2. WHAT DID I THINK?_____

3. HOW DID I FEEL?_____

4. WHAT DID I WANT TO DO?_____

5. WHAT DID I DO?_____

6. WHAT WAS THE RESULT?_____

It doesn't matter whether your answer to a question fills several pages or half a line. The important thing is that you log your thoughts, feelings, and behaviors so that later you can recall them clearly.

Some people carry around a notebook all the time and make entries as they go. Others sit down for a half hour every evening and fill in their log either from memory or from little notes that they've been scribbling all day. No matter how you do it, be diligent and consistent.

To many people, keeping a log sounds like a lot of work, especially if you are so preoccupied with your lover that you think you'll be filling volumes. Also, it's hard to find the energy to do something like this if you're depressed and don't feel like doing anything but crawling into bed and pulling the covers over your head.

But keeping your log will *make you feel better*. If you want to get your life out of its obsessive rut, you've got to be willing to make this effort on your own behalf.

UNDERSTANDING YOUR LOG QUESTIONS

Each of your log questions refers to a different aspect of obsession and its effect on your life. Because these aspects are so interconnected, they have a tendency to become confused with one another. In using your log, you will learn to differentiate the thoughts, feelings, and behaviors of obsession. This differentiation will help you gain the clear understanding you need to begin to get your obsessive patterns under control.

Here's what you need to keep in mind when you answer your log questions:

1. WHAT CAUSED THE THOUGHTS?

To answer this question you must become aware of your individual "triggers"—those specific sights, sounds, smells, tastes, sensations, places, and things that prompt thoughts of your target. A trigger could be a love song, a whiff of perfume, a favorite restaurant, a certain time of day, a romantic movie, the sound of a doorbell, a meaningful date on the calendar, a photograph, sexual yearnings, a gift that your lover once gave you . . . anything that makes you think of your lover.

2. WHAT DID I THINK?

This question sounds easier than it is because when you start thinking about your lover, you may go on for hours. The key here is to try to condense your complex thoughts into a few sentences, whether they involve memories, fantasies, wishes, or ideas. You can be as specific ("I remember him drinking champagne from that coffee cup") or as general ("I wonder what she's doing right now") as you like.

3. HOW DID I FEEL?

Feelings can always be described in one or two words— "happy," "sad," "angry," "guilty," "loving," "jealous," "sexy," "anxious," "excited," "ecstatic," "afraid," or "humiliated," to name a few. But feelings are not always simple. You can have a number of feelings simultaneously. Try to become aware of the complete range of your feelings when you answer this question.

4. WHAT DID I WANT TO DO?

Invariably, when you start thinking about your lover, you want to do something. You may want to see him or her. You may want to get drunk. You may want to get even. Whatever you feel like doing, write it down. You may find this question embarrassing if you have an urge to do something irrational or shameful. Please don't let that stop you from answering it honestly.

5. WHAT DID I DO?

When you answer this question, keep in mind that I'm not only talking about pursuit behavior. I'm referring to any behavior that results from thoughts or feelings about your lover. That could consist of eating a gallon of ice cream or driving by his or her house or watching a romantic movie or burying yourself in work or simply staring at the walls. You should write down whatever your obsessive thoughts and feelings prompt you to do.

6. WHAT WAS THE RESULT?

This answer should have more than one part. If you have any contact with your target, there is your target's reaction. Did your target hang up on you? start crying? call the police? Then there is any physical outcome: a smashed car, a hangover, a neglected job. And finally, there are the feelings you are left with as a result of what you did: sadness, humiliation, relief, rage—whatever is true for you. Behavior always has physical and emotional consequences, and I want you to focus on both.

AN IMPORTANT DISTINCTION

Almost all my clients get confused when they first try to fill in their log questions because they, like most of us, sometimes have a hard time distinguishing between thoughts and feelings.

Thoughts and feelings are so closely interwoven in our consciousness that the difference between them is often muddy. But there *is* a simple way to tell them apart. This may sound like merely an intellectual exercise, but—as anyone who has read my other books already knows—I consider the relationship between thoughts and feelings to be a central factor in changing behavior.

Most of us make the common mistake of expressing thoughts as if they were feelings. We constantly say things like "I felt the movie was too long." But there is no such feeling as "The movie was too long." That is a thought. The *feelings* the film goer is trying to express are probably restlessness, boredom, or disappointment.

Thoughts, unlike feelings, are generally expressed in complete sentences. They embody ideas, perceptions, and opinions. To clarify this point, let's look at some examples of things I've heard obsessive lovers say:

"I feel like my lover never means what he says."
   THOUGHT: My lover never means what he says.
   FEELINGS: Anxiety, fear, insecurity

"I feel like we're going to spend the rest of our lives together."
   THOUGHT: We're going to spend the rest of our lives together.
   FEELINGS: Hope, excitement, joy, love

"I feel that my lover is seeing somebody else."
   THOUGHT: My lover is seeing somebody else.
   FEELINGS: Fear, jealousy, anger, humiliation

In everyday speech the distinction between thoughts and feelings isn't particularly important. But when your thoughts and feelings are part of an obsessive pattern that you want to get under control, separating and identifying them is essential.

THE BEHAVIOR COMPONENT

If you find yourself having trouble answering the question "What did I do?" it may be because you are acting in passive rather than active ways. There are some obsessive behaviors that are obviously active—incessant calling, drive-bys, and stalking, for example. There are others that are less obviously but equally active—like overeating or abusing drugs or alcohol. And then there are passive behaviors.

Passive behaviors are often behaviors of *omission* rather than *commission*, behaviors characterized by what you're *not* doing rather than by what you *are* doing. Passive obsessors often stay in bed all day, stop calling their friends, stop going to work, and neglect their personal needs. Obsessors who turn to passive behaviors invariably withdraw into depression.

You might not think these passive behaviors are behaviors at all, but let me assure you that they are. Staring at the walls is as much a behavior as incessant calling. Both are specific reactions to obsessive thoughts and feelings, and they can be equally damaging to your emotional health.

If you tend to be a passive obsessor, don't overlook what you actually did, even if that means writing, "I slept all day." You'll discover that as you begin to really focus on your passive behaviors, they will become clearer to you and your log work will become easier with each entry.

Some Sample Logs

Most of my clients are initially daunted by the idea of keeping a log, especially before they make that ice-breaking first entry. Nora was a prime example.

Nora
I hated writing in high school and I don't like it any better now. I work too hard all day to do homework. I'm depressed, I'm exhausted. By the time I get

home I just want to collapse. I don't have the energy
for this shit.

Nora came into therapy, as many people do, hoping I had
some sort of magic wand to make her feel better. But the
truth is, no one can deal with major personal problems in
an hour or two a week. Even if I could have seen her every
day, she still had a whole life outside of therapy. If Nora
wanted anything to change, she had to begin integrating
the things we were doing in therapy into her life.

I wasn't surprised that she felt too exhausted to work on
her log—she was pouring an enormous amount of energy
into her preoccupation with Tom. But I promised her that
if she would just give the log a try, we could begin to
recycle some of that wasted energy into positive life changes.

I reminded Nora that she didn't have to write down
every tiny thought or action. The amount of detail and
number of entries in people's logs differ greatly. She only
needed to keep a log sufficiently complete to allow her, in
a few weeks, to objectively reconstruct a picture of her
obsessive patterns. After a bit more grousing, Nora agreed
to give it a try. The following week she came in with a
handful of loose-leaf pages. Here are a few of her entries:

MONDAY, 8:20 A.M.
    WHAT CAUSED THE THOUGHTS? the phone
rang
    WHAT DID I THINK? it might be him
    HOW DID I FEEL? hopeful, excited, nervous
    WHAT DID I WANT TO DO? talk to him
    WHAT DID I DO? answered the phone
    WHAT WAS THE RESULT? it was my Mom
instead of him—I got mad at her for no reason

MONDAY, 8:30 [ten minutes after the last entry]
    WHAT CAUSED THE THOUGHTS? it wasn't him

WHAT DID I THINK? I had to hear his voice
HOW DID I FEEL? disappointed
WHAT DID I WANT TO DO? talk to him
WHAT DID I DO? call him
WHAT WAS THE RESULT? I knew he'd be pissed off so when he answered I hung up and felt like a jerk

MONDAY, 8:30–11:00 A.M.
WHAT CAUSED THE THOUGHTS? once I started thinking about him I couldn't stop
WHAT DID I THINK? he knows it was me on the phone and he hates me for bugging him
HOW DID I FEEL? humiliated, sad, hopeless
WHAT DID I WANT TO DO? crawl back into bed and cry
WHAT DID I DO? ate ice cream for breakfast
WHAT WAS THE RESULT? I thought about him all morning—even after I got to work

You may notice a significant difference between the first two entries and the third. The first two referred specifically to incidents: the phone call that raised her expectations and the call she made as a result. The third entry was a much more general one, referring to a period of time during which she was flooded by so many different thoughts about her former lover that it was impossible for her to be specific about them.

Nora told me she felt bad about answering the question "What caused the thoughts?" with "once I started thinking about him I couldn't stop" because she thought that she hadn't really answered the question right. I told her what I tell all my clients: there is no right or wrong. Don't let this log make you anxious, no one's going to grade you on it.

STYLE DOESN'T COUNT

Nora's writing style was spare. Ray, the movie camera-man, tended to write longer entries. Despite his busy work schedule, Ray looked forward to writing his log because he knew he was doing something to fight the obsessive tendencies that were sabotaging his relationship with Karen.

When Ray and Karen came in for their consultation, they had been living apart for two weeks. Although they wanted to go into couples therapy, I preferred to work with Ray alone for a few months because he was the one whose obsessive patterns were out of control. At the same time, I referred Karen to a women's support group where the focus was on learning to set limits, to communicate clearly, and to be assertive. I assured them that couples therapy would be much more constructive after they took some time apart to deal with some of their individual issues. They both agreed and set to work.

Ray was highly motivated and soon began his log. Here is an example of one of his entries:

SUNDAY, breakfast time

WHAT CAUSED THE THOUGHTS? The smell of coffee always reminds me of Karen because she makes this mocha-java that is out of this world.

WHAT DID I THINK? I'm thinking about how much happier I would be if only Karen was here to be with me. The coffee would taste better, I'd have someone to talk to, maybe we could wind up making love. We always used to read the Sunday paper together. I really miss her. I wonder what she's doing right now. I'm afraid that she's with some other guy. She's so beautiful, any other guy would jump at the chance. If she was with some other guy I'd want to break his neck. I wish she was here.

HOW DID I FEEL? I feel lonely and I feel frustrated because there's nothing I can do about it right now. I feel mad at myself for not being able to control my jealousy and my temper. I feel mad at her for kicking me out. I feel depressed.

WHAT DID I WANT TO DO? I want to go over to her place and see her and make sure she's alone and make passionate love to her.

WHAT DID I DO? I drove by her place and saw that her car wasn't there.

WHAT WAS THE RESULT? I was too depressed to go to the gym like I usually do, so instead I sat home, watched football, and felt sorry for myself.

Something as minor as the smell of coffee was enough to trigger such intense memories and wishes that Ray was moved to drive by Karen's house, and ultimately to become depressed for the rest of the day.

Notice that the first four questions are written in the present tense and the last two in the past. Ray wrote about how he was feeling while he was drinking his morning coffee. But when he was moved to drive by Karen's house, he left his log behind. Then he completed his entry later. This method of breaking entries into different parts is fine, as long as you get down all the information.

Ray was still spending time with Karen. This meant that, unlike Nora, Ray had entries to make based on his interactions with his lover. Here is an example:

THURSDAY, evening
WHAT CAUSED THE THOUGHTS? We're going out for dinner. I've been thinking about it since I woke up.

WHAT DID I THINK? I'm worried about what kind of mood she's going to be in. I spent about 20 minutes just picking a shirt, I'm so worried about how I'm going to look.

When we went out I kept thinking she was looking at this other guy in the restaurant. Everything I said was just small talk, I really just wanted to ask her if she was going to come home with me after dinner or not, but I didn't because when I put pressure on her she gets mad. I wasn't sure how to act because now that we're both in therapy I'm not sure what the rules are anymore. She seemed like she didn't even want to be there. After dinner she made me take her home and I couldn't stop thinking that she didn't want to sleep with me anymore because she didn't love me anymore.

HOW DID I FEEL? I feel really nervous and uncomfortable because things are changing and I'm not sure it's for the better. I feel scared that I'm losing her and I feel like a wimp because I can't seem to do anything about it.

When she wouldn't come home with me, I felt rejected and horny.

WHAT DID I WANT TO DO? I wanted to talk her into coming home with me.

WHAT DID I DO? I tried to talk her into coming home with me.

WHAT WAS THE RESULT? She got mad and I felt like an idiot.

You may have noticed that Ray took an entire evening and boiled it down to one entry (again starting the entry at one time and completing it at another). Nora, on the other hand, took a single incident and broke it into three distinct entries. Use whatever style makes you feel most comfortable. There are only two things that matter in your log:

1. a real effort to isolate and identify your thoughts, feelings, and behaviors
2. the courage to accurately describe your behavior regardless of how embarrassing that behavior may be

Please don't try to analyze or interpret your entries at this point. There will be plenty of time for that later. It is important that you have the freedom to make entries without feeling self-conscious about what they mean or what they may say about you. The less you try to analyze your entries, the less likely you are to censor them.

This log is for your eyes only (or to be shared with your therapist), so there's no reason to be anything less than totally honest. Once you've gotten over any resistance you might have, you'll discover this record is a blueprint of that part of your life that needs changing, and the more accurate the blueprint, the easier it will be to design corrections.

TEN

Dismantling the Obsessive System

There is only one way to escape the pain of obsessive love: shut down the "obsessive system." This system has three components—obsessive thoughts, obsessive feelings, and obsessive behaviors. These three components feed on and nourish one another and, like the cogs of a machine, if you slow down any one, the others will inevitably follow suit.

The interconnected, interdependent parts of the obsessive system affect each other in a predictable and repetitive way.

> THOUGHTS CREATE FEELINGS
> which
> LEAD TO BEHAVIORS
> which
> TRIGGER MORE THOUGHTS
> which
> START THE CYCLE ALL OVER AGAIN

We're going to begin the process of interrupting your obsessive system by focusing first on changing your thoughts and behaviors. You may wonder why I am not going to work directly on feelings at this point. I certainly don't mean to diminish the importance of feelings, but I've had too many clients over the years who were convinced that before they could begin to do this work they had to feel stronger and less anxious. In other words, they used their feelings as an excuse to put off doing what they needed to do.

The fact is, this work will make you feel stronger, it will make you feel calmer. When you change your thoughts and behaviors, your feelings, as part of the system, will have to change with them. So there's no reason to wait. We'll have plenty of time to deal with your feelings in depth in Chapters Eleven and Twelve.

All the hours you have poured into your log over the past two weeks will now begin to pay off as your entries help you understand how your personal obsessive system works. Sit down with your log and read it through.

Pay close attention to how the answers to the question "What did I think?" led to the feelings you described in your answers to "How did I feel?"

Then look at how those feelings have been driving you to repeat the behaviors you reported in response to "What did I do?"

Finally, consider how these behaviors have been creating problems in your life, by reviewing your answers to "What was the result?" Obsessive behavior does not exist in a vacuum; it has consequences, and those consequences are generally hurtful to both the obsessor and the target.

Once your log gives you access to the inner workings of your obsessive system, you can begin the process of dismantling it.

Taking an Emotional Vacation

Obsessive behavior patterns disorient you like a relentless psychological sandstorm. If you want to regain your emotional balance, you've got to get out of the storm. So I'm going to ask you to do something courageous: take time out from your obsessive behaviors and thoughts. This is what I call an "emotional vacation," a time away from your lover and/or your pursuit tactics. During this time you will focus on yourself, learn some techniques to control your obsessive patterns, and gain some realistic perspective on your situation.

If you're in a relationship, I know it sounds frightening to take time off from your lover—which is why I'm asking you to do it for only two weeks. I'm also going to give you a lot of constructive emotional and cognitive work to help you to find the strength for this and to fill the emptiness that you will probably feel.

Don't expect yourself to make deep, dramatic changes in your life in only two weeks. Simply by interrupting your self-defeating patterns you will begin a chain of small, progressive changes that can ultimately lead you out of the destructive maze of obsession.

"ANYTHING BUT THAT!"

For my obsessive clients, the idea of giving up a lover, or the pursuit of a former lover, even for a short time, seems inconceivable. It's as if they were being asked to give up breathing.

I'm reminded of an alcoholic who came to me for help many years ago bemoaning the fact that his wife had left him, his children had cut off contact, he had been fired from his job, he had gone through his life savings, and his liver was shot. When I told him the first thing he had to do was stop drinking, his response was "Anything but that"—anything but the thing he most needed to do.

"Anything but that." I've heard this answer echoed by hundreds of obsessive lovers over the years when I've asked them to take an emotional vacation.

When Margaret contemplated two weeks without hearing her lover's voice, without seeing his face, without knowing what he was doing, she panicked. Margaret is the woman whose relationship with her lover Phil had deteriorated into a purely sexual one.

Margaret

I'll do whatever you want, as long as I don't have to stop seeing him. I feel him slipping away already. I'm afraid if I do this "vacation" thing he won't be there after two weeks. I couldn't stand that.

Susan

I'm not sure there's anything left to salvage in your relationship with Phil, but if there is, the only chance you have is to let go of your obsession. If your relationship can't endure a two-week break, it's doomed anyway. And if that's the case, you've got to let go of your obsession in order to survive emotionally. Either way, you've got nothing to lose except a lot of pain.

By the end of the session, Margaret's resistance had softened. Her emotional vacation was to become a major turning point for her.

THE SAVIOR'S DILEMMA

Saviors have an additional problem in planning an emotional vacation because their lovers have become so dependent on them. Kirk was afraid that if he were to leave his lover Loretta alone for two weeks, she wouldn't be able to survive.

Kirk

What if I come home and find her dead? Then how am I going to feel? I mean, I'm all that's standing between her and the gutter.

Susan

Then you'd better be prepared to stand there for the rest of your life, because you're not helping her, you're just allowing her to prolong her problem. She has the same resources available to her that you had when *you* went on the wagon. You can't help Loretta until she's ready to help herself. You have to take responsibility for yourself and you have to let Loretta do the same thing. It's as simple as that.

Kirk

But I can't.

Susan

I don't see how I can help you until you do.

Kirk was astounded by the finality of my statement. As Saviors always do, he was hoping I could make him feel better while at the same time giving him permission to keep on rescuing. But I was not willing to collude in his and Loretta's mutually destructive behavior. If he wanted to feel better, he had to start breaking the patterns that were making him feel so bad. And chief among them was the fact that he was shackling himself with Loretta's problems—problems that were impossible for him to solve.

Kirk understood what I was saying. He had been hearing the same message several times a week in his AA meetings. But in real life, an understanding of the truth does not always make appropriate action any easier.

Kirk only agreed to take his emotional vacation after he found a way to get Loretta out of his life for the allotted time without relinquishing his feelings of responsibility for her. His compromise solution was to persuade Loretta to visit her mother for two weeks. Though he was not yet ready to stop being a caretaker, this solution at least freed him to begin his vacation, and at this early stage of our work, that was all he needed to do.

Planning Your Emotional Vacation

The arrangements you have to make for an emotional vacation will vary according to how much or how little contact you have with your lover or former lover.

If you're currently living with (or married to) your lover, it's obviously going to be more difficult to get away for two weeks. But it's still important that you tell your lover that you need to take a vacation from the relationship, and then you must find a way to do so. Some people stay with relatives or friends. Others move into a motel. You can even travel, as long as you are willing to take time out from your tour schedule to do the work I'm going to give you. If your lover is living in *your* house or apartment, you may choose to ask him or her to move out for two weeks instead of leaving yourself. This is up to you. But ultimately, *you* have the responsibility for finding a way to physically separate from your lover.

Whether you live with your lover, see your lover regularly, or only see him or her sporadically, you need to briefly but firmly explain three things to him or her:

1. You realize the relationship is not working.

2. You need to take a two-week break to clear your head and make some decisions.

3. You want your lover to respect the fact that this work is important to you, and you need him or her to honor this two-week hiatus by not contacting you.

You can tell your lover this in person, over the telephone, or in a note or letter—it doesn't matter as long as the message gets across. Then, for two weeks you need to go cold turkey—no contact of any kind.

It's easy to fall into the trap of fantasizing that your sudden withdrawal is going to reawaken your lover's interest. Guard against this. This vacation is not an exercise in playing hard to get. The purpose of your two-week emotional vacation is to focus on your own personal growth and change. If you become preoccupied with the fantasy that your lover is going to become lonely and desperate for you, you're not going to be able to concentrate on the work you have to do.

The truth is, most targets will be relieved. Some targets will be supportive, others will be indifferent, and some (especially targets of Saviors) might even be hostile. But whatever your lover's reaction, don't let it undermine your determination. If your lover attempts to talk you out of doing this, assuring you that the two of you can work out your problems together, you must hold firm. You must do this work on yourself, for yourself, and by yourself.

There are some situations where a two-week physical separation is simply not possible—there may be children involved, there may be financial constraints, there may be medical complications. If a separation is genuinely out of the question, the work we're going to do in this chapter *can* still be effective. But it will be considerably more difficult and take considerably more time. It is extremely hard to disentangle yourself psychologically from an obsessive bond when you are still physically connected. Where you need clarity, you find confusion. The physical presence of the target feeds the obsession at the same time that you're trying to starve it.

If you can't separate physically, it's almost mandatory that you get professional support to overcome the obstacle of your lover's presence. But consider your situation carefully to make sure that you truly are a captive of circumstances, not of excuses.

Of course, if, as in so many of the cases here, your target has already told you he or she doesn't want to see you anymore or has simply disappeared, you have a head start—you don't have to figure out a way to tell him or her about your plans for a two-week hiatus. But the fact that you already have a physical separation from your lover does not mean you have a psychological separation. You still need to take an emotional vacation to cool down the overheated machinery of your obsessive system.

Jamming the First Cog: Behavior

Though you can't just will your obsessive thoughts away, you *can* use willpower to take a break from obsessive behaviors. In this way you can give yourself the emotional breathing space you need to work on controlling your thoughts and feelings.

I'm a strong believer in starting with behavior because it is external, it is tangible, it is overt—it is the easiest of the three components to identify. You may be able to deny that a lot of your *thoughts* are obsessive, but it is hard to kid yourself about such *behaviors* as driving by your lover's house or dialing your lover's phone number when you know that he or she doesn't want to see or hear from you.

Before you can stop your obsessive behaviors, you have to acknowledge exactly what they are. Use the "What did I do?" entries in your logbook to help you clearly identify these behaviors. List them, and make note of pursuit tactics and revenge tactics.

During this period, you are going to take a moratorium from all of these behaviors. For the next two weeks:

NO showing up unannounced

NO phone calls

NO hang-ups

NO spying

NO drive-bys

NO letters

NO gifts

NO anything

If you are a passive obsessor, you may not believe you have much overt behavior to stop. For you, the focus will be on avoiding self-punishing behaviors. If you are using food, drugs, or alcohol to deaden the pain of rejection, now is an excellent time to find a twelve-step program, support group, or therapist.

Whatever your behaviors, once you have experienced choosing to *not* act in ways that seemed irresistible, you will feel a new sense of empowerment. You *can* choose nonobsessive behavior if you want to. It's not always easy and it's often in direct opposition to your desires, but if you make the extra effort, you'll be surprised at how much stronger and calmer it can make you feel.

THE OBSESSOR'S FALLACY:
"I CAN'T HELP MYSELF"

Your obsessive behavior isn't really out of your control, it just feels that way. The belief that you can't help yourself is a seductive form of denial that has allowed you to avoid taking personal responsibility for your actions. But in the process, this belief has cost you self-esteem, happiness, dignity, and perhaps the possibility of a healthy relationship. The key to controlling your obsessive behavior is to recognize that it is not something that happens to you, it is something you have *chosen*.

The concept of obsessive behavior as a choice is hard for many obsessors to accept. Most of my clients describe their obsessive behavior in terms like these:

"Before I knew it I had already done it."

"I felt like I was watching someone else."

"I tried to stop myself but I couldn't."

"Something just took control of me."

"There was nothing I could do about it."

The general theme of these statements is that the obsessors have no choice, that they act purely on impulse, as if they were in some sort of altered state. But obsessive behavior for the most part is not impulsive. When someone gets angry and smashes a plate without thinking, that's impulsive. When someone on a restricted diet reflexively grabs a cookie off a dessert tray and eats it, that's impulsive. Impulsive action is sudden, with little or no thought between the impulse and the action.

Most obsessive behavior, on the other hand, is the end product of lengthy rumination. What may start out as an impulse usually gets bogged down in obsessive preoccupation before it emerges as an action. This is a crucial distinction, because if you think about something before you do it, you are not acting on impulse, you are acting by choice. When you do something after thinking about it, you have chosen one of at least two alternatives, even if you believe that you have no alternative.

Remember when Nora talked about renting cars so that her lover Tom wouldn't recognize hers when she drove by his house? When I told her she had made the choice to do what she did, she didn't believe me.

Nora

I didn't think about it, I just did it. It was like I was the puppet and someone else was pulling the strings.

Susan

I know it felt that way, but let's look at what you did. If you had driven over there impulsively, you would have done it as soon as you had the desire. Instead, you thought about how you'd feel if Tom recognized you. You *chose* not to drive your own car to his house. You *chose* to leave your house. You *chose* to go to the rental car place. You *chose* to spend money to rent a car. You *chose* to fill out the application. You *chose* to drive the rental car by his house. And then later, you *chose* several times to drive by again. Those were all *choices* you were making, and at any time during the process, you could have made the choice to stop—something you can't do when you act on impulse. Every time you think about doing something, you automatically give yourself the alternative not to do it.

Nora, like all obsessive lovers, had to stop hiding behind the fallacy that she was helpless in the face of her obsession. And, in fact, when she became more conscious of her choices, she began to make increasingly healthier ones.

How to Change Your Behavior

When you become aware that you have choices you begin to wrest control of your behavior from your obsessive system. To help you continue this progress, I'm going to show you how to interrupt many of your obsessive behavior patterns. If you use these strategies every day, they can go a long way toward putting you back in the driver's seat of your own life.

PUTTING YOUR BEHAVIOR ON NOTICE

Your behavior is like a difficult child—it needs to be warned that you will not tolerate any more disobedience, and it needs to be given firm limits so that it knows exactly how far it can go. Don't be afraid to read the riot act to your behavior for all the trouble it's caused you. I want you to put your behavior on notice, just as you might a disobedient child, detailing exactly what your frustrations, limits, and expectations are.

To do this, find a quiet time and place, disconnect your phone for a little while, and place an empty chair in front of you. Imagine your behavior as an unruly child sitting in that chair. Imagine yourself as that child's loving but firm parent. The child has been creating havoc, and you are finally at the end of your rope. What would you tell that child?

I'll never forget the day I asked Anne to do this exercise. Anne is the hairdresser who trashed her own apartment in an attempt to keep her lover John from leaving. Later, when John broke off all contact with her, she swallowed a bottle of painkillers and then called John to tell him what she'd done. She hoped he would come running to save her, but instead, he called the paramedics.

When I first asked Anne to talk to her behavior she, like many people, had trouble taking the empty chair seriously. But as she began to talk, she became more and more involved, berating her behavior for what it had done to her in the past. By the time she got to her suicide attempt, she was on her feet, pointing her finger accusingly at that chair like a prosecuting attorney.

Anne

You almost killed me, do you know that? I couldn't believe it. I woke up in County General, not knowing how the hell I got there . . . behind bars, strapped in. . . . I was stunned. My girlfriend came to see me and all she would say was that John had called her because he could not be anyway involved with anything like that whatsoever. The shame of that was devastating for me, and it's all your fault. But that's over now. I'm not going to let you control me or humiliate me anymore. *I'm* in control of you from now on. No more hurting myself, no more breaking things. And for the next two weeks, you're not going to pick up that phone and call John. You're not going to get in your car and drive by his place. You're not even going to call his friends to see how he's doing. Do you understand?

Anne was so convincing that I half expected the empty chair to reply. I applauded her conviction and assured her that even though she might not be feeling as brave as she sounded, within the two weeks, her feelings would begin to catch up to her words. When she came back the next week, she told me that every day, after she sat that child back down in a chair to reiterate her rules, she felt a little stronger.

I urge you to do this exercise every day, as Anne did. It doesn't take very long, and it will help you reinforce your commitment to yourself. The important thing is to let "your behavior" *hear* what you will no longer tolerate. When you say the words out loud, the goals they embody have a much greater impact on your inner world than does mere wishful thinking.

Turning Impulses Into Options

As we've seen, the mere act of *thinking* about what you're doing turns an impulse into a conscious choice. In effect, you are adding an on-off switch to the wire between your impulse and your behavior. Ideally, this switch would be equipped with an alarm bell that would sound every time you had an impulse to act obsessively. Of course there is no such thing, but you *can* use visual reminders to do the job of that bell.

One of the most powerful symbols of restraint in our culture is the simple stop sign. Most of us are programmed to stop at stop signs. We practice this on a daily basis when we drive. So, for the next two weeks, take advantage of this programming and surround yourself with miniature stop signs to serve as visual alarms whenever you feel the urge to act out in impulsive ways.

My clients have found these stop signs very effective for interrupting their obsessive impulses. You can draw them with red marker or crayon on self-stick notes and put them anywhere you might go to act out your behavior. This usually means putting them on your telephones, your steering wheel, and inside your front door. You might also want to put one on your bathroom mirror, on your purse, on your refrigerator, on your pillow, and on your desk at work. For the next two weeks, every time you see a stop sign, remind yourself that you have made the commitment to stop your obsessive behavior and think about what you are doing right now.

This may sound simplistic, but a great deal of research on the unconscious has shown that visual symbols often have a far greater impact on us than words do. These stop signs are going to help you turn your impulses into options, reminding you that you *do* have the power to interrupt your obsessive patterns.

FINDING AN EMOTIONAL ANCHOR

Twelve-step programs like Alcoholics Anonymous provide "sponsors" who are available to members when they feel the need for support and encouragement. When AA members feel that they're losing the battle, their sponsor is the cavalry riding to their rescue. The same technique can be extremely effective in fighting obsessive love.

If you have a close friend or relative with whom you feel safe enough to confide the details of your situation, reach out to him or her during this two-week period. Ask this person to be an anchor for you, an emotional mooring to help keep you from drifting into trouble.

(NOTE: If you are in a twelve-step program, your sponsor is probably already acting as your anchor. You may want to ask your sponsor if he or she would prefer that you ask someone else to be your anchor in dealing specifically with your obsessive relationship. But quite often the roles of sponsor and anchor overlap too much to divide.)

Your anchor's main job is to be available to talk to you, either in person or by phone, at those times when you feel yourself dangerously close to doing something obsessive. I know how hard it is to stop acting out when you can't think of any other way to siphon off some of the unbearable pressures that have built up inside you, but if you want to break the cycle, you've got to stop your self-defeating behaviors. When your willpower starts to slip, call your anchor.

**When you *talk* things out
you're less likely to *act* them out.**

You may feel reluctant to ask a friend to make a commitment like this for you. It may seem like a lot to ask of someone, depending on how much anchoring you are going to need. But a surprising number of friends or relatives will gladly volunteer. After all, many of them have seen how your obsession is making you suffer and might welcome the chance to help you get past it.

It is sometimes especially hard for men to enlist an anchor because so many men have been socialized to keep their emotions to themselves. Men often believe that to ask for help is a sign of weakness. Many of my male clients wind up doing the work during their emotional vacation *without* an anchor. An anchor is certainly not a necessity, but the support of a caring friend or relative can make the job of resisting obsessive behavior infinitely easier.

Your anchor is not there only to listen, but also to do his or her best to talk you out of doing anything obsessive. That means you must tell your anchor what your obsessive behavior patterns have been in the past and how you are attempting to interrupt them during your emotional vacation. Explain your concerns about being tempted to repeat some of your past behavior during the next two weeks and ask your anchor to do whatever seems appropriate to help you through those moments of vulnerability.

Nora had lots of trouble asking her best friend Anita for help, because she was embarrassed by how absurd her behavior seemed in light of the fact that she'd gone out with Tom only a few times.

Nora

I hadn't been real honest with Anita about my feelings because I knew she'd just say I was being ridiculous, so it was hard to ask her to be my anchor. But when I finally leveled with her, she wasn't all that surprised. I guess she knew what I was going through more than I thought she did. But I don't know how I would have made it through the two weeks without her. I remember the first Saturday night I was dying to drive by and just know where he was. So I called her and she talked to me for a while, but that didn't do a lot of good, so she came over and we watched TV and talked till about midnight. When she got up to go home, she asked me if I wanted her to take my car keys overnight, but I really didn't feel like I needed that anymore. All that talk had kind of put out the fire.

By spending an evening with her anchor instead of going over to Tom's, Nora was able to experience what it felt like to resist her impulses. And she also found that after she made the choice to resist, the impulse actually faded. Before her emotional vacation Nora had been convinced that it was useless to resist her obsession. Now she could see that she did, indeed, have that choice.

Nora told me she was concerned that by using her friend as a crutch, she was not learning how to change her own behavior. I assured her that there was nothing wrong with using a crutch during her two-week vacation. Just as a crutch helps you through the beginning of the healing process when you break your leg, your anchor can help you through your emotional vacation and beyond, at least until you're strong enough to stand on your own two feet.

COMING OUT OF ISOLATION

Obsession is a lonely and isolating condition. When obsessors become preoccupied with a lover, they often alienate friends, relatives, and co-workers. Obsessors typically do this by neglecting these people, making them feel unappreciated, breaking dates, or being consistently unavailable. Many obsessors burden or even bore the people in their lives with endless monologues about their lover, their pain, or their frustration.

During your emotional vacation, you're going to reverse that trend. Invite old friends out for a meal, a concert, or a movie. Renew old acquaintances with a friendly phone call. Visit a neglected relative.

If friends and relatives have become wary of spending time with you because for the past several weeks, months, or years you've sounded like a broken record, assure them that you don't want to talk about your lover—in fact, you specifically want to avoid talking about your lover. You're trying to rediscover other interests.

Reinitiate that weekly tennis game, yoga class, volunteer work, or bridge game that you may have let lapse during the course of your obsessive relationship.

Don't think of these activities as things you're doing temporarily because you can't see your lover. Outside activities and friends are essential to your emotional well-being whether you're in a love relationship or not. In a healthy relationship, there is room for both a love partnership and a life of your own. Only obsessive love demands the kind of fixation that cuts you off from the rest of your life.

If your obsessive behavior has been primarily passive,

you may have a tendency to be passive in other areas of your life. The idea of withdrawing from the world to mourn your relationship sounds much more appealing than getting involved in new activities. As comforting as withdrawal may be, the only way to fight isolation and loneliness is to push yourself to get out and spend time with other people.

You might be surprised to find that it *is* possible to have a good time without your lover if you're willing to emerge from the cocoon of your obsession. A lot of things can make you feel better. Give yourself some flowers, head for the beach, buy yourself some new clothes, go to the ball game with a pal, enroll in a class, take up a hobby—whatever you like. Try to reconnect with the memories and sensations that gave you pleasure before your relationship took over your life.

DIVERTING YOUR BEHAVIOR

When you find yourself hounded by a desire to do something obsessive it is often helpful to have a strategy ready to divert that emotional energy into a more productive activity. If you make a contract with yourself to do some physical exercise when you have an impulse to do a drive-by or to contact your lover, you can divert much of your obsessive drive into activities that not only will be good for you physically, but will make you feel better emotionally.

Your brain releases chemicals called endorphins when you exert yourself physically. These chemicals are part of the body's natural painkilling system and, like many artificial painkillers, have the effect of raising your spirits. But, unlike artificial painkillers, endorphins have no down side—they make you feel good without side effects and without bringing you down when their effects wear off.

Take five minutes to write down all the physical activi-

ties you enjoy (or at least put up with to get exercise).
These can include anything from racquetball to aerobics to
jogging to pumping iron—my personal favorite is my tap-
dancing class. I've had several clients who, like me, had
an aversion to organized exercise, but they still enjoyed
riding bicycles, taking nature hikes, or going out dancing.
Anything that makes you work up a sweat will suffice.

Once you've listed your favorite forms of exercise,
make a deal with yourself that once a day, when you feel
an impulse to do something obsessive, you will divert that
impulse into exercise. Instead of calling your lover, take a
swim. Instead of driving by, skip rope. Do something
physical just once a day as an alternative to calling your
anchor or engaging in some of the thought-changing techniques I'll be showing you later in this chapter. In addition
to activating your endorphins, you'll be learning yet another way to defeat your obsessive impulses. By the time
these two weeks are up you will have quite a repertoire.

How to Control Your Obsessive Thoughts

If you can change your obsessive thoughts, you can change
your life. You've already begun the process by cutting
back on your obsessive behavior. By slowing down this
cog in your obsessive system you trigger fewer obsessive
thoughts. The fewer obsessive thoughts you have, the
easier it is to get a handle on controlling them. The more
control you have over them, the easier it is for you to
transform them into nonobsessive thoughts. The more you
transform your thoughts this way, the less desperate you
feel and the less obsessively you act.

AVOIDING OBSESSION'S TRIGGERS

The easiest way to cut down on obsessive thoughts is to avoid as many triggers as possible. You identified many of your triggers when you answered the question "What caused the thoughts?"

Take a few minutes to go through your log and make a list of these triggers. Then, using your list as a guide, hide or throw away as many triggers as you can. These may include photographs of the two of you, gifts from your lover, tapes or albums the two of you enjoyed together, perfume or cologne you wore to please him or her—anything you associate with your lover. Try to steer clear of restaurants or other special places the two of you used to frequent. Don't go to romantic movies. Don't listen to love songs. And empty your refrigerator of any foods you stocked for your lover. Do whatever you can—within reason—to remove these personal triggers from your life.

The triggers we've considered so far have been external. But some triggers are generated from within us. For example, if you feel sad, that can trigger thoughts of your lover because you wish he or she were with you to comfort you. If you feel angry, you may think about screaming at your lover. If you feel sexual yearnings, you may wish he or she were there to make love to you.

Unavoidable life situations can also act as triggers. There's nothing like having a fight with your mother, or having the dry cleaner ruin your favorite shirt, or having your boss bawl you out, to make you long for your lover's embrace.

You can't possibly eliminate every external trigger from your life. And you can't avoid internal triggers any more than you can protect yourself against unavoidable life situations. But no matter how inescapable some triggers may be, they are only as powerful as the thoughts they invoke, and you *can* do something about those.

IDENTIFYING OBSESSIVE THOUGHTS

Before you can control your obsessive thoughts, you have to be clear about what they are. Again, your log can help you obtain this clarity. Read through the "What did I think?" entries and try to separate your obsessive thoughts into three basic categories:

1. memories

2. fantasies

3. internal monologues

A memory is any thought about the past involving your lover. It can be painful or pleasant. It can be of anything from a particularly thrilling sexual encounter to a particularly painful rejection.

A fantasy is a mental picture of some place and time (either past, present, or future) in which you imagine being with your lover. Obsessive fantasies are often long imaginary conversations with your lover in which you get your thoughts and feelings off your chest. Fantasies may be revised versions of the past in which the ending turns out better. They may be simple loving interludes. Or they may even be visions of revenge.

An internal monologue is a conversation you have with yourself, either in your head or out loud. It can be about how you wish things were between you and your lover, about self-recrimination, about pursuit, or about revenge. These monologues often begin with phrases like:

"If only he would . . ."

"Why did (or didn't) I . . ."

"Someday he'll realize . . ."

"Why can't she see . . ."

"She doesn't know what she really wants . . ."

"He can't do this to me . . ."

Internal monologues can easily masquerade as insights into your situation, but they are usually just mind games—excuses, justifications, or rationalizations designed to help you avoid facing up to your obsession.

Another type of internal monologue stems from impulses to act. These types of thoughts can be culled from your answers to the question "What did I want to do?" They include thoughts like:

"I've got to see her."

"I'll give him a call."

"Maybe I'll just drive by her house."

"I'm going to make him pay."

Whatever the nature of your obsessive thoughts, you've got to learn to control them if you want to stop them from controlling you.

Techniques to stop or change your thoughts are not all-or-nothing propositions. Many of my clients think they have to fight their thoughts to the death, like mental gladiators. But thought-stopping and -changing is much less daunting if you approach it gradually. Don't expect instant success the first time you try any of the following exercises. They become increasingly effective with practice.

LABELING OBSESSIVE THOUGHTS

If your doctor tells you ice cream may cause your arteries to clog, you will never look at another dish of ice cream without thinking about its potential danger. Once you see ice cream differently, you label it differently in your mind. What you once enjoyed without worrying about consequences becomes forever stigmatized as "harmful." In the same way, labeling can help you stigmatize your obsessive thoughts.

Once you have identified your obsessive thoughts, think of the label "obsessive" whenever they occur to you. When you realize you're thinking about how badly you need to hear your lover's voice, or how happy he could be if he'd just let himself love you, just say to yourself: "This is obsessive."

Now that you've accepted the fact that your obsessive thoughts are working against you, the label "obsessive" will make them less tempting. They will never occur to you again without reminding you that they represent something self-defeating. Labeling is a surprisingly easy way of throwing cold water on your obsessive thoughts.

TIME LIMITING

When I first mention the idea of stopping obsessive thoughts to my clients, they invariably complain that once the thought pops into their mind, they can't just will it away. They are usually surprised to learn that I don't expect them to. Instead, I introduce them to "time limiting."

Time limiting is a simple technique in which you give yourself permission, once a day, to give your obsessive thoughts free rein—but only for a specific amount of time.

Find a quiet time for this exercise—I usually recommend that my clients do it right before they go to sleep. Then just lie down and let your obsessive thoughts fly. Make sure you have a stopwatch, clock, or timer nearby and that you keep careful track of the time. When your time runs out, you tell your thoughts out loud to go away.

Most of my clients develop a little monologue to do this. Anne called hers her mantra:

Anne

"All right, time's up. It's time for you to go away. I'll see you tomorrow at the same time. I know you're not good for me, and I don't want to waste any more time with you right now. If you insist on coming back, you'll just have to wait until tomorrow because I'm not willing to indulge in you anymore today."

When Anne first began time limiting, she thought it was a ridiculous and simplistic exercise. She pointed out that she still had other obsessive thoughts during the day, no matter how much time limiting she did before going to sleep. I assured her that this exercise was not meant to prevent obsessive thoughts altogether, but that it would considerably reduce their duration and frequency by the time her two weeks were up.

On the first day of your emotional vacation, give your thoughts fourteen minutes. On the second day, give them thirteen minutes; on the third day, twelve; and so on. By the end of your vacation you will be surprised at your ability to fence in the psychological wild horses that have been stampeding through your mind.

DIVERTING YOUR THOUGHTS

Just as you learned to divert your behavior by doing something active when you felt like behaving obsessively, you can divert your obsessive thoughts by engaging in activities that require concentration. If there is ever a time to learn a foreign language, paint the apartment, organize your address book, or do a crossword puzzle, this is it.

When you begin having an obsessive thought, force yourself to do something that requires you to shift your focus. Make sure the activity is easily available when you need it. If you've taken up painting, keep your easel standing. If you're into home video games, keep your system hooked up. If you're into chess, invite a friend over to play or get a chess computer.

Whatever activity you choose, if it forces you to concentrate, it will help push your obsessive thoughts out of your mind. The concept is simple, but effective.

PULVERIZING YOUR OBSESSIVE THOUGHTS

In psychology, as in journalism, a picture can be worth a thousand words. The last technique I'm going to give you to control your obsessive thoughts is a visualization exercise in which you are going to picture yourself actually destroying those thoughts.

This visualization is a powerful way to gain some psychological distance from your obsession. It will help you come to see your obsessive thoughts as entities separate and distinct from yourself. Though you must acknowledge personal responsibility for your obsession and for keeping it alive, it is not embedded in the core of your being. Your obsessive thoughts are not pieces of you—they are your burdens, your enemies.

Though this exercise only takes a few minutes, to minimize distractions you should find a quiet time and a comfortable place to sit. Take a few deep breaths to relax before you start, then close your eyes. . . .

Picture your obsessive thoughts as a huge boulder crushing your hunched-over shoulders. Now imagine standing up straight to throw off your burden. Watch your boulder fall to the ground with a resounding crash. Feel the sense of relief as you stretch your muscles and appreciate how light you feel without your burden.

Now look at your boulder and feel the rage as you realize how it has been weighing you down and making you ache. Imagine taking a giant sledgehammer to your boulder and smashing it to bits. With every blow, you release a little more rage.

When you've reduced the boulder to fragments, picture yourself collecting the fragments in a bucket.

Take your bucket of fragments to a tropical island. As you wade into the surf, cast the remnants of what were once your obsessive thoughts into the sea. Watch the fragments sink down to the ocean floor and slowly decompose until they disappear into the sand.

As the surf laps your ankles, feel the sun, smell the salt air, hear the sea gulls, and enjoy the experience of triumph, relief, and freedom. You have overthrown your personal tyrant.

Anytime you feel the boulder of obsession weighing you down, you can come back to this visualization to find some relief. The more you use your visualization, the more effective it will become in pushing obsessive thoughts from your mind.

This particular visualization is one I have used with clients for many years. But that does not mean you have to follow it exactly. You may prefer to throw your obsessive thoughts off a mountaintop, toss them into a bonfire, or bury them in a coffin. Feel free to use whatever images are most effective for you.

Through visualization, you can harness the power of images to profoundly affect your thoughts, both conscious and unconscious.

•   •   •

Some of the techniques in this chapter will work better for
you than others. Try them all and then adopt whatever
does the job. It doesn't matter whether you surround yourself with stop signs, rely on an anchor, become a crossword fanatic, or wear a clove of garlic around your neck—as
long as you throw a monkey wrench into your obsessive
system. Once you find effective ways to ward off your
obsessive thoughts and behaviors, your obsessive patterns
will change and you will have proved to yourself that they
are not the all-powerful demons that they've always seemed.

I know that I've given you a great deal to do and to
think about during your two-week vacation, but overcoming obsession entails hard work and commitment. If you
feel overloaded, feel free to stretch your vacation out for
another week or two to get a better handle on these techniques. And if you slip now and then, don't beat up on
yourself. Obsession is a powerful force, and if you can
take two steps forward for every one step back, you're still
making progress. If you can succeed even slightly in loos-
ening the stranglehold that obsession has on you, these few
weeks will pay off for a long time to come.

ELEVEN

Dealing with the Truth About Your Relationship

We're about to build a bridge from your emotional vacation to the rest of your life. But in order for this bridge to carry you over the dark waters of obsessive love, you must be willing to take an honest look at your relationship—or lack thereof—and to deal squarely with what you find.

I know how frightening this can be. I know how important it may be for you to hold on to whatever glimmer of hope you can find to persuade yourself that you have a future with your lover. But too often that hope is false, and false hope is a trap that can keep you from moving on with your life.

The Fourteenth Day

The last day of your emotional vacation is a day of evaluation. If possible, plan your vacation so that this day falls on a day off from work. Don't make any dates with friends; plan to spend this day on your own. You've got a lot of thinking to do about the true nature of your relationship.

If you are like most obsessive lovers, taking a tough, candid look at your relationship is the last thing in the world you want to do because you know in your heart of hearts that this will inevitably result in some painful revelations.

Many of you have already lost your lover. Others are in a relationship that seems hopeless and is probably doomed. And a few of you are in a relationship that might have a chance of survival if only you can stop the obsessive behavior that is driving your lover away. Now that you've spent two weeks putting some distance between yourself and your obsession, you are ready to gain some real perspective about which of these situations applies to you.

STATUS CHECK

To help you gain this perspective, I have devised the following relationship status check. Even though some of the items on these two lists may appear self-evident, I've known scores of obsessive lovers whose denial was so great that they were blinded to even the most obvious of these signs. Don't let this happen to you.

YOUR RELATIONSHIP IS ALREADY OVER IF . . .
1. your lover has cut off all contact with you.

YOUR RELATIONSHIP CANNOT CONTINUE AS IT IS IF . . .
1. you have to initiate almost all contact with your lover.

2. your lover rarely returns your phone calls.

3. after having had an exclusive relationship with you, your lover wants to begin, or has begun, dating other people.

4. the only way to get your lover to spend time with you is to make him or her feel guilty or sorry for you.

5. your jealousy, possessiveness, violence, or pursuit behavior repeatedly angers or frightens your lover.

6. sex is the only thing you and your lover enjoy together or the only thing you do together.

7. your lover is married to someone else and, despite promises, makes no move to separate or get a divorce.

8. your lover is financially irresponsible and expects you to repeatedly bail him or her out of financial difficulties.

9. your lover has problems with alcohol, drugs, gambling, or other compulsive behaviors and is unwilling to take any personal responsibility for these problems.

The first checklist has only one item—it is self-explanatory. If you answered "yes" but have not given up the fantasy that you are still in a relationship with your lover, it is time to face the truth. No matter how painful this may be, it will ultimately hurt less than the pain and humiliation you've been suffering by continuing to pursue a lover who rejects you.

If you answered "yes" to even one of the items on the second checklist, you must be willing to give up on your relationship *as it now exists*, even if that means losing it forever. The only chance you have for a healthy relationship is if you are willing to do what it takes to change your obsessive behavior *and* if you have a partner who is willing to give you the time and opportunity to make those changes.

If you found yourself answering any of these items with a "yes, *but*" followed by some kind of defensive explanation, you are rationalizing. For example, you may have answered the question about whether you have to initiate almost all contact with your lover by saying something like, "Yes, *but* I know he's busy." If so, you are reluctant to face the painful but more likely explanation: that your lover simply does not want to spend time with you.

Please don't let rationalization—or any other form of denial—keep you from being honest with yourself. Denial can only stand in your way.

Now that your two-week vacation is at an end, you are in a position to consider your relationship more objectively than you ever have before. Between your log, the exercises done during your time out from obsessive love, and your status check, you should have a much clearer perspective on the nature, if not the future, of your relationship. With this perspective, you are ready to deal with the loss of your relationship, if you no longer have one, or to reenter your relationship on new terms, if that's still possible.

Your Emotional Vacation Ends: Now What?

For two weeks you've been living in a state of emotional suspended animation. You've artificially isolated yourself from your target and from your obsessive patterns. During this time you've learned various ways to control the thoughts, feelings, and behaviors that make up your obsessive system. I know a lot of you may have slipped a few times during this two-week period, but even so, you made progress and you deserve to congratulate yourself for it. But the changes you've made have been temporary.

Now the permanent healing must begin—no more Band-Aid solutions. If your relationship has ended, I'll help you to come to grips with that painful truth and to continue work on controlling your obsessive tendencies. If you are returning to a relationship, I'll help you maintain control of your obsessive love in the presence of your lover—your most irresistible trigger.

It's day fifteen. Your suspended animation is over. It's time to *accept* what you've learned about your situation and your obsessive behavior and actually start to *integrate it into your everyday life*.

When Your Relationship Is Over

If your status check convinced you that your relationship is over, you are ending your emotional vacation on a very sad note. But the good news is, the confusion, doubt, and speculation that have been making you feel crazy are now behind you. With this new clarity, you can begin to develop a sense of stability in your life and to move out of the rut of your obsessive love.

I realize that people sometimes get back together again long after they've broken up, but for the purposes of this work, it is important that you don't cling to that small ray of hope. You'd be surprised at how many clients I see who have absolutely no relationship and yet are still convinced that they do.

The hope that your lover will turn out to be that one-in-a-million who comes back after having decisively broken off the relationship can only serve to keep you stuck in a quagmire of obsessive thoughts. It will also postpone your recovery from the emotional pain that is the inevitable result of any loss.

GRIEVING A LOST RELATIONSHIP

The end of a love relationship is a death. It is—at least for a time—the death of hopes, of expectations, of passions, of dreams, and, in some cases, of love. Giving up on an obsessive relationship is an extremely painful thing to do. Your sense of loss can be tremendous, even if the relationship was a brief one or you were miserable in it. But—as with the death of a person—the demise of a relationship can be worked through by the powerful healing process of grieving.

Nora was finding it especially difficult to let go of her dreams about Tom, even though when she did her status check, she only needed to go as far as the first item. She hadn't heard from Tom in more than two months, yet she still expected him to call and tell her how he'd been missing her and how he wanted to start over.

Nora and I went through her log together and I pointed out how every entry about Tom was a reflection either of her thoughts about not having heard from him or of her unfulfilled wishes to be with him. It was clear that the relationship was nothing more than a fantasy kept alive by memories of a few exciting evenings.

When Nora finally accepted the fact that Tom was probably not going to call her again, she became very upset.

Nora

I've got no relationship, no Tom. . . . I've just got the pain. What am I supposed to do?

Susan

Looking at your relationship, Tom, and your pain— your pain is the only thing you have the power to do something about. You can't create a relationship out of thin air . . . nobody can. And you can't force Tom to care about you if he's not interested. But you *can* do some work to get rid of your pain.

To help Nora, I asked her to do what people have been doing for thousands of years when they've needed to accept the finality of a loss: conduct a funeral ceremony.

A EULOGY FOR YOUR RELATIONSHIP

I often ask my clients to express their grief by delivering a eulogy for their relationship and for all of its attendant fantasies and dreams. Over the years, I've found this ritual to be extremely effective.

If you, like Nora, come to the realization that you have no relationship left, take a few minutes to sit down with a pencil and paper and memorialize what your relationship meant to you and how its death is going to affect you. Then read your eulogy out loud as you visualize your relationship being lowered into a grave.

When I asked Nora to do this, we staged a memorial service in my office using a chair as a podium. Nora was a little self-conscious at first as she stood behind the chair, but by the time she finished her improvised eulogy she was surprised at how much she had had to say. Here is an excerpt:

Nora

I used to believe that Tom was the answer to all my prayers, but today I'm here to bury all that. Let it rest in peace. All the love I felt for him, all the dreams I had for us, all the good times we had . . . they're gone now and I have to accept that. I really thought we had a future together, but today I'm laying that future to rest because that son of a bitch just doesn't care. I guess I expected too much too fast but now . . . I'll never see those expectations again. I thought it was love but it was just a brief romance . . . it died before it even began, and that makes me really sad. But it's time to move on and think about the living, namely, me. I'm strong and I can get over this. I just need to lay this relationship to rest.

Nora was crying by the time she finished. She told me that it would take her more than a few words to get over Tom but that she did feel much better now. I assured her that this was exactly what her eulogy was supposed to accomplish. It gave her an opportunity to externalize the sadness, anger, and frustration that make up grief. By symbolically burying the thoughts and feelings that were bogging her down, she was reinforcing her commitment to get beyond them. It was not a magical incantation—it was an expression of goals. Her eulogy was not an ending—it was a beginning.

You might feel skeptical, but please don't underestimate the value of symbolic rituals like this one. The expression of grief has a powerful effect on the unconscious, and rituals like this are very effective tools for expressing grief. Your eulogy can be a vital part of your healing process.

GRIEF HAS NO RULES

There are no rules about how to grieve or how long it takes. Contrary to popular theories about a "grieving process" made up of specific universal stages, recent studies have shown that everybody works through grief differently. The only thing about grief that *is* universal is that it must be acknowledged and expressed in some direct way or it will burrow into your unconscious and express itself indirectly as depression, anger, physical illness, or self-defeating behavior.

I told Nora that she might be spending a lot of time

crying during the next few weeks but this was sadness that had a purpose and a direction. It was far more productive than turning her pain into stomachaches, depression, and problems with overeating and alcohol. The sadness she was now experiencing had an end in sight. Active grieving always does.

Now that Nora's eulogy had initiated her grieving process, it was up to Nora to continue it. Nora discovered that what worked best for her was to discuss the end of the relationship with her friends. Every time she talked about it, it became a little more real to her.

Some people need to talk about their feelings. Others need a shoulder to cry on until their sadness subsides. Still others grieve by themselves, working through their pain by writing in a journal, expressing themselves through art or music, or engaging in strenuous physical activity. Some people deal with grief quickly; others need more time. In the end, it doesn't matter how you grieve—as long as you don't avoid it.

When Your Relationship Cannot Continue as It Is

I'm well aware that many of you will end your two-week vacation and go right back to your lover, even if you've only got a shadow of a relationship. But if you answered "yes" to any of the items in the second part of the status check, you cannot go back to business as usual. If you do, you will wind up right back where you started, mired in an obsessive, unhappy relationship.

Once you acknowledge that your relationship cannot continue as it is, you must take responsibility for doing something about it. If you are like most obsessors, you probably realized a long time ago that your relationship must change, but your solution has been to try to get your lover to change. The fact is, you can't change your lover, you can only change yourself. And in changing yourself, you will change your relationship. Either the relationship will get better or you will grow strong enough to leave it behind.

Reestablishing Contact

Whether you live with your lover, see your lover once or twice a week, or see your lover only sporadically, returning to your relationship can be very precarious for you.

Coming off two weeks without obsessive behavior—for the most part—you are like a dieter who has just come off a crash program. Now that the diet is over, you find yourself surrounded by temptation, and you may feel that because you've been virtuous, you can afford to drop your guard. But as with dieting, you must keep up the good work you began and remain vigilant against the temptation to fall back into your old, familiar behavior patterns.

Your partner has every reason to be gun-shy in light of the oppressiveness of your obsessive tactics in the past. You used to react to your lover's triggers in predictably obsessive ways. Now, in returning to your relationship, you will be returning to an environment filled with those same triggers. Though you have done much work on your own behavior during the past two weeks, chances are your partner will pick up just where he or she left off. If he or she had been rejecting before, or had been giving you double messages, or had been emotionally unavailable, that probably won't be different.

When you learned to control your behavior during your emotional vacation, it was like learning to swim in the shallow end of a pool. Now you're diving into the ocean.

The same skills may keep you afloat, but the waves and currents will be working against you, making it much more challenging to swim.

MARGARET AND PHIL

By the time Margaret resumed contact with her policeman lover Phil, she knew she was not returning to much of a relationship. She had identified with five of the nine items on the second part of her status check. When she called him the day her emotional vacation ended, she did so with a new outlook.

Margaret

He came over that night around eleven o'clock, just like he used to, and the first thing he wanted to do—as usual—was go to bed. I told him I didn't want to do that right now. I was shaking when I said it, I was so scared that he'd just leave. But you know what? I'm worth more than a roll in the hay twice a month, and I told him if he wasn't willing to give me more than that, I didn't want to go on. He got really confused. This was the last thing he ever expected to hear from me. He said he'd think about it and give me a call. Then he left. The minute the door closed I had this incredible urge to run after him. It was like all the work I'd done and all the thought I'd put into what I was going to say went down the drain and I was ready to do anything to stop him from leaving. But I didn't! I don't know why, but I didn't. So now it's been a week and I still haven't heard word one. But I know if I call him, I'll fall right back into it and that's just too hard for me, so I'm not going to do it. It really hurts when I think about what we had at the beginning, but I

know I'll never get it back anyway, and the bottom
line is—I really stood up for myself. I really did.

Though Margaret was convinced that she had pushed Phil
to leave her, the truth is he had left her, in an emotional
sense, a long time before.

Margaret had gained a new clarity about her situation
with Phil through her log and her status check, and that
clarity gave her the courage to refuse to continue her
emotionally unnourishing relationship. The real test came
when Phil walked out and she was flooded with obsessive
impulses to follow him. But the work she had done during
her emotional vacation gave her the strength to hold her
ground and, after working through her grief over losing
him, she has never looked back.

RAY AND KAREN

When Ray returned to Karen, he was, unlike Margaret,
returning to a mutual relationship. Ray and Karen had both
been working hard in their separate therapies on learning
to overcome the obsessive aspects of their interactions. But
Ray still found himself reacting to the same triggers that
had driven him crazy before. He still felt rejected when
she closed the bathroom door, he still felt jealous when he
heard men's voices on her answering machine, and he still
felt desperate when he didn't know where she was.

But now Ray was aware of how these triggers affected
him. And he was armed against them with new behavioral
strategies. Slowly but surely, Ray was chipping away at
the obstacle of his obsession.

Ray
I thought it was tough being without her for two
weeks, but being back with her is even harder. I

thought I had this stuff under control, but now that I'm seeing her again . . . I have to be on guard twenty-four hours a day against my own feelings. I'm really self-conscious . . . I examine every thought, every move I make . . . but at least she's still hanging in there with me. The toughest thing is the not knowing. I still have this urge to know everywhere she's been and everything she's been doing, but I know that I'd just be pushing her away. So instead of badgering her, I say this little phrase over and over, "If I do this I'm going to lose her, if I do this I'm going to lose her," and it seems to work. It doesn't make the feelings go away, but they don't eat at my insides so much. I know I've got a long way to go, but I can tell I'm making progress, and that's what counts.

For the first time, Ray was taking responsibility for his obsessive behavior. In the past he had always blamed Karen for his jealousy and possessiveness. *She* made him feel insecure. *She* made him feel rejected. He had always thought that his tantrums and his interrogations were justified. He had always seen his behavior as a perfectly natural reaction to Karen's withdrawal. But as a result of his log and two weeks of taking a hard look at his own behavior, Ray finally came to see his own role in creating the turmoil that was making him suffer so.

Even though Ray's introspection was making him feel self-conscious, for the first time he was developing an awareness of what made him tick. It was exciting to see this happening to him. For two weeks we had been working on applying external controls to his behavior, but now those controls were becoming self-generated. Where his obsessive thoughts used to incite him to action, they now triggered new thoughts about exercising control. Though

Ray still had a long way to go, he was clearly heading in the right direction.

THE VIOLENT OBSESSOR

If you have crossed the line to violence against either your target or your target's property, I strongly advise against reestablishing contact with your lover under any circumstances. I realize this injunction may make you feel angry and frustrated, especially if you're working hard to conquer your obsessive behavior, but the fact is, violence has a tendency to repeat itself.

I am well aware that some people who resort to violence manage to overcome their particular demons and return to relationships without further incident, but that's the exception not the rule. Your relationship with your target has triggered your violence before. Though there is no guarantee that it will do so again, you can reduce the odds against you by avoiding a situation that is fraught with known risks. You have enough difficult emotional work to do without increasing your burden in a relationship with proven triggers.

But it is not enough to do the work in this book if you are struggling with violent tendencies as well as with obsession. Violent tendencies are very deeply, firmly rooted. I can't emphasize strongly enough that your violence is outside of your conscious control, and all the wishing, willpower, promises, and resolutions in the world are not going to change that. You owe it to yourself, to everyone around you, and to everyone in your future to enter therapy with someone who has specific experience with violent clients and who will work with you both on behavioral controls and on dealing with your childhood rage.

THE SAVIOR'S RETURN: KIRK AND LORETTA

If you are a Savior, you cannot go back to your lover without demanding behavioral changes unless you are prepared to continue rescuing and taking care of your lover for the rest of your relationship. If you *insist* on continuing your caretaker role, you must also be prepared to continue enduring the frustration and emotional deprivation that have characterized your relationship. Until your partner takes personal responsibility for his or her own problems, nothing will change between the two of you.

You must set firm limits on your partner's behavior. If your partner responds positively to these limits and makes some real changes, you *may* have a chance to salvage your relationship. But if your partner refuses to respect the limits, your relationship will continue to be self-destructive for both of you. In this case, you *must* end the relationship for the sake of your own emotional survival.

Kirk had repeatedly asked his addicted lover Loretta to go with him to AA meetings, but she had always found an excuse to avoid them. His own involvement with the twelve-step program had already prepared him for the fact that he had to stop taking responsibility for Loretta, but it wasn't until his two-week vacation gave him the tools to deal with his obsessive feelings for her that he resolved to take a hard line.

With encouragement from his AA sponsor on one side and me on the other, Kirk finally found the strength to set very specific limits. He told Loretta that he would no longer tolerate any drug or alcohol use in his house and he would no longer tolerate her staying out all night. He also insisted that she become involved in a twelve-step or detox program. He told her that if she wasn't willing to do something about her problem, she would have to move out.

Kirk

She pulled out all the stops—she argued, she cried, she manipulated, she seduced, she guilt-tripped—but I'd heard it all too many times before. I refused to be sidetracked. She finally told me to go fuck myself and she split. I've got to tell you, I didn't feel exactly victorious. In fact, I felt like she'd kicked me in the balls. But I knew I had to hang tough because there was just no way we could be together if I was in recovery and she was in the gutter.

Kirk knew that when he confronted Loretta in this way, he ran the risk of her leaving him. When you set firm limits on a target who is refusing to take responsibility for serious life problems, any or all of three things can happen:

1. Your lover will become enraged.

2. Your lover will make empty promises to change.

3. Your lover will agree to seek help.

You must recognize that, if your lover chooses not to make the healthy choice to seek help, you have not only the right but the responsibility to refuse to continue rescuing him or her. This is not an act of betrayal; it is an act of personal survival. This is a difficult truth for most Saviors to accept because they are so heavily burdened with guilt. But, as we've already seen, caretakers and rescuers are part of the problem, not part of the solution. You can't dig your way out of obsession if you're buried under someone else's troubles.

NATALIE AND RICK

The limits Kirk set were clear-cut. For Natalie, who went through her savings bailing her lover Rick out of money troubles, setting limits was more complicated.

Natalie could hardly insist that Rick stop dreaming or improve his financial track record. But, after taking her emotional vacation, she did insist that he set up a schedule to begin paying off his debts to her. She also asked him to start paying his part of household expenses.

Rick surprised Natalie by responding positively to her new ground rules. He told her he was fed up with feeling like a failure and agreed with her that things had to change. All he asked was that she give him a thirty-day grace period so that he could find a job. Natalie agreed.

Natalie

He went out every day with the classifieds under his arm, but somehow nothing ever panned out. I don't know why. Maybe he wasn't really looking. Maybe he was blowing the interviews. But whatever it was, I fought the impulse to make it my problem. I refused to look through the ads for him, I refused to compose letters for him, I wouldn't even let him borrow my car for job interviews. After a month of excuses, he still hadn't found anything, so I finally forced myself to tell him he had to move out. It killed me to do it because I still really believed he had potential, but I also knew I couldn't make him fulfill it. So I never saw him again. And I never saw my money again, either. But at least I cut my losses, both moneywise and peace-of-mind-wise.

Natalie found herself in a position typical of Saviors whose lovers have chronic financial problems: if she were to end the relationship, she stood a good chance of forfeiting all the money she'd lent him. But the alternative of prolonging the relationship would only serve to prolong her pain and further deplete her resources.

Natalie made the only healthy choice she had under the circumstances, even though it was tough and took a lot of courage. And though it was finally over, she was still saddled with a lot of pain and guilt. As her therapy continued, the deeper source of these feelings became clear.

YOUR THREE-MONTH REALITY CHECK

If you have been fighting obsessive love, your perception of your relationship may still be clouded, even after you've begun applying your newfound strategies. It's one thing to know that your relationship must change, but it's quite another to determine, over time, whether those changes have occurred.

Having grown used to tolerating rejection and humiliation in pursuit of your target, it is easy to make too much of small improvements and to decide to tolerate a fundamentally bad relationship. Because of this, I'm going to ask you to candidly judge whether, as a result of the work you have been doing, your relationship has a future.

I call this the "three-month reality check." It's very simple: three months after your reentry into your relationship, just repeat your status check. If you are still answering "yes" to even one of the items, you are still in a seriously troubled relationship, and you would be well advised to end it.

THERE IS NO CRYSTAL BALL

Almost all of my clients in failing obsessive relationships come to me looking for the reassurance that if they change their behavior they can save their relationship. I can't make that promise. Each situation is different.

Your lover may have rejected you for reasons that have little or nothing to do with your behavior. Even if your obsessive tendencies were solely responsible for turning off your lover, your change in behavior may be coming too late to reverse his or her feelings. Your target may not be willing to risk trusting you again, period. If you are a Savior, your target may refuse to take personal responsibility for his or her own problems. And if your target has truly lost interest, no amount of change on your part will make a dent in his or her indifference.

It is vital that you don't put all your emotional eggs in the frail basket of your relationship. Your emotional well-being is too important to entrust to a lover who, for whatever reason, has already rejected you.

Your relationship *must* take a backseat to your emotional health. If your relationship gets better as a result of the work you do on yourself, more power to it. If it doesn't, you'll still be walking away from your lover feeling infinitely better about yourself and you'll have gained new skills for building healthy relationships in the future. Either way, you come out a winner.

TWELVE

Exorcising Old Ghosts

Rejection opens a Pandora's box inside every obsessive lover, unleashing all of your worst anxieties about being unloved and unlovable: the toxic twins of low self-worth. Rejection makes you feel horribly flawed—not pretty enough, not smart enough, not sexy enough, not witty enough, not talented enough, not enough of anything.

As we've seen, the power of these negative feelings about yourself stems, for the most part, from the pain of having felt rejected as a child. This is what drives your connection compulsion. When you get rejected as an adult, your deepest childhood fears and anxieties are reactivated, so you must deal with two rejections at once: present and past. The pain of rejection comes not only from how a lover feels about you, but also from how you feel about yourself. This is the emotional one-two punch that makes rejection seem so unbearable.

The difficult, courageous work you've done so far has gone a long way toward interrupting and changing many of your obsessive patterns. If you want to internalize those changes, if you want them to become part of you instead

288

of something you have to force yourself to do, you've got to root out the old emotional demons that still drive your connection compulsion. It's time to exorcise the ghosts from your past.

Confronting Childhood Rejection

It will come as no surprise to those of you who've read any of my other books that I am going to take you back into your childhood to deal with relationship problems that have been plaguing you as an adult.

People who deal with their deep-rooted childhood issues usually do so with the help of a professional therapist. But many obsessive lovers—especially those whose childhoods were not marred by extreme abuse—are able to do this work on their own. If you decide to attempt this work without a therapist, be prepared to stir up a lot of old feelings that may be significantly stronger than you anticipate. Make sure that you have a friend or relative—perhaps your anchor—who can be there to offer you support. If you still find yourself thrown off balance by the intensity of your feelings, I urge you to seek the support and guidance that a trained therapist can provide.

"WHAT IF I HAD GOOD PARENTS?"

I know that some of you will insist that your parents were generally loving and never rejected you as a child. And in many cases, I'm sure this is true. But that doesn't mean you never *experienced* childhood rejection. As we've seen, children do not need to actually *be* rejected in order to *feel* rejected.

Anne certainly believed her parents loved her. Although

she talked to me at length about how they had inadvertently neglected her when they became preoccupied with her brother's drug problem, she still considered them good parents. She didn't see how her parents' inattention could possibly have had anything to do with her attempted suicide.

Anne

They did the best they could. I just don't feel right blaming them. Sure I felt left out, but they always loved me. That's not being rejected. I'm very close to them now and I don't want to do anything to wreck that. I feel like you're trying to make me get mad at them when I'm not. I have nothing to get mad about.

It was true that compared with many obsessive lovers I've worked with, Anne had little to complain about as far as her childhood was concerned. She wasn't abandoned; she wasn't physically, sexually, or verbally abused; and neither of her parents was alcoholic or addicted to drugs. Anne loved her parents and resented the implication that they might have been deficient or cruel.

Susan

Look, you may understand *now* that your brother's problems took your parents away from you, but as a little kid, you were too young to understand. You've told me a number of times how invisible and neglected you used to feel.

Anne

But I wasn't rejected. Rejection is when people don't want you. Only bad parents reject their own children. My folks just had their hands full.

I assured Anne that I was not trying to accuse her parents of being bad people, or even of being inadequate. But the fact remained that Anne had been describing the experience of feeling neglected as a child. The difference between feeling "neglected" and feeling "rejected" is merely a difference in terminology. The underlying feelings are identical.

As we worked together, Anne grew to understand that what had happened to her was indeed a form of childhood rejection. Armed with this acknowledgment, she was finally able to see the link between her past and her obsession, and once she saw that link, she was able to take steps to reduce the obsession's power over her.

Anne's story illustrates how the experience of childhood rejection can be quite subtle. This is even true for some Saviors, especially if their parents were physically or mentally ill as opposed to being alcoholic or drug addicted. But it doesn't matter whether your wounds are obvious or obscured—if you want to heal them you need to face them.

A LETTER TO YOUR REJECTING PARENT

Through her work in therapy, Margaret came to understand that her pain was caused not only by her failed relationship with Phil, but also by the way that relationship reopened wounds from her childhood. Not only had Margaret's father left her, but he had added insult to injury by failing to maintain contact with her after he left.

I asked Margaret what she had done about all the pain she had left over from her father's rejection. She replied that she'd never really done anything about it. To Margaret—as to most people—childhood trauma was something to just get through and then try to forget. But that approach left the trauma buried within her where it continued to cause her pain. I told her that if she wanted to get the pain out of her system once and for all, she had to stop suppressing it.

To help Margaret do this, I asked her to write a letter to her rejecting father, telling him how she felt when he left the family. She would have to somehow face her pain once she had committed her feelings to paper. Here is what she wrote:

Dear Daddy,

When you went away you broke my heart. I felt so horrible. I can understand why you left Mom, lots of people get divorced. But why did you leave me too? Why didn't you come and see me once in a while? Why didn't you call? Why didn't you write? I always thought it was because you didn't love me anymore. Or maybe I'd done something bad and you were mad at me. When I saw other kids with their fathers it just made me hurt more. I guess you just never cared how much I loved you. I'll never understand how you could just turn your back on me like that. I didn't deserve to be treated like that. All I did was love you.

Margaret

When Margaret brought her letter into group, she told us it had taken her four days just to get herself to sit down to start it. This resistance was a clear demonstration of how afraid she was to face her unresolved pain.

When she read the letter aloud to us, she was forced to stop several times as her voice choked with tears. But as she uncovered the pain she had previously stuffed into her unconscious, she realized that, though uncomfortable, it wasn't as devastating as she had feared it would be. This was an exciting discovery for her—her pain hurt, but she could handle it.

I urge you to write a letter of your own. It can help you clarify, identify, and focus on your feelings of childhood rejection in order to begin the process of exorcising these particularly tenacious ghosts. Begin your letter with the words that best describe the specifics of your situation. For example:

"When you left me it made me feel . . ."

"When you neglected me it made me feel . . ."

"When you put me down all the time it made me feel . . ."

"When you hit me it made me feel . . ."

"When I had to take care of you and be *your* parent it made me feel . . ."

"When you got drunk it made me feel . . ."

Try to recall and express as many of your childhood feelings as you can. Don't judge them and don't hold back. You have a right to the full range of your feelings, whatever they are.

ROBERT'S RAGE

While Margaret's letter expressed a great deal of hurt, other letters—for example, Robert's—focus on different feelings altogether.

Robert was the stereo salesman who, after attacking his girlfriend's car with a hammer, came to see me because he was afraid that unless he got a handle on his temper he was eventually going to hurt someone. Robert was unusual in that most people who act out their rage or revenge fantasies through violence lack the courage or insight to seek help. Robert seemed genuinely motivated to get a handle on his anger.

I asked Robert to write a letter to his father so he could constructively express the feelings he'd had as a child when his father left his mother for another woman—the same feelings he had been *destructively* reenacting in his obsessive relationship with Sarah. Here is an excerpt from a five-page letter he brought in the following week:

> Dad,
>   The night you left me standing on that road and drove off with that woman, I felt like a bug who'd just been stomped on. I wish I could have stomped you right back. . . .
>   What the hell kind of father cares more about some bimbo than he does about his own son? A real asshole, that's who. . . .
>   I'll never forgive you for doing that to me. And I'll never forgive you for doing that to Mom. You treated us like dirt and I hate you for it.
>
>   Your son,
>   Robert

In contrast to Margaret's letter, Robert's focused on his anger at his father instead of on his sadness. But in reality, Robert and Margaret were more alike than different. Anger and sadness go hand in hand when they're rooted in childhood rejection.

Robert's anger and Margaret's sadness reflected the same pain; it's just that they expressed it in different ways. Their particular patterns of expressing pain were typical of the way in which our culture tends to channel us. In our society—in fact, in most societies—women are often more comfortable expressing sadness than anger, while men tend to be just the opposite. Robert was unconsciously using his anger to cover up a "feminine" emotion with which he felt uncomfortable: sadness. Margaret, on the other hand, unconsciously used sadness to avoid her rage.

Though both Robert and Margaret needed to get in touch with their more deeply hidden emotions, that was something we could work on in other exercises. For the purposes of this particular letter, there is no right or wrong, no good or bad. The object is to write down whatever feelings you can reach to take the lid off your internal pressure cooker.

If you choose to do this exercise, *writing* the letter is only half the job. When you finish writing, you need to *read* your letter aloud, either to someone with whom you feel safe or to yourself. It is the reading of it that fully drives home the reality of the emotions you've been stuffing for so long.

Reread your letter as often as you like. The more often you do, the more effective it will be. Actually *hearing* the words you've been denying has a powerful effect on your unconscious.

Many of my clients choose to actually send their letter to their rejecting parent. If you decide to do this, I encourage you to go ahead. But I should warn you that this may unleash extremely strong emotions and conflicts between you and your parents.

This sort of confrontation is a major life decision that should not be taken without adequate emotional preparation. However, an effective confrontation is one of the most healing, empowering things you can do for yourself. This process is outlined and explored in depth in my previous book, *Toxic Parents*.

ROBERT'S SADNESS

Because of his violent tendencies, I thought it was essential that Robert dig deeper into his unconscious to explore other emotions that were certain to be lurking beneath his rage. So I assigned him another letter to his father, only this time I asked him to refrain from expressing anger in order to see what other feelings he might connect with. When he brought his letter in a week later, it was only half a page long—a far cry from the five pages of his first letter.

> Dear Dad,
>   When you left me it made me feel like a piece of shit. I felt like you didn't love me, you didn't care about me, you didn't want me, you didn't need me, and you didn't like me. I cried so hard I thought I'd never stop. I still feel like crying sometimes. I still feel like shit sometimes.
>
> Your son,
Robert

Rage had always been accessible to Robert, but now he had connected with the emotions that lay beneath his rage—less "masculine" emotions like sadness, helplessness, and humiliation, emotions that had been making him feel weak and ashamed since childhood.

These were the same emotions Robert felt whenever a woman rejected him. As a child he was too helpless to do anything but suffer them, but as an adult he could explode into violence, which would momentarily flood him with feelings of strength and power to mask the emotions that made him feel so inadequate.

Robert's second letter allowed him to reexperience his "softer" feelings in a context that didn't make him anxious. He could begin to accept them as a normal part of his humanness. This, in turn, made the feelings much less threatening to Robert, reducing his need to defend against them with violent behavior. In getting in touch with the emotions beneath his rage, Robert was essentially eliminating one of the major triggers for his violence (though by no means the only one).

As he progressed in therapy, Robert continued to work to control both his violent tendencies and his obsessive ones. In time, he let go of his obsession for Sarah. He has since become involved with another woman in what appears to be a stable relationship. He has not had a violent episode in over a year.

AN OVERDUE APOLOGY

We all carry within us an active bundle of emotions and memories that have remained unchanged since childhood—our "inner child." When obsessive lovers reenact their old struggles in their adult relationships, they drag this small, helpless child along with them. Through obsession, their inner child is forced repeatedly to relive the pain of parental rejection.

When I explained this to Nora—whose mother beat her with a razor strop and accused her of being seductive with her stepfather—she acknowledged that she had been putting her inner child through hell. I asked Nora if she wanted to apologize to her inner child, and she liked the idea.

I asked Nora to picture herself as a little girl, and to put that little girl in the empty chair that I placed before her. Then I asked her to tell that little girl—her inner child—how sorry she was for subjecting her to so much pain and turmoil. Nora took a few moments to think. Then she began haltingly.

Nora
Honey, I'm so sorry. I've really done a number on you and I just keep doing it. I'm so sorry for making

you feel like nobody loves you, for making you feel
like nobody even cares how much you hurt. And I'm
especially sorry for putting you through that again
and again and again, just because I couldn't handle
letting go of Tom. But he's out of our life now and
I'm not going to let that happen with anybody else—at
least I'm going to try not to—for both our sakes.

Nora's touching apology did more than just assuage her
feelings of remorse for how she had been treating her inner
child. It solidified her sense of being able to do something
about her childhood feelings of rejection. She was learning
that she had the ability to ease her own pain.

This realization came as a big surprise to her. Until now
she had been looking to someone else—most recently
Tom—to make the pain go away. But now, for the first
time, she was coming to believe that it was within her own
power to soothe and comfort her inner child. And she was
getting very excited about it.

NORA'S "GOOD MOTHER" EXERCISE

The following week, when Nora came in for her session,
she was bursting to tell me about an exercise she had come
up with on her own. She called it her "good mother"
exercise, and she was doing it every morning before going
to work.

Nora

I was thinking about how my mother never said
anything nice to me and how things would have been
different if she had. I used to have this teacher who
was really nice to me and I used to dream about
what it would be like if she was my mother. So what
I do is picture myself as a little girl with this teacher

walking across the room to me with this big smile on her face, and I imagine that she *is* my mother. She sits down next to me and puts her arm around me and tells me all the things that I always wanted my mother to say to me. I imagine her saying all these nice things to me and I say them out loud.

I was anxious to hear what Nora had come up with, so I asked her to do the exercise for me. This is what her visualized "good mother" said to her:

Nora

I really love you. You're so pretty, you're so smart. I'm so proud of you. Everything you do is so fine. You're such a terrific kid I wouldn't trade you for anybody. I'm so glad you're my child because you make me so happy. And that's all I ever want to do for you—make you as happy as you make me.

When Nora finished her eyes were wet with tears—and so were mine. She had needed a loving parent to replace the abusive one she'd had, and through her wonderfully imaginative exercise she had dug within herself to find one. This powerful healing process is called "reparenting." Through her good mother exercise, Nora was starting to push out the negative messages that her mother had planted in her unconscious and to replace them with the loving, validating messages that she had always wanted and deserved.

Nora provides an excellent example of how to use the skills you're learning in these visualization and role-playing exercises to create new exercises of your own. She was delighted when I told her I would like to use this exercise with other clients. I have since made the "good parent" exercise (adapted to include "good fathers") a standard part of my therapeutic repertoire and have used it effectively for years.

You can't expect any one exercise to undo years of hurt, especially if you do it only once. Some of these exercises need to be repeated as regularly as physical exercise. Others need to be done only once or twice. For example, you certainly don't need to write a different letter to your rejecting parent every week, but you can reread your original letter as often as you like. And you probably don't need to apologize to your inner child more than once or twice, but you can calm and comfort that child whenever you feel agitated and frightened. There's no limit to how often you can do the good parent exercise—it's an emotional vitamin.

Giving Up the Childhood Struggle

As you do these exercises you will feel a new sense of strength and purpose. You will feel yourself slowly wresting from your unconscious the power to control your own life. But before you can really free yourself from the chains of obsession, you've got to give up, once and for all, the childhood struggle to change your rejecting parent.

After writing her letter to her father and doing a good father exercise, Margaret was feeling better than she had in years. But before she could really give up her struggle, she had to uncover the anger that still lay buried beneath her more accessible sadness, just as Robert had had to get to the sadness that lay beneath his anger.

To help Margaret do this, I asked her to imagine she was in a play, cast as her own father. The play was an improvisation in which her father would read the letter she had written and then respond as he might if he were here today.

When Margaret began, she portrayed a man who seemed truly sorry for the pain he had caused. Considering how her father had treated her, this was an unrealistically sympathetic image. So I stopped Margaret and asked her to play her father, not as she wanted him to be, but instead, as her worse fears might depict him. This was much harder for her.

Margaret (as her father)

I don't know what you want me to say about your letter. It's all ancient history as far as I'm concerned. I couldn't stand your mother anymore so I split, and you were part of the package. I didn't call because I didn't want to. I had nothing to say to you and I didn't have any interest in hearing what you had to say. I didn't care about you then. And now, you're part of a past that I'd just as soon forget.

Susan

Okay. There it is. Your worst fears put into words. What's going on with you right now?

Margaret

I don't know because those were really *my* words, not his. Those were *my* fears. I don't believe he'd really say those things to me.

Susan

But, Margaret . . . he *did* say those things to you. With his behavior.

For a moment, Margaret looked like she was about to cry. But as the truth sank in, she became angry instead.

Margaret

You're right. That's exactly what he said! That bastard! He didn't care! He just didn't care! And Phil was exactly the same way! I've got to stop doing this to myself. I've got to stop chasing these bastards who don't love me. I've just got to stop!

In accepting the fact that her father's behavior articulated his feelings for her, Margaret was letting go of one of the core beliefs that had been driving her obsessive patterns: that her father really loved her and somehow she could still connect with that love. By getting in touch with the anger she felt about that behavior, she was able to realize how much she resented Phil's rejection as well.

Margaret was also angry at herself, for permitting herself to be mistreated. This helped her clarify for herself what she was and was not willing to tolerate in a relationship. She was finally ready to set limits, both on her lover and on herself—a major victory in her fight against obsession.

Armed with a new awareness, Margaret discovered one of the most powerful ways to release the pain of childhood rejection: giving up the struggle to rewrite history.

CHILDHOOD REJECTION
AND PERSONAL RESPONSIBILITY

You are not accountable for any form of rejection that you experienced as a child. I can't emphasize this strongly or often enough.

You are in no way responsible for any form of rejection that you experienced as a child.

This is a basic truth that can have an enormous impact on how you feel about yourself and on the way you treat yourself and others.

BUT . . . now that you see some of the connections between childhood rejection and obsessive love, you may be tempted to use this understanding to justify how you have been treating your target.

Ray yielded to this temptation. Ray was the movie cameraman who came into therapy with his lover Karen. As we explored his childhood issues, Ray came to appreciate how much he was still suffering from rejection by his alcoholic mother. He grew increasingly resentful toward Karen for not being more sympathetic to his plight.

Ray

Of course I'm a little overbearing. I've got a lot of stuff to deal with. When you had a childhood like mine, you don't grow up to be the mental health poster boy. Why can't she see that? Why doesn't she cut me a little slack?

Ray's rationalizing threatened to become an impediment to our work together. I told him he was using the classic "I-can't-help-being-obsessive-I-was-rejected-as-a-child" excuse. I pointed out that Karen was not responsible for the emotional pain he may have suffered in childhood and she had no obligation to put up with his unacceptable behavior just because he was still hurting.

I urge you not to fall into the same trap that Ray did. The truth is, you are totally responsible for any pain you have inflicted on your target and for finding ways to stop doing it.

Understanding the power of the connection between childhood rejection and adult obsessive patterns is no reason to believe your obsession is beyond your control. Nor is the fact that you were not responsible for what happened to you as a child any justification for avoiding responsibility now for changing those patterns.

DESYMBOLIZING YOUR LOVER

As an obsessive lover, you have been expecting your symbolic parent to make up for whatever rejection you experienced from your real parent. This only serves to keep your childhood struggle alive. You cannot bring that struggle to a resolution until you desymbolize your lover.

Ray was having a particularly difficult time separating Karen from his mother. On an intellectual level he understood how he had turned Karen into his symbolic mother, but on an emotional level he was still doing it. To help him stop, I asked him to bring in two photographs, one of his mother and one of Karen.

At his next therapy session, I had him place the photos side by side on one of two empty chairs. Then I told him to explain to Karen—through her photo—exactly how he had been trying to make her undo the emotional damage that his mother had done to him.

Ray

I'm sorry that I got you and my mother all mixed up together. You're two separate people, but I sure haven't been treating you that way.

At this point I stopped him and told him to separate the photos as a way of symbolically separating the people. He took his mother's photograph and moved it to the other empty chair. When he resumed talking to Karen he found himself turning to the other chair whenever he referred to his mother. This helped reinforce for him the goal of the exercise—to see that Karen was not his mother.

Ray

My mother made me crazy and I was always trying to make her see how much I loved her so she'd stop. When I met you, I started doing the same thing, only this time I made *you* crazy and that was a crappy thing to do. She was an alcoholic; you're not. She always yelled at me; you don't. I had to take care of her; you can take care of yourself. It was her job to take care of me; it's not your job. She always made me feel helpless and scared. I feel that way with you, too, sometimes, but I know that's coming from me, not from you, and I've got to remember that whenever I feel that way. She's her and you're you, and I'm really sorry I haven't been keeping that straight.

In doing this exercise, Ray was *feeling*, as well as understanding, the difference between his mother and Karen. He told me he was surprised at how deeply this exercise moved him. This was an important emotional experience for Ray, something he could think back on whenever he started to react to Karen in the ways he had reacted to his mother in childhood.

Ray had been projecting onto Karen all of his obsessive fantasies about changing his mother. But by desymbolizing Karen, he was freeing her of those impossible expectations.

No lover can heal the wounds of childhood rejection.

You, and *only* you, have the ability, the motivation, and the responsibility to accomplish that task.

The emotional pain of childhood rejection won't go away overnight. It took a long time to form, and it will take time to dismantle. But if you make these exercises an ongoing part of your life, you will continue to diminish the power that childhood rejection has over you and over your behavior in love relationships. You are no longer a helpless child. You are an adult with not only the responsibility but the power to deal with the ghosts from your past.

THIRTEEN

Keeping Your Balance

You've done a lot of hard work. You've discovered ways of changing many of your obsessive behavior patterns, and you've worked on controlling your obsessive thoughts and feelings. You've either finally given up on the target of your obsessive love or purged much of the obsession from your relationship. And you've confronted the childhood rejection that laid the groundwork for your obsessive love in the first place.

There's just one thing left to do: reinforce these changes to make sure they don't slip away in future relationships or in your remodeled current relationship.

Whether you're in or looking for a relationship, some form of rejection—even if only momentary—is virtually inevitable. This is not as tragic as it sounds; it is simply the way things are in normal human interaction.

If you're in a relationship, no matter how good it is, your partner may withdraw, he or she may use words in anger that make you feel unwanted, or a misunderstanding may seem like a rejection. The two of you may even grow apart and decide to separate. Human feelings ebb and flow. No relationship comes with an ironclad guarantee.

If you're looking for a relationship, you may very well be jilted a few times before you find one. Your new love interest may not be attracted to you, he or she may be terrified of intimacy, the timing may be wrong, there may be family complications, your prospective lover may hate your dog . . . there's no end to the possibilities. Even if you have your obsessive behavior completely within your control, you may be rejected for reasons that are completely *beyond* your control.

I don't mean to imply that your love life is destined to be one rejection after another. You are *not* programmed to be attracted only to people who will hurt you. You are *not* doomed to a life of romantic disappointment and pain. You have *not* been singled out by some greater power to be obsessive for all eternity.

However, a little preventive medicine can't hurt. And having the skills to deal with rejection will make you feel safer and more confident in any relationship. In this chapter I'm going to show you how to be prepared by changing your perceptions of rejection and learning new ways to respond to it.

Old Triggers, New Perceptions

As an obsessive lover you were often oblivious to the damage your behavior was doing to your relationship. You may have seen yourself as the innocent victim of a heartless lover. Now, as an ex–obsessive lover, you may be so sensitive to your former blind spots, and so determined to avoid repeating past mistakes, that you take *too much* responsibility for any troubles that may arise in your relationships.

This is especially easy to do when a new lover rejects you without clearly communicating why. After all, it's not unusual for people to have a difficult time being straight-forward about their reasons for leaving a relationship. Or your lover may simply leave or stop calling without explanation. Some people don't even know why they're dissatisfied; they just know they want to get out. When ex–obsessive lovers are faced with this gaping unknown, they typically assume that if they had done something differently the relationship could have been saved.

IT ISN'T ALWAYS YOU

Nora resorted to this sort of unjustified self-blame as she was nearing the end of her work with me. About a year after Nora finally gave up her fantasies about Tom, she met a new man. They saw each other exclusively for several months and then he suddenly called it off.

Nora

I can't believe he did it. Everything was going so good. And it felt so different from before. I swear to you, Susan, it was different. I didn't feel pressured about it at all. I didn't even call every day. He asked me out maybe twice a week and that was just fine with me. I really didn't want to push. And then he just dropped this bomb. He said he didn't love me anymore. I couldn't believe it. I asked him what I did wrong, but he just kept talking in circles without saying anything. What the hell did I do?

I told Nora that there was no reason to suspect she'd done anything wrong and that it was self-defeating to keep speculating about it. If she tried hard enough she was bound to come up with something self-blaming, but simply coming up with possibilities doesn't make them true.

To help Nora see her situation from a more positive perspective, I asked her to make a list of all the non-self-blaming reasons she could think of to explain why this man might have rejected her.

This was Nora's list:

He's too scared to commit to a relationship.

He doesn't trust women.

He has a wife and 12 kids in Peoria.

He's decided to become a monk.

He's emotionally constipated.

He only has six weeks to live.

He only likes stupid women.

He's intimidated by intimacy.

He's on the lam from the Mafia.

He's on the lam from the law.

He's on the lam from his wife and 12 kids.

He's ashamed of the fact that he can't afford to go out anymore.

He's an alien from another planet.

I was pleased that Nora was able to find some humor in this exercise. Therapy doesn't have to be relentlessly grim and serious any more than life does. Love relationships are often flavored by irony and absurdity, and it helps make the pain of rejection less overwhelming if you can use laughter to soften the blow. While I don't mean to discount the pain or sadness of the end of a relationship, finding the humor in a difficult situation always makes it easier to endure.

Nora's humor helped her put a damper on some of her disappointment and did nothing to undermine the effectiveness of her list. Even her playful entries helped her gain an important understanding: that her lover could have rejected her for reasons that had nothing to do with her.

Between the extremes of taking too little and too much responsibility for problems in love relationships, there lies a middle ground—reality. When you finally find that middle ground, you will appreciate that there are two people in a relationship, both of whom have their own internal conflicts and agendas.

If you accept the fact that rejection is not necessarily a reflection on you, your life doesn't have to turn upside down every time you're rejected. This new perspective can help you let go of a lot of your feelings of low self-worth and self-reproach that rejection has previously triggered. By letting go of these feelings, you will undermine many of your self-defeating fears, making it easier for you to face and to handle the emotional risks of new relationships.

Old Triggers, New Responses

We all know the horrible frustration of finding ourselves in a painful, humiliating situation and not being able to think of anything to say. In the car on the way home, we invariably come up with a million things we wish we'd said, but in the heat of panic, the words that come to our lips tend to be inadequate or regrettable.

Because of this, it helps to have more than insight and awareness at your fingertips should you need to deal with rejection. It helps to be ready to articulate that insight and awareness. If you're armed with specific verbal responses you can minimize your feelings of powerlessness and maintain your dignity. Let me illustrate.

About four months after breaking up with Phil, Margaret came into her group session with a dilemma.

Margaret

I've been seeing this new guy for a few weeks now and I'm really starting to like him. But I'm so scared it won't work out that I'm afraid to go out with him again. I don't know if I could take the humiliation of another rejection. The thing with Phil just about did me in.

Margaret had already made considerable progress in controlling her obsessive behavior. And she had taken giant strides in repairing the childhood damage of her father's rejection. But she was still feeling the emotional wounds from her experience with Phil. She was afraid that a new rejection would once again trigger her old familiar pains and that she would react in her old demeaning ways.

DIGNITY DESTROYERS

In the past, Margaret had reacted to rejection as most obsessive lovers do, with what I call "dignity destroyers."

The most common dignity destroyers are:

- pleading for another chance
- refusing to accept that the relationship is over
- threatening harm to the other person or to yourself
- predicting that you will not be able to survive a breakup
- offering to do anything to keep your lover

In the past, Margaret's dignity destroyers had made her feel foolish, desperate, and sometimes crazy. To alleviate her fears of repeating these behaviors in the future, I suggested that she practice some new responses to her old triggers.

DIGNITY PRESERVERS

One of the ways I help people learn new responses to rejection is to simulate their worst case scenario in a nonthreatening setting.

Before I took Margaret through this exercise, I demonstrated for her by asking each member of her group to say something rejecting to me as if we were ending a relationship. Margaret's group was made up of men and women who were trying to overcome obsessive patterns. Since rejection was an issue for all of them, they had no trouble coming up with rejecting statements that had served as triggers for their own obsession. I then showed Margaret how she might respond to these triggers with new responses.

I call these kinds of responses "dignity preservers":

OLD TRIGGER: "I don't ever want to see you again."

NEW RESPONSE: "It hurts to hear you say that but I'll respect your decision."

OLD TRIGGER: "I can't take it anymore. You're too needy for me."

NEW RESPONSE: "I know I'm needy but I'm working on it. I'm sorry you're not willing to give me the time to change."

OLD TRIGGER: "I don't love you anymore."

NEW RESPONSE: "I appreciate your honesty. I'm sorry things didn't work out."

OLD TRIGGER: "I'm just not physically attracted to you. Let's just be friends."

NEW RESPONSE: "We obviously want different things out of this relationship, so I think it would be best if we don't see each other anymore."

OLD TRIGGER: "I don't want to hurt your feelings but you're not my type."

NEW RESPONSE: "I wish things could have been different but I accept the fact that they're not."

After my exercise, I handed out this list of dignity-preserving responses to everyone in the group. Then we did the exercise again, with Margaret in the hot seat. As each member said something rejecting, she replied with one of the new responses from the list, or with a response of her own that she adapted from the list. When she had finished, Margaret realized how different her responses to rejection had been in the past.

The secret to making a response dignity preserving is to make it nonargumentative and nondefensive. In that way, you don't find yourself backed into the impossible position of trying to beg or persuade someone to love you.

Of course, no matter how well you understand the principle of dignity preservers, you may still find yourself tongue-tied if you are ever again confronted by rejection. Because of this, I urge you to *memorize* some of these dignity-preserving responses so they will be available to you when you need them. You don't have to be in group therapy to learn or to practice them. You can use a tape recorder just as effectively.

To do this, record a group of rejecting statements on tape, leaving a pause between them for your response. You can use the triggers that Margaret's group members came up with and add any other rejecting statements from your own experience. When you play the tape back, respond with one or more of the dignity preservers above. You'll find that almost all of them can work as a response to almost any form of rejection.

Having a repertoire of new responses to old triggers prevents you from yielding to the desperation that has typically driven you to say and do things you've come to regret. These dignity-preserving responses are like emotional life preservers. They keep you afloat when your emotional tides threaten to drag you under.

CONFRONTING DOUBLE MESSAGES

Another way to avoid triggering obsessive behavior is to learn to clarify any double messages that a current or future lover may give you. As we've seen, double messages can really throw you off balance. You cling desperately to the part of the message that says or implies that your lover wants you, while at the same time you're terrified of the part that says or implies that he or she doesn't. The easiest way to cut through the fog is to *refuse to be confused*. If you find that your lover is saying one thing and doing another, don't try to guess what's going on—*ask*.

Here are a few examples of the kinds of questions you can ask your lover:

> "I don't understand something. You say you love me but you don't make any time for me. Doesn't that seem contradictory to you?"

> "I'm getting very mixed signals from you. We see each other three times a week, but you're still going out with other people. What kind of a relationship do you want?"

"You *act* like you want to make a real commitment to me, but every time I bring it up, you get very distant. Am I wasting my time in this relationship?"

"You *talk* about wanting to make a real commitment to me but you never seem to *do* anything about it. What's really going on?"

"When we're alone you act like we really have something special, but when we're out with your friends you act like I'm just a casual date. That makes me feel like sex is the only thing you want out of this relationship. Is that true?"

Obviously, this list could go on and on. But the central strategy is to ask the kinds of questions that will bring the hidden issues in your relationship out into the open. Even though you risk getting answers you may not like, you're always better off knowing the truth than you are retreating into the murky world of fears and speculations.

Is There Love after Obsession?

Even though, if you have done the work in this book, you are almost certainly feeling better about yourself, you may still feel a bit rocky about entering new relationships. After all, your obsession was such a dominant part of you for so long that it's hard to imagine a love relationship without it.

You now have a lot of the tools you need to be in relationships in a new, healthier, and more satisfying way. However, that doesn't necessarily mean that you're ready to use these tools. Before you can feel comfortable and safe with a new partner, you've got to learn to feel comfortable and safe with yourself.

LEARNING TO TRUST YOURSELF

Many ex-obsessors enter new relationships with such a terror of repeating past mistakes that they walk on eggshells around their new lover. This makes them seem nervous, withdrawn, and secretive to the person they're trying to get to know. They are afraid to trust themselves to be themselves.

When Anne got involved in her first post-John relationship, she was very concerned that if she allowed herself to be spontaneous, she would lose the control she had gained over her obsessive behavior.

I assured Anne that her trust in herself would increase over time if she could relax enough to permit herself to take some emotional risks. Even if things didn't always work out, she could learn from her setbacks as well as from her successes. Being constantly on your emotional guard can be extremely taxing both on you and on your lover.

Anne agreed to make an effort to be less restrained around her new boyfriend. By the time she and her lover celebrated their six-month anniversary, she was feeling much less anxious about being open and genuine with him.

Anne

I don't know whether I trust him more now or I trust myself more now, but I feel a lot more philosophical about this relationship than I ever did before. It's like, I don't feel like I'm going to go off the deep end again so I don't worry about it too much anymore. If this relationship doesn't work out, it doesn't work out. It has to be good for me, too, you know. I never paid attention to that before. I was always so intent on getting him to love me that I never cared that I was miserable in the relationship. Now I know

that if I'm not happy I can walk away from it. I'll be
disappointed, but I'll live. And that's really freed me
to be myself. It's an incredible feeling. If you had
asked me six months ago if I ever thought I'd feel
like this I would have said "no way." Maybe I'm
kidding myself, but all I know is I'm not going crazy
worrying about my relationship right now, and that
in itself is a miracle.

Anne had done far more than just relax into this new
relationship. She had made changes in her attitudes and
expectations that helped keep her relationship and her life
in perspective. She realized that a relationship needed to
work for her in the here and now, not in some fantasy
future. To help her keep her perspective, she resumed
friendships and activities that she had dropped when she
became obsessed with pursuing John. She was integrating
her relationship into her life instead of making her relationship the be-all and end-all of her existence.

As time passed, Anne discovered that it took less and
less work to control her obsessive behavior. The obsession-
stopping techniques she had worked so hard to learn during her emotional vacation became increasingly automatic.
She learned to trust herself more, her fear of her own
obsessive tendencies faded, and her relationship flourished.

CELEBRATING A NEW WAY TO LOVE

Ray and Karen had been together for a stormy two years
when they started therapy. A year later they were still
together, but now they were united in a progressively
different kind of relationship. Ray was learning to control
much of his obsessive behavior, and Karen was learning to
set clear, firm limits on what kind of behavior she was
willing to accept from him.

As Ray neared the end of his work with me, he brought in a very poignant letter he had given Karen:

My darling Karen,

Though we've known each other for three years, I mark the beginning of our relationship from that moment, exactly one year ago today, when I came back to you after two of the most grueling but eye-opening weeks of my life. I know that the things I learned during my emotional vacation have saved our relationship, and I thank God for that every day.

It still hurts me to think of all the torture I put you through. Every time I think about it I'm appalled all over again at how insensitive I was. I was demeaning to you and emotionally cruel and thought that I was righting some wrong that you were doing. I was acting exactly the opposite of how I feel for you, not respecting and honoring that most important of all things to me, your dignity and individuality. I grieve for the lost love and wasted time.

I know now that the anger and pain inside of me has nothing to do with you, and every day my love for you helps me remember that. I know that we will thrive as long as I can continue to act consistently out of respect and out of love.

I know in my heart that it will not be easy. There are still a lot of things to learn and a lot of habits to break. But I love you for sticking this out with me, despite the pain and suffering I caused you in the past. And I love you for not letting me get away with any of my old crap anymore. And I especially love you for giving me a chance to change when a lot of other women might have given up on me. But most of all, I love you for being exactly who you are.

Happy anniversary, baby. I love you.

Ray

Ray's anniversary letter was a joyous way of celebrating not only his renunciation of obsessive patterns, but his discovery of a new way of loving which freed him from the fear and anger that had dominated his life with Karen in the past.

As a result of the work he had done to understand how he had invaded Karen's boundaries, Ray now accepted the fact that Karen was a separate individual. That meant that she had a right to her own feelings, thoughts, and interests, and that he had to respect that right.

Obsession can't coexist with this kind of respect for a lover's personal rights, and a good relationship can't exist without it.

TRADING TURMOIL FOR REAL INTIMACY

But how do you know a good relationship when it comes your way? How do you know when it's the real thing? The answer is, you can't—at first. If you go into a new relationship "knowing that it's the real thing," you're loading up that relationship with the same kinds of fantasies and magical expectations that have sabotaged you in the past.

New relationships are, by nature, filled with unknowns. Until you've allowed a relationship enough time to develop, until you and your lover have grown with each other long enough to see that you're growing in the same direction, until you've had the opportunity to explore your lover's deepest fears and dreams and to reveal your own, you *cannot* know if your love is the real thing. Mutual exploration and discovery is what intimacy is all about.

If you're like most ex–obsessors, you may have a tough time believing that a safe, comfortable relationship based on genuine intimacy can possibly be passionate and exciting. Because the only love you've ever known has been fueled by high drama, passion without turmoil may not seem like real passion to you at all.

But giving up obsession does not mean giving up passion. It means giving up suffering, anxiety, chaos, humiliation, jealousy, and possessiveness. Once you let go of these obstacles to a healthy relationship, you will free yourself to discover the deep joy of genuine intimacy—the only basis for a love that is truly satisfying.

SUGGESTED READING

Bradshaw, John. *Homecoming*. New York: Bantam Books, 1990.

Branden, Nathaniel. *The Psychology of Romantic Love*. New York: Bantam Books, 1981.

Delis, Dean C., Ph.D., with Phillips, Cassandra. *The Passion Paradox*. New York: Bantam Books, 1990.

Diamond, Jed, L.C.S.W. *Looking for Love in All the Wrong Places*. New York: Avon Books, 1989.

Edward, Joyce, M.S.S.A., Ruskin, Nathene, M.S.S., and Turrini, Patsy, M.S.S. *Separation/Individuation*. New York: Gardner Press, 1981.

Halpern, Howard M., Ph.D. *How to Break Your Addiction to a Person*. New York: Bantam Books, 1983.

Hayes, Jody. *Smart Love*. Los Angeles: Jeremy P. Tarcher, 1988.

Katz, Dr. Stan J. and Liu, Aimee E. *False Love*. New York: Ticknor & Fields, 1988.

Norwood, Robin. *Women Who Love Too Much*. New York: Pocket Books, 1986.

Tennov, Dorothy. *Love and Limerance*. New York: Stein & Day, 1978.

About the Authors

Susan Forward, Ph.D., is an internationally renowned therapist, lecturer, and author of the number-one *New York Times* bestsellers *Toxic Parents* and *Men Who Hate Women and the Women Who Love Them,* as well as *Betrayal of Innocence: Incest and Its Devastation.* In addition to her private practice, for five years she hosted a daily ABC Talkradio program. She has also served widely as a group therapist, instructor, and consultant in many Southern California medical and psychiatric facilities, and she formed the first private sexual abuse treatment center in California. She lives in Los Angeles and has two grown children.

Dr. Forward maintains offices in Encino and Tustin, California. She has established a national helpline counseling service for persons interested in her methods. For further information, call (818) 905-5292 or (714) 838-4444.

Craig Buck, a film and television writer and producer, also written extensively on human behavior for many tional magazines and newspapers. He is the coauthor, Susan Forward, of *Toxic Parents* and *Betrayal of I cence.* He lives in Los Angeles with his wife and four-y old daughter.

"*Don't Call It Love* should be required for anyone in any kind of recovery program, whether or not they are dealing with sexual addiction."—Melody Beattie, author of *Codependent No More*

| DON'T |
CALL IT
| LOVE |

Recovery From
Sexual Addiction

Patrick Carnes, Ph.D.

Here is groundbreaking work by the nation's leading professional expert on sexual addiction, based on the candid testimony of more than 1,000 recovering sexual addicts in the first major scientific study of the disorder. This essential volume includes not only the findings of Dr. Carnes's research but also advice from the addicts and co-addicts themselves as they work to overcome their compulsive behavior. Positive, hopeful, and practical, *Don't Call It Love* is a landmark book that helps us better understand all addictions, their causes, and the difficult path to recovery.
